BOB

ACCOUNTING CHANGES

Chronicles of Convergence,
Crisis, and Complexity in
Financial Reporting

AICPA®

Robert H. Herz, CPA, FCA, CGMA

Notice to Readers

Accounting Changes: Chronicles of Convergence, Crisis, and Complexity in Financial Reporting does not represent an official position of the American Institute of Certified Public Accountants, and it is distributed with the understanding that the author and publisher are not rendering legal, accounting, or other professional services in the publication. This book is intended to be an overview of the topics discussed within, and the author has made every attempt to verify the completeness and accuracy of the information herein. However, neither the author nor publisher can guarantee the applicability of the information found herein. If legal advice or other expert assistance is required, the services of a competent professional should be sought.

Copyright © Robert H. Herz, 2013.

All rights reserved. For information about the procedure for requesting permission to make copies of any part of this work, please email copyright@aicpa.org with your request. Otherwise, requests should be written and mailed to the Permissions Department, AICPA, 220 Leigh Farm Road, Durham, NC 27707-8110.

1 2 3 4 5 6 7 8 9 0 PIP 1 9 8 7 6 5 4 3

ISBN: 978-1-93735-210-3 paperback
ISBN: 978-1-93735-212-7 casebound
ISBN: 978-1-93735-211-0 ebook

Publisher: Linda Prentice Cohen
Acquisitions Editor: Martin Censor
Developmental Editor: Andrew Grow
Project Manager: Amy Sykes

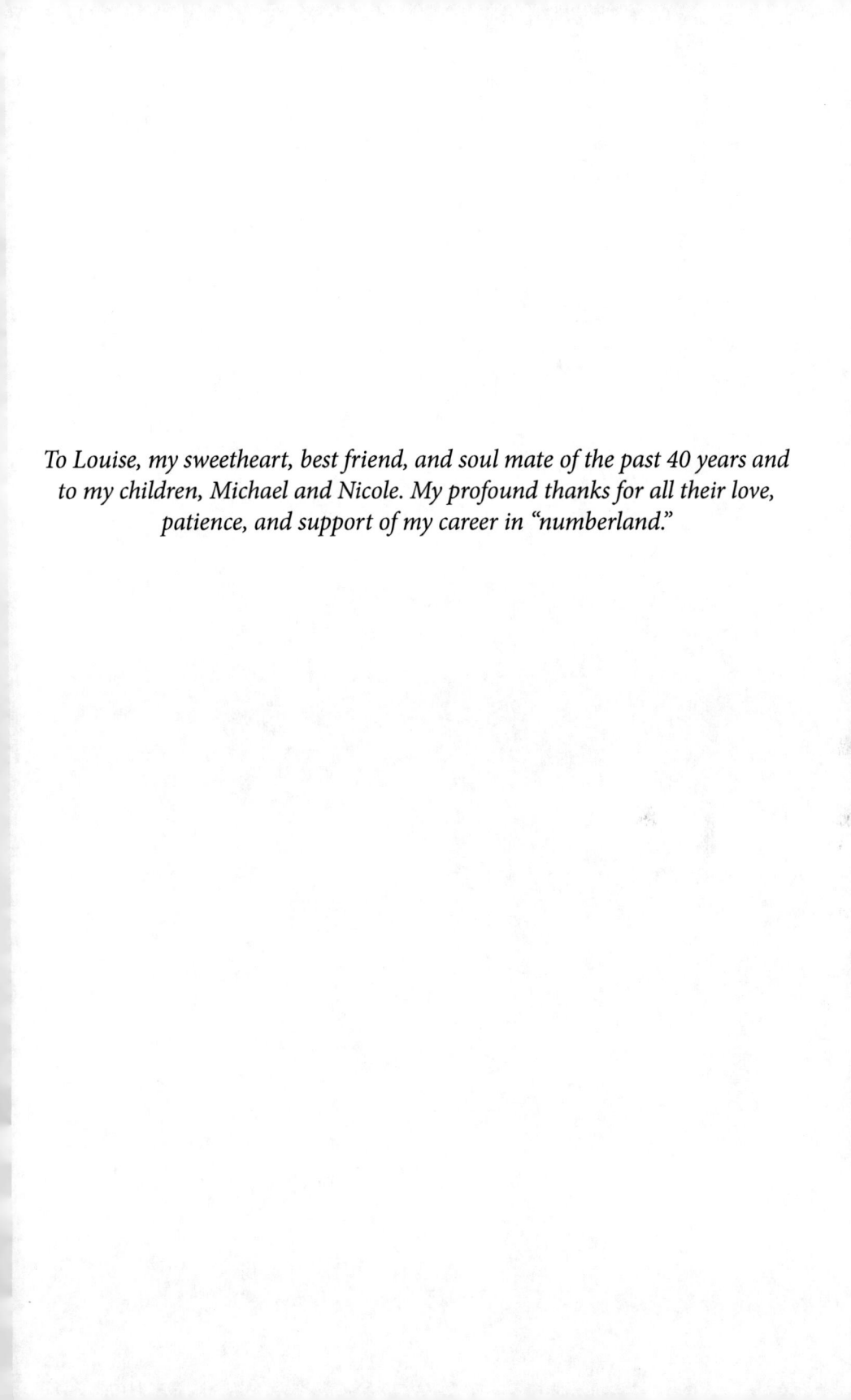

To Louise, my sweetheart, best friend, and soul mate of the past 40 years and to my children, Michael and Nicole. My profound thanks for all their love, patience, and support of my career in "numberland."

TABLE OF CONTENTS

Chapter		Page
	Foreword	ix
	Preface	xiii
	Acknowledgments	xvii
1	My First 49 Years	1
	Jersey Boy	1
	Don't Cry for Me Argentina	3
	Rule Britannia	5
	The Early Accountant	6
	Hello Miami, Goodbye Miami (and PW), and Hello Boston (and Coopers & Lybrand)	9
	Return of the Prodigal Son	10
	The Roaring '80s and Bad Bob	11
	Poacher Turned Gamekeeper	15
	Professional Affairs	18
	A Merger of Equals and "the Dream Team"	21
	Could You See It Coming?	23
	International Bob	23
	Unforgettable Events and a Fork in the Road	25
	Some Basics About the FASB	28
2	Charting Course	33
	Improving Standard Setting	39
	Can We Make Things Simpler?	42
	Rationalizing the Structure of U.S. Accounting Standard Setting	44
	The Accounting Standards Codification—Reorganizing and Codifying U.S. GAAP	45
	Addressing Complexity and Improving the Understandability of Standards	48
	International Convergence	49
	Setting Course	50

Table of Contents

Chapter		Page
3	Stock Option Controversies—Take Two	53
	What's the Problem?	56
	Addressing the Accounting Issues in the Face of Pressure Politics	63
4	International Convergence	83
	The Urge to Converge and Wherefore IFRS?	83
	What Does the Law Require?	84
	Views of Standard Setters on International Convergence	84
	The Norwalk Agreement	87
	Short-Term Convergence Projects	90
	Undertaking Major Joint Projects	93
	The 2005 SEC Staff "Roadmap" and the 2006 FASB-IASB MoU	95
	Conceptual Framework	100
	The SEC Eliminates the Reconciliation Requirement and Explores Potential Adoption of IFRS in the United States	102
	Improve and Adopt IFRS	109
	The SEC Proposes a New Roadmap for IFRS Adoption; the FASB and IASB Update the MoU	110
	Mixed Responses to the SEC Roadmap	112
	Some Begin to Question America's Commitment to Global Accounting Standards	114
	The G20 Leaders Push for Rapid International Convergence of Accounting Standards	115
	The FASB and IASB Respond to the G20 Call by More Than Redoubling the Convergence Effort	116
	A Necessary Change in Plans	118
	In the Meantime, Back at the SEC	125
	So, Bob, What Do You Really Think About Convergence and IFRS?	131
	Nobody Said This Would Be Easy	135
	Now Where?	137
	Conclusion	144

Chapter		Page
5	The Financial Crisis	145
	Accounting Did Not Cause the Financial Crisis, and Accounting Will Not End It	145
	Were There Warning Signs?	146
	The Addiction to Off-Balance Sheet Accounting	147
	Off-Balance Accounting 101	149
	Did They Qualify?	150
	SIVs, Conduits, and Other VIEs	152
	The Lehman Repo 105 and 108 Transactions	153
	Fair Value, Mark-to-Market Accounting, and Impairment of Financial Assets	156
	Some History	156
	Then Came the Crisis	159
	The Year 2008 Draws to a Close	166
	Into 2009—Congress Weighs In	168
	Our Response	174
	The World Goes On, but It's Not the Same	176
	Some Lessons Learned	177
	Measuring Financial Instruments—Amortized Cost Versus Fair Value	182
	Some Arguments for Using Amortized Cost	183
	Some Arguments for Using Fair Value	184
	So, Who Is Right?	185
	Another Alternative	186
	Continuing Conceptual Challenges	191
6	Complexity	193
	Does It Need to Be So Complex?	193
	The Reporting Scandals and the Sarbanes-Oxley Act of 2002	194
	Conceptual Controversy and Complexity	196
	Asset and Liability View	197
	Revenue and Expense View	197
	My Opinion	200
	An Example	201
	Back to Concepts	201

Table of Contents

Chapter		Page
6	Complexity—continued	
	Theory and Practice	202
	Suggestions on an Overhaul of the Accounting Framework	203
	Can We Handle a More Principles-Based System?	206
	A Call to Action	208
	CIFiR	210
	Disclosure Overload	215
	Can Technology Help?	218
	Private Company Reporting	219
	The Private Company Financial Reporting Committee, IFRS for Small and Medium Enterprises, and Other Initiatives	221
	Blue-Ribbon Panel	224
	FAF Working Group and Increased FASB Focus on Private Companies	225
	FAF Proposes Establishing a Private Company Standards Improvement Council	226
	The FAF Establishes the Private Company Council and a New Process for Setting Private Company Accounting Standards	228
	So Where Are We on Complexity?	230
	Conclusion	235
7	Looking Back and Moving Forward	237
	Proud Accomplishments	244
	Opportunities for Further Improvement	247
	Some Regrets, Mistakes, and Disappointments	249
	Changes in Financial Reporting—A Challenging but Necessary Process	250
	Some Words of Advice to Colleagues and Successors	253
	So, What Now, Bob?	256
	People Mentioned in This Book	263

Foreword

Prepared by
Daniel L. Jensen, PhD

Bob was a leader on the forefront of financial reporting during a time of unprecedented challenge for accounting, auditing, and financial reporting. Born in New York City in 1953 and raised in New Jersey for much of his childhood, his father was a well-known commodities trader who moved the family to Buenos Aires, Argentina, when he was fourteen years old. He attended an Anglo-Argentine school built on the English public school model; that led him to England and the University of Manchester where he took a degree in economics, graduating at the top of his class in 1974 with first class honors—and a full head of long hair. During his three years at Manchester, he also studied accounting under the direction of Sir Bryan Carsberg, later Secretary General of the International Accounting Standards Committee, and Professors John Arnold and Tony Hope, all of whom encouraged him to pursue a career in accounting.

Following graduation he joined Price Waterhouse in Manchester, where he qualified as a Chartered Accountant. He reports that the United Kingdom's low salaries and highly progressive taxes convinced him and his wife, Louise, to move to the United States in 1978. The following year, he joined the Boston office of Coopers & Lybrand and shortly thereafter passed the CPA Exam, winning the Gold Medal for the highest score in Massachusetts and the Elijah Watt Sells Award nationally. In 1980, he was transferred to the national office in New York City where he was immersed in both client engagements and technical research projects. He was named a partner in 1985, becoming senior technical partner in 1996 and continuing in a similar position at the merged firm of PricewaterhouseCoopers in 1998.

Accounting Changes: Chronicles of Convergence, Crisis, and Complexity

Bob's passion for accounting and for improving the information provided to financial markets led to his appointment in 2002 as Chairman of the Financial Accounting Standards Board, following the term of Edmund L. Jenkins. Enron Corporation had collapsed in a financial reporting scandal, WorldCom would shortly follow, and the Sarbanes-Oxley Act was in the works. The latter led the Securities and Exchange Commission to formally re-designate the FASB as the recognized U.S. accounting standard-setter. As the new FASB Chairman, Bob led a concerted effort to improve and simplify both the standards and the process by which they are developed and to pursue convergence of U.S. and international standards. A central outcome of this effort was the comprehensive reorganization of U.S. accounting standards which brought together in a coherent codification some 2000 individual authoritative pronouncements issued by various organizations and agencies over more than half a century.

A second important outcome was the signing of the "Norwalk Agreement" in October 2002, in which the FASB and the IASB agreed in principle to work toward convergence of their standards. In the years that followed, joint teams made progress on accounting for stock-based compensation, business combinations, financial instruments, consolidations, revenue recognition, lease accounting, financial statement presentation, as well as other standards.

A third among the many important outcomes under Bob's watch as chairman was the issuance of a major standard to clarify the general meaning of fair value in financial reporting. The new standard described the different techniques for measuring fair value and provided a framework for related disclosure in the financial statements. The new standard was intended to improve fair value reporting in areas where it was already required or permitted and to augment long-existing rules on lower-of-cost-or-market and asset impairment and has also now become the basis of the international standard on fair value measurement.

During this period Bob appeared repeatedly before Congressional committees and was a highly effective spokesman for an independent accounting standard-setting process, free from inappropriate political intervention or override. In addition, he worked extensively with the SEC, the PCAOB, the Treasury Department, other national accounting standard setters, and both U.S. and international bank regulators. Together with his fellow Board members, he enhanced the outreach to investors and the input the FASB receives from investors, small and private companies, not-for-profit entities, and the academic community.

His tenure with the FASB caps a long and extraordinary record of service to his firm, to the accounting profession, to the capital markets, and to the public interest. He served as a founding member of the IASB, a member of the Emerging Issues Task Force, and as chair and member of many other AICPA committees and task forces. He was the first Chairman of the Transnational Auditors Committee of the International Federation of Accountants and served as a member of numerous other committees and advisory boards including the New York Stock Exchange International Capital Markets Advisory Committee, various SEC and U.S. Treasury advisory committees, and the Prince of Wales' International Integrated Reporting Committee.

As an audit partner and leader of his firm's Corporate Finance Advisory Services, he worked extensively with major corporations, investment banks, and private equity funds. As the senior technical partner of Coopers & Lybrand and PwC, he was responsible for firm policies on accounting, auditing, and professional matters, resolution of client practice issues, risk management and practice quality, and firm publications and communications on accounting, auditing, and professional developments. He also served as a member of PwC's U.S. and Global Boards, and as president of the C&L and PwC Foundations, and as a member of the investment, compensation, finance, and human capital committees.

Bob has also written extensively on accounting, auditing, finance, and business subjects. He has authored or coauthored five books and monographs and over 40 articles published in professional and academic journals. His books include the influential *The ValueReporting Revolution: Moving Beyond the Earnings*, coauthored with Robert Eccles, E. Mary Keegan, and David Phillips and published in 2001. In addition, he has delivered over 40 invited lectures at universities throughout the United States and in many other countries.

His honors and awards include an honorary doctorate from his alma mater, the University of Manchester, and recognitions of his distinguished contributions to accounting and financial management by many other organizations and institutions.

Currently, he is Executive in Residence on the faculty of Columbia University Business School. In 2011, he joined the Board of Directors of Fannie Mae and serves on their audit , nominating and corporate governance, and strategic initiatives committees and has recently joined the board of directors and audit committee of Morgan Stanley. In addition, he serves on many other boards and advisory groups including, the Accounting Standards Oversight Council of Canada, the Financial Reporting Faculty of the Institute of Chartered Accountants in England and Wales, the Standing Advisory Group of the PCAOB, WebFilings LLC, AccountAbility, and the Kessler Foundation.

He and his wife, Louise, have two grown children, Michael and Nicole, and live in South Orange, New Jersey, where he has participated in civic and school district budgetary administration. He is the 89th member of The Accounting Hall of Fame: Robert Henry Herz.

Prepared by Professor Daniel L. Jensen, *Deloitte & Touche Emeritus Professor of Accounting,* Department of Accounting & MIS, Fisher College of Business, Ohio State University, Columbus, Ohio, in honor of the induction of Robert Herz to the Accounting Hall of Fame.

Professor Jensen is the Director of the Master of Accounting Program in the Fisher College of Business. His research on cost accounting and auditing topics has been published in various journals including *The Accounting Review* and the *Journal of Accounting Research*. He has co-authored two textbooks and edited various books and collections including six volumes of collected writings in the Accounting Hall of Fame Series in Accounting History.

From 1993 to 1995, Professor Jensen was Director of Publications for the American Accounting Association, chaired the Association's Committee on Publications, and served on its Executive Committee. He has served as editor of *Issues in Accounting Education* and on the editorial boards of various scholarly journals; in addition, he is a Trustee of the Academy of Accounting Historians and has served as its president. He has taught cost accounting and management control courses in the Ohio State Accounting Honors Program for over twenty years in addition to other graduate and undergraduate accounting courses, and has chaired the Accounting Hall of Fame Committee since 1994.

Before joining The Ohio State University in 1980 as the Ernst & Young Professor of Accounting, Professor Jensen was a member of the accounting faculties at the University of Illinois at Urbana-Champaign and at Purdue University and served as a visiting professor at Indiana University at Bloomington. A Certified Public Accountant, he received his bachelors and masters degrees from the University of Minnesota (1962, 1964). In 1991, Professor Jensen received the Outstanding Ohio Accounting Educator Award.

Preface

I retired as Chairman of the Financial Accounting Standards Board (FASB) on September 30, 2010. For me, it marked the end of nearly a decade in accounting standard setting at the highest level, first as a member of the newly created International Accounting Standards Board (IASB) in 2001–02 and then for more than eight years at the FASB. It was a fascinating, challenging, and personally very satisfying part of my career and my life and, more importantly, a period of significant change, challenge, and opportunity for financial reporting, both in the United States and internationally.

Soon after leaving the FASB, I was encouraged by a number of parties to write a book about my years as an accounting standard setter. My perspective on these matters, they said, would be both informative and interesting, as I had been involved in and had a "front row seat" on many of the major developments affecting accounting and financial reporting during this period: the reporting scandals of 2001 and 2002, the recent global financial crisis, and efforts at international convergence of accounting standards. Some even went so far as to say I had a responsibility to accounting history to share my insights and views on these events and developments.

Although such encouragement was both flattering and may have had the intended effect of engendering a bit of a sense of responsibility (or perhaps better said, guilt), I thought long and hard before committing to write this book. My prior experiences in authoring books, papers, and articles had taught me that publishing can be a lengthy and consuming process. Moreover, upon leaving the FASB, I had quickly undertaken several new roles and activities in pursuit of new and different challenges. I wrestled for a while with any trade-offs that could arise in terms of my personal, professional, and business activities, but in the end, I decided to give this book a go, believing I could provide a relevant and interesting chronicle of some of the major events, developments, and forces in the world of accounting and financial reporting during the past decade, along with my perspectives on these matters.

Having made that decision, I then asked myself whether the book should cover more than my tenure at the FASB and IASB. In other words, should I get really ambitious and write about my entire personal life and career to date? On the one hand, I could share adventures from my childhood in the United States, my teenage years in Argentina, my years as a student and budding accountant in England, then as a partner with Coopers & Lybrand and PricewaterhouseCoopers (PwC), and as a husband, and father. On the other hand, such an autobiography would clearly be a major undertaking, and some of these experiences, though interesting, would probably be of little relevance to most of the likely readers of a book authored by me.

So, I settled on a middle ground. I wrote chapter 1, "My First 49 Years," with the intent to summarize my life before accounting—although it is hard to imagine such a time existed—and my almost three decades in the profession prior to joining the IASB and FASB. My goal was to describe some of the key forces, experiences, and people that I believe have shaped a number of my perspectives as a professional and as a person. I believe we are, at least in part, products of our background and experiences, so understanding where a person has been before is important in understanding where he is now in terms of views, actions, and dealings with others. Certainly, my international background and many years in the accounting profession have affected my thinking and perspectives. I must confess, however, that writing the first chapter was rather enjoyable. It gave me an opportunity to fondly reminisce about where I have been, the tremendous professional opportunities I have been afforded, and the many wonderful people with whom I have been blessed to share life's journey.

I then moved on to the core chapters of this book, which cover what I regard as the more noteworthy events and developments in accounting standard setting and financial reporting during my years as Chairman of the FASB. In doing so, and in order to try to communicate key aspects of these matters, I selected numerous passages from my own speeches and Congressional testimony and those of many others, as well excerpts from relevant articles and media accounts and other publicly available sources.

FASB board and staff members have a common statement in the opening of speeches and presentations: "The views are my own and do not represent official positions of the Financial Accounting Standards Board that are arrived at only after extensive public due process and deliberations." Throughout the book, I provide my perspectives on various developments, events, and key issues. It is important for readers to understand that, to the extent I have expressed personal views, those views are my own. As well, in order to be even-handed, I have included the perspectives of others on some key issues. I have certainly found throughout my years that informed and reasonable people can and often do have differing views on particular matters. So, I apologize in advance to those readers who may have a different point of view than mine if you think I have not fully or fairly captured your perspectives on those issues.

The FASB's activities are covered on a regular basis by a variety of media, and its meetings are conducted "in the sunshine" through webcasts, meeting minutes, project descriptions, summaries of Board decisions, FASB standards and proposals, and comment letters on Board projects, all of which are available on FASB's website. Although the matters discussed in chapters 2–6 are matters of public information and not intended to provide a comprehensive history of the activities of the FASB during my years there or of financial reporting developments over that period, my hope is that this book will contribute to the historical understanding of this period in accounting and financial reporting. I hope that it also makes for interesting reading.

So, which of the multitude of standard-setting activities of the FASB and events and developments in financial reporting have I chosen to write about? Chapter 2, "Charting Course," deals with the key strategic objectives and resulting initiatives we developed early on in my tenure as Chairman of the FASB. Chapter 3, "Stock Option Controversies—Take Two," recounts the background, controversy, and principal events relating to our exploration of the issues surrounding the accounting for employee stock options. Chapter 4, "International Convergence," covers the many facets and milestones in our convergence efforts with the IASB, as well as some of the key events in the Securities and Exchange Commission's (SEC's) ongoing consideration of International Financial Reporting Standards. In chapter 5, "The Financial Crisis," I discuss the global financial crisis, focusing on the financial reporting issues emanating from it and our standard-setting actions in response to those issues. Chapter 6, "Complexity," attempts to address the complexity inherent in accounting and financial reporting. Finally, in chapter 7, "Looking Back and Moving Forward," I review what has been, and what I believe will continue to be, a period of challenge, change, and opportunity in accounting and financial reporting and in my life after accounting standard setting. In doing so, I could not resist the temptation to offer a few modest suggestions to those with continuing responsibility for accounting standards and the financial reporting system.

Acknowledgments

As expected, writing this book turned out to be quite an undertaking. I am indebted to many people at the AICPA who contributed to the effort, including Arleen Rodda Thomas, Senior Vice President, a long-time colleague in the profession, and one of the first to encourage me to write this book; Amy Plent, Director of Publications Product Development; Martin Censor; Andrew Grow, whose excellent comments and suggestions on my initial draft of the manuscript helped improve it greatly; Suzanne Morgen, who located numerous articles and other citations that added to the relevance and contemporaneous feel of my chronicles; and to the talented copyeditors and graphic designers at the AICPA.

Beyond the people directly involved with this book, I need to thank scores of people who were my mentors, colleagues, and friends during my career. In terms of my years at the FASB, that starts with those who served with me as FASB board members—George Batavick, G. Michael Crooch, John (Neal) Foster, Thomas Linsmeier, Katherine Schipper, Gary Schieneman, Leslie Seidman, Marc Siegel, Lawrence Smith, Edward Trott, Donald Young, and John Wulff—and those who served as FASB staff directors and assistant directors during this period: Suzanne Bielstein, Susan Cosper, Russell Golden, Ronald Lott, Linda MacDonald, Jeffrey Mechanick, Kim Petrone, Peter Proestakes, Lawrence Smith, and Kevin Stoklosa. Perhaps most of all, I want to express my heartfelt thanks to the members of the FASB technical staff for all their dedication and hard work. They include some of the finest professionals I have had the honor and pleasure of working with over my career. I'd like to personally thank each of them, but let me just mention some of the lead managers on key projects during my years at the FASB: Holly Barker, Ken Bement, Bob Bhave, Ron Bossio, Halsey Bullen, Jules Cassel, Regina Cafini, Nick Cappiello, Pat Donoghue, Phil Hood, Jeff Johnson, Todd Johnson, Nobu Kawanishi, Kim Petrone, Peter

Proestakes, Brooke Richards, Chris Roberge, Kevin Stoklosa, Jenny Sullivan, Jill Switter, Michael Tovey, Bob Wilkins, Jeff Wilks, and Danielle Zeyher. I also need to thank the two FASB senior investor liaisons, Chandy Smith and Jeff Brickman, who work hard to make sure the Board receives input from investors and users of financial information on standard-setting projects. There were also many Fellows from the major accounting firms, industry, and academia who greatly contributed to the standard-setting efforts of the FASB and the Emerging Issues Task Force and the many post-graduate technical assistants who spent a year at the FASB after graduating from major universities with top accounting programs.

A very special thanks to Michele Kilcran, my absolutely invaluable and extremely capable assistant throughout my more than eight years at the FASB; to other key members of the FASB support staff, including Len Tatore, Jane Gabriele, Judy Solo, Joanne Romas, Karen Kosminoff, Patty Lapolla, Mary Hyudic, Debby Monroe, Stacey Sutay, Joe Damico, Eileen Mishley, Steve Jaroszynski, J.R. Richter, and Joe Vernuccio; and to Jeff Mahoney, Chris Allen, Grace Hinchman, and Allen Weltmann in Washington, D.C., and Ned Regan who also provided help and advice on a variety of matters. With great memories of being a member of our Financial Accounting Foundation (FAF) softball and volleyball teams, I also want to thank everyone who participated in those after-work activities. We had some good years and some not so good years in terms of results but always a fun time and wonderful camaraderie. I had known Ed Trott for many years before joining the FASB but had not realized that, in addition to his accounting skills, he is also an excellent softball pitcher.

My sincere appreciation to Richard Swift and Dennis Chookaszian for very ably chairing FASB's principal advisory group, the Financial Accounting Standards Advisory Council, during my years at the FASB and to Terri Polley, Alicia Posta, Karen Guasp, and Roberta Small who coordinated the activities of our many advisory groups. Thanks to all who served on these advisory groups.

My thanks and appreciation to those who helped guide the FAF by serving as trustees, under the leadership of Manley Johnson, Robert Denham, and John Brennan and to those who served as trustees of IASC (now IFRS) Foundation, which was chaired by Paul Volcker during my time on the IASB. Your public service, support, and stewardship of the FAF, FASB, the Governmental Accounting Standards Board (GASB), and IASB are vital to private-sector accounting standard setting. Thank you to the terrific staff of the FAF, including Terri Polley, the late Joe La Gambina, Bob DeSantis, Jodi Dottori, Janet Brody, Roseann Plank, Ron Guerrette, Steve Getz, Doris Rogers, Elaine Blackman, Bob Kalina, Ginny Cintron, Charry Boris, Miriam Solomon,

Laura Ferrera, Peter Spencer, Lisa Pittu, John Dreibelbis, John Alusik, Neal McGarity, Christine Klimek, and Gerard Carney. Thanks also to members of the IFRS Foundation staff under the leadership of Tom Seidenstein. Many thanks to all who worked on the Codification and eXtensible Business Reporting Language projects, including Tom Hoey, Ellen Crowhurst, Scott Logan, Denise Moritz, Jim Green, Debby Monroe, Susan Miller, Mary Hyudic, Vickie Lusniak, Neal Hannon, and Louis Matherne. I also very much appreciated the ability to interact with members and staff of GASB, our sister standard setter in Norwalk, Connecticut, including Tom Allen, Bob Attmore, and David Bean.

Throughout my years at the FASB, we worked closely with our colleagues at the IASB. So, my thanks to my good friend David Tweedie and all his fellow IASB Board members, many of whom I served with on that board when it was first established, and to the directors and staff of the IASB, whose hard work, collegiality, and spirit of teamwork with our staff greatly contributed to the joint standard-setting activities of the FASB and IASB. I owe a very special thanks to Jim Leisenring, who has been a colleague and friend for many years and who, during my years as Chairman of the FASB, served as the liaison between the two boards. Jim, together with some of the veterans of accounting standard setting at the FASB and the IASB, such as Jules Cassel, Todd Johnson, Ron Bossio, Bob Wilkins, and Wayne Upton, were often invaluable to me and others in putting things in a historical context. From time to time, I would seek and receive wise counsel from former FASB Chairmen Ed Jenkins, Denny Beresford, and Don Kirk and from other former FASB members, such as Walter Schuetze and Bob Swieringa.

During my years at the FASB, I had the opportunity and pleasure to work with many people in various departments and agencies of the U.S. government, probably most notably with commissioners and staff of the SEC. I thank them for their dedication to investor protection and for their help and support of the FASB's mission and activities. I also thank the members and staff of the Public Company Accounting Oversight Board (PCAOB) with whom we worked on many matters involving the financial reporting system.

The first chapter of this book briefly covers my career at PwC and predecessor firms. I owe hundreds of people so much for whatever success I achieved at the firm and in the profession. Although there are far too many to acknowledge and thank in this preface, I am glad I was able to mention a number of them in chapter 1 and pleased and proud that many of them continue as my friends to this day. My special thanks to my long-term colleagues and friends, Sam DiPiazza and Dan Jensen, for their very kind words that were excerpted from their "Remarks" at my induction to the Accounting Hall of Fame in August,

2012. Chapter 7 notes some of some of my current activities with many fine organizations and terrific people.

Last and most importantly, I owe my deepest thanks to my family. That begins with my loving father and mother, both of whom passed away many years ago. They ensured that I received a good upbringing and solid education and enabled me to experience living in different countries. By far, my most profound thanks need to go to my wife, Louise, and our two children, Michael and Nicole. For nearly 30 years, my work had me on the road much of the time. Even when I was at home or on family vacations, work was a constant companion because I would frequently have to disappear into, and devote my attention to, as they termed it, "numberland." Their patience, understanding, and constant support and encouragement have been my greatest source of strength over the years. Now, being able to spend more time with my family is my greatest source of happiness and satisfaction in life.

Chapter 1: My First 49 Years

In this book, I focus primarily on the work and key activities of the FASB during my chairmanship from July 2002 to September 2010 and I offer my perspectives on these matters and the major forces affecting the FASB's work during that period. However, because our background and experiences help shape our perspectives, actions, and dealings with others, knowing where a person has come from is important in understanding that person's outlook.

So, in this chapter, I will offer a high level sketch of the first 49 years of my life: the years before accounting—though it's hard now to imagine such a time existed—and then the nearly 3 decades I spent in the profession before joining the FASB. Along with giving readers insight to my perspectives, this gives me an opportunity to reminisce a bit about some of the key experiences, forces, and people that have shaped my life and thinking. I have fond recollections of those years and I feel blessed to have been afforded tremendous opportunities in life, to have a wonderful family, and, in the course of my life's journey, to have formed many lasting friendships.

Jersey Boy

I was born on June 18, 1953, at Lenox Hill Hospital in New York City. My father, James Herz, was a native New Yorker and fairly well-known commodity trader. My mother, Susan Herz, the daughter of a rabbi, grew up in Germany in the 1920s and 1930s, fled with her older brother to Manchester, England, in 1939, and later joined her parents in Argentina, where, in 1946, she met my dad who was in Buenos Aires working for the U.S. government. They were soon married and moved to the United States.

I am an only child. My birth was uneventful, except for the following anecdote my father would ritualistically recount each year on my birthday. My dad was a lifelong Yankees fan. Back in 1953, it was rare for husbands to be present at the births of their children. So, on the evening of my birth, my dad travelled uptown from his work on Wall Street to Lenox Hill to visit my mom and his new son. Well, Lenox Hill was the official hospital of the Yankees, and as luck would have it, Joe DiMaggio, who had retired a couple years prior, was there that evening. When he saw Mr. DiMaggio, my father, never the bashful one, went up to him, got his autograph, and briefly chatted with him. From then on, my birthday became known as the greatest day in the life of my dad, not because of the birth of his only son but because it was the day he met the "Yankee Clipper."

So it was with that twist of fate and good fortune for my dad that my life began. We lived in New York City until I was about two years old. Then, as was the case for so many in those days, we moved out to the suburbs in Maplewood, NJ. I would say we were upper middle class, and Maplewood was one of the nicer suburbs close to New York City. It had a lovely village center that has a New England look and feel, a good school system, and lots of nice tree-lined streets and big houses. We lived in a five-bedroom colonial on a quiet street. My readers will soon come to recognize that a lot of my life has revolved around three places, the New York City area, including Maplewood and its sister town South Orange; Buenos Aires, Argentina; and Manchester, England. But I'm getting ahead of myself.

We lived in that house in Maplewood for the next 12 years. I went to the Maplewood-South Orange public schools and had loads of friends. On our block alone, one of less than 20 houses, were about a dozen boys within 2 years each side of my age. We were constant after-school and weekend companions, playing softball, touch-football, half-court basketball, and other sports and games, depending on the season and weather. We went to Yankees games, first with our dads but later on our own, and to Knicks and Rangers games at Madison Square Garden. We went to Radio City Music Hall and to rock concerts. (I was at the Beatles concert in Shea Stadium.) We were on the town little league teams and would go fishing and hunting for salamanders in the "Reservation" (the 2,000 acre county forest that was only a short walking distance from our block).

In summer, most of us went to camp. First, it was day camp a bit further out in New Jersey, and later, I and a number of my classmates from school went to sleep-away camp (Camp Mah-Kee-Nac in the Berkshires in western Massachusetts) for eight weeks each summer.

Chapter 1: My First 49 Years

Before and after the weeks of camp, it was, as words of the Billy Joel song "Allentown" go, "weekends on the Jersey Shore"—day trips to Deal, Asbury Park, Point Pleasant, and Long Beach Island; long weekends in Atlantic City, Wildwood, and Cape May; and February school breaks in Miami Beach.

Then there was school. Modesty aside, from third grade on, I was always either top of my class or in the top 2 or 3. I guess I was always somewhat risk averse (perhaps an early sign of the accountant in me) and would try to stay ahead of things: doing my homework before going out to play and reading ahead in textbooks. My mother was always a source of encouragement and help—verbally testing me the evening before a big test. In junior high, I got straight As (even some A+s), was always on the honor roll, and represented the school in math bowls against neighboring schools. Most of us were Jewish but of the Reform or Conservative variety, far less observant than orthodox Jews. We went to Sunday School and midweek Hebrew classes through the age of 13, until our Bar Mitzvahs liberated us. As was the custom of the time among our crowd, we all had big Bar and Bat Mitzvah parties, not only in celebration of our passage into adulthood (or at least the very early stages of it) but also as a necessary and expected business and social affair for our parents.

Such was my life until the age of 14; nothing out of the ordinary for the times and many other such Jersey boys who grew up in the suburbs during the 1950s and 1960s. I have very fond memories of it, and ultimately, it was something I wanted and chose to try to replicate for my kids. But big changes in my life were soon to occur.

Don't Cry for Me Argentina

One evening in 1968 my father and mother told me we were moving to Buenos Aires, Argentina. My father, who now worked at Bunge, a company with large operations in Argentina, was being transferred there. I think, however, that it also had something to do with my mother and her desire to be with her parents while they were still alive (and indeed both her parents died in 1969). I guess the move had been in the works for a while, but it took me by surprise. I had been to Argentina a couple times to visit my mom's family—her parents and her brother and his wife and some other aunts, uncles, and cousins all lived there. So, although I was familiar with Buenos Aires and had some good memories of times with my mom's family, the news was crushing. Leaving my lifelong buddies and the home and life that were so familiar and comfortable was daunting. I did not speak Spanish (and, in fact, had been taking French lessons in junior high). I did not play soccer, and there would be no more Yankees games or going to the Jersey Shore.

Accounting Changes: Chronicles of Convergence, Crisis, and Complexity

But off we went. We quickly settled into an apartment in a high-rise building in the Belgrano section of Buenos Aires. It was a large two-bedroom apartment in a nice area, but it wasn't Maplewood. Moreover, I was enrolled in an Anglo-Argentine School—St. Andrews Scots School in terms of the Anglo part and San Andres in terms of the Argentine part—that was very much like an English "public" (to Americans, private) school, and I had to wear a school jacket and tie every day. Worse yet, it was outside the city and unlike Maplewood where I walked to school, I now had to take two buses (*collectivos*) each way to get to school.

Faced with such a change, one can choose to sink or swim. I chose to swim. With regard to learning Spanish (or *Castellano*, the Argentinian version of Spanish), I guess I went through something similar to what infants go through. When I arrived in Argentina, I could barely speak a few words of Spanish. By six months I could get by, and within one year, I was virtually fluent at a conversational level. At first, school was a challenge: the curriculum was new and foreign, and the classes were very different than I was used to. Over time, I adjusted. I made lots of new friends at school and in a co-ed Jewish youth group my relatives introduced me to.

Buenos Aires is a beautiful and vibrant city. To this day, along with London, it is one of my two favorite cities in the world. Perhaps that is because I have very fond memories of my time there—my "wonder years" so to speak. The activities of the youth group (*el grupo*) became the center of my new life. Again, to this day, I continue some of the friendships I formed in those years, periodically visiting Buenos Aires and catching up with friends and their growing families, as well as my relatives. On weekends, we would go by bus to a club outside the city in a town called Banfield. It was something like a country club, with a large swimming pool, tennis courts, soccer, basketball, and volleyball and a somewhat dilapidated clubhouse with a restaurant. Soccer and volleyball replaced touch football and softball. During the week, we would meet at a facility in the city and go out to eat and to movies and other events—all as a group. We also went on camping trips to various parts of Argentina, including beautiful locations such as Bariloche in the southern Andes. In 1971, my final year there, my steady girlfriend was a member of the group, as were my two best friends and their steady girlfriends who they went on to marry.

I also travelled to various places in Argentina with my parents: Cordoba, Mendoza, and the beaches south of Buenos Aires that are in every way as nice as the New Jersey beaches, such as Mar del Plata, Miramar, and Villa Gesell. I became a fan of the *futbol* (to Americans, soccer) team Boca Juniors and would go to games in La Bombonera stadium.

Chapter 1: My First 49 Years

Throughout my years in Argentina, the country experienced chronic and severe hyperinflation and constant devaluations of the currency. Although painful to observe, it gave me an early understanding of, and grounding in, a number of economic and financial concepts that would serve me well in my career.

In short, after several years there, I began to feel like an Argentinian, a *porteño* as the inhabitants of Buenos Aires call themselves. But time was moving on, and another round of change was in store for me.

Rule Britannia

In school in Argentina, my studies were based on the British system, and I took what are called the "O" (ordinary) and "A" (advanced) level examinations that are required to get into British universities. So it was that in August 1971, I left Argentina and went to England to attend the University of Manchester. I had dabbled with the idea of staying in Argentina and going to university there, but despite my fondness for Buenos Aires, my Argentinian friends, and my girlfriend, after some soul searching, I realized my future did not lie in Argentina. I had also considered returning to the United States for college and had taken the SATs, but perhaps largely due to encouragement from my father who believed a British education and European experience would be good for my future (not to mention that it would be a lot cheaper than a U.S. college education—a major plus from my father's point of view), I decided to give England a go. I chose Manchester for a few reasons. First, I was interested in "reading" (studying) economics. My understanding was that, at that time, the top three English universities in economics were Cambridge, the London School of Economics, and the University of Manchester. Getting into Cambridge would have required another round of examinations and a delay of one year in starting university. I chose Manchester because of its history as the cradle of the Industrial Revolution, its reputation for free thinking, and because my mother had some relatives there.

My father had retired, so my parents accompanied their only child to Manchester. We settled into a two-bedroom apartment on the second floor of a house in the Didsbury section of Manchester. I began classes at the university in September 1971. One of my classmates was a fellow named Stephen Moss, who would become and remain one of my best friends in life. Like me, he lived with his parents in an apartment on the same street in Didsbury. He had lived in Manchester for many years and, unlike me, he had a car. So, with his help and that of my relatives, I soon got into the Manchester scene.

Then, in March of 1972, I met the most important person in my life, Louise, who later became my wife. We met at a youth group whose stated purpose was to do voluntary charitable services, but like *el grupo* in Buenos Aires, it had a major social aspect to it as well. Stephen Moss also met his first wife, Leah, Louise's best friend, that night. By June, I was going steady with Louise, and Stephen was going steady with Leah. The four of us became inseparable. I was the best man at Stephen's wedding to Leah, and he was the best man at Louise's and mine. We all remain close friends to this day, despite Stephen and Leah's breakup in 1990. I was in England until April 1978 when Louise and I moved to Miami as newlyweds. But again, I'm getting ahead of myself.

I had fun during my three years in university but I also received a solid education. I did well academically, achieving the prize for top student each year. In my second year, I took some classes in accounting and found that I liked the subject and was good at it. My economics courses gave me a solid grounding in both macro- and microeconomics and finance, and I saw accounting as a real-world process of capturing the financial and economic activities of enterprises. In my third year at university, three influences shaped my decision to take more accounting courses: the onset of the recession of 1973–74, better job prospects in accounting than in economics, and encouragement from key faculty members, such as Bryan Carsberg, John Arnold, and Tony Hope.

In addition to my academic pursuits, I travelled around England and Europe, both with Stephen and as a member of the University of Manchester volleyball team—we won the U.K. equivalent of the NCAA championship in 1972–73. We went to "football" (soccer) games: Stephen and Leah were "supporters" (fans) of Manchester City, but Louise was a Manchester United fan. We went to rock concerts and spent many evenings, if not most, in pubs, some of them local and some more far afield in the Lancashire, Yorkshire, and Derbyshire countryside.

The Early Accountant

I graduated from the University of Manchester in June 1974 and joined the Manchester office of Price Waterhouse (PW) soon after. The British system is one in which you join as an articled clerk, similar to an apprenticeship. I spent the first 3 years on a variety of audit engagements. Some were large (Shell Oil, Courtaulds, Ingersoll-Rand, and Carborundum) and some much smaller (William Birtwistle Damasks Ltd. and Edgar Pickering Looms Ltd—in those days, Manchester and the surrounding area were the textile capital of England). I was also learning how to prepare company tax returns. Though I was paid very little—my salary the first year was £800, or under $1,500—the firm sent me for 8 weeks a year to full-time training courses in preparation for the chartered accountant (CA) examinations. Those exams are, in my

Chapter 1: My First 49 Years

opinion, much harder and deeper than the U.S. CPA exams. I believe the early training I received at PW Manchester made me a solid accountant and sound professional, notwithstanding the frequent liquid lunches at work.

Looking back on my time with PW in England, some aspects of it now seem rather quaint and almost Dickensian. As an articled clerk, one enters into an employment and training contract under a partner. My partner was a fellow named Charles Godwin, who one year or so after I joined PW became head of the Manchester office. In addressing or referring to a partner, we used their initials, not their first or second names. So, Charles Godwin was CRG, not Charles or Mr. Godwin. All of the audit managers were male and we generally addressed and referred to them as Mr. _____. The partners were all on one floor, with managers and staff on other floors. Two of the more senior career managers in the Manchester office were Mr. Beech and Mr. Halsall. I seem to recall that Mr. Beech's first name was Alan, and Mr. Halsall's was Tom, but I could be wrong because we rarely referred to them by their first names. They were very experienced, salt of the earth individuals who seemed to have great pride in the profession.

Back in those days, most of the accounting records were kept manually in large bound books. In some cases, companies had mechanical ledger card systems, and in a few larger companies and financial institutions, there were the beginnings of computerized systems. We would leave tick marks on certain company records as evidence they had been officially audited or inspected. Our audit working papers were written in ink, and if you made a mistake, you were not supposed to cross it out or white it out; instead, you had to rewrite the entire page.

I can still remember quite vividly some of the more colorful experiences and characters I met while working as a young accountant in England. I could recount many, but I will spare you by telling about only one of them. One year, on December 31, I was assigned to observe the year-end stock taking (inventory count) at a distribution depot of a company that made ceramic pipes. The depot was in southern Scotland, just across the English border. I "motored up" the M6 motorway, arriving at the depot in the middle of the afternoon in what was becoming something of a raging blizzard. Upon arriving, I was greeted by the manager of the depot who informed me that because many of the ceramic pipes were stored outside in the depot yard and due to the impending snowstorm, they had done the stock take that morning. After finishing the stock take, the rest of the depot staff had gone to the local pub to get an early jump on New Year's Eve celebrations. This presented an obvious problem for this erstwhile junior auditor. Undaunted, I explained to the depot manager that I really needed to get some audit assurance on the accuracy of the stock take, so I told

7

him that I would need do a sample of test counts, recounting particular items of inventory myself and comparing my count with that noted on the count sheets done by the depot staff. Somewhat grudgingly, the depot manager, a rather crusty Scotsman, acceded to my request. So I proceeded to do my test counts, finding that the depot staff had in almost every instance properly tallied up the number of items. After approximately one hour, the depot manager, quite impatient with all this, asked me in a sharp tone of voice, "Had enough yet, lad?"

I politely told him, "Almost done, sir," and pointing to a large pile of s-bend pipes that were stacked up in the yard, I said I would make that pile my final count. Just one minor problem: the pile was covered in snow, and many of the pipes were partially frozen together. So I asked that we brush off the snow and try to lay out the individual pipes to facilitate my count. We began doing that. Inevitably, as we tried to separate pipes, some of them cracked. The depot manager was not amused, expressing his anger in words I shall not repeat here. In the end, I counted 220 s-bends in the pile, a total that exactly matched that in the stock take sheets. I did, however, note in my working papers that approximately 50 of the pipes appeared damaged and should be evaluated for write-off. An early lesson in the law of unintended consequences!

In 1977, I passed the final parts of the exams and became a CA. I had steadily risen through the staff ranks and was now an assistant manager. I also spent some time working in London, principally as a part-time computer auditor in what were the very early days of computer auditing.

Soon after I passed the exams, Louise and I vacationed in Fuengirola, Spain. It was there I asked her to marry me, and she said "Yes." At that time, I was making the princely sum of £4,500 per year. Louise was earning a bit less working at a freight forwarding firm. Taxes took much of what we earned. I was keenly aware that in the United States, accountants at my level of experience were making multiples of what I was earning. So, after discussion with Louise, we agreed we would move to the United States—the land of opportunity—once we were married. For Louise, it could not have been an easy decision to leave her homeland, family, and lifelong friends. I am forever in her debt.

Hello Miami, Goodbye Miami (and PW), and Hello Boston (and Coopers & Lybrand)

We were married on April 2, 1978, in Manchester and left England a few days later for Miami. I had asked PW for a transfer to the United States, stating New York or an office in the Northeast as my preference. PW offered me Miami because it needed bilingual people there, and I spoke Spanish. The Miami office of PW was a relatively small one. Its largest clients were Eastern Airlines and Dade County. I worked on the audits of Dade County, Eastern Airlines Credit Union, and some smaller clients. We rented a small but nice apartment in North Miami, and Louise went to work for a small freight forwarding firm.

We were to be in Miami less than 9 months. I was a qualified English CA, but the Florida professional licensing laws were such that not only would I have to take the CPA exam, but I would have do over much of my university education because it was not accredited in Florida. The prospect of spending 5–7 years in night school did not appeal to me, so I asked the folks at PW Miami for a transfer to another office in a state that recognized a British college education, so I could take the CPA exam without the need to take additional classes. When the local leadership of the Miami office refused to facilitate such a transfer, I wrote 7 letters, one to each of the other Big Eight accounting firms. Within a few weeks of writing those letters, I had agreed to join the Boston office of Coopers & Lybrand (C&L) as an audit supervisor. I recall the disbelief and disdain of the personnel partner of PW Miami when I told him I was leaving to join C&L, a firm he clearly regarded as inferior to PW. Little did we both know that 20 years later, the 2 firms would merge and that I would be higher in the ranks of the merged firm than he.

In fact, the Boston office of C&L was a powerhouse. It was almost as large as the New York office and had a dominant position in most segments of the marketplace. There was a clear "work hard, play hard" ethos and an overriding sense of pride in being there. Louise and I moved into a townhouse in a development in Norwood, a suburb of Boston.

Despite my U.K. training and work at PW, C&L welcomed me, and I got some very good assignments and experience, including the audits of Stone and Webster, Hills Department Stores, and several "Route 128" technology firms. In November 1979, I took the CPA exam. I not only passed all parts, but I got the Gold Medal for the highest score in Massachusetts and the Elijah Watts Sells award nationally from the AICPA.

Unsolicited job offers began pouring in. One intrigued me: an offer to join the FASB, the U.S. accounting standards setter.

I went down to Stamford, CT, spent a day interviewing, and the FASB offered me a job as an assistant project manager. I was about to take the job, but when I informed the powers that be at C&L Boston, they quickly responded. In particular, two senior partners, Don Moran and Vin O'Reilly, seemed to recognize my potential and took me under their wings, counseled me, and persuaded me that if technical accounting work was my primary interest, a better option would be for me to join the C&L national office in New York City. They would promote me to manager and I would have a larger salary than I would at FASB. It would also allow me to move back to New Jersey, which was an important consideration because Louise was pregnant with our first child and my parents were living in Hackensack.

Return of the Prodigal Son

We bought a lovely three-bedroom colonial in Maplewood, my hometown, and we moved there in October 1980. I worked in the national office in the Exxon building on Avenue of the Americas in midtown Manhattan. Like my father before me, I became a commuter into New York City. The work was great. I was involved in following projects at the FASB, often observing their public meetings and writing up minutes that were then distributed to the practice. I was involved in writing comment letters to the FASB and SEC and I wrote alerts, practice guidance, and firm publications on accounting developments. The partners in the national office were some of the finest professionals I have worked with—Jim Quinn, Ron Murray, Fred Spindel, George Fritz, Bob Mooney, and Rick Steinberg to name a few, all leaders in the profession. I was soon able to gain a reputation within the firm as an expert in some subjects, most notably in accounting for foreign currency transactions and financial instruments. In 1981, I also took on some audit assignments in the New York office, including the audit of Dun & Bradstreet (D&B).

Our son, Michael, was born in February 1981. We would frequently visit my parents and periodically travel back to Manchester to visit family and friends, and our English friends and Louise's family would visit us in Maplewood. Life was good, but then, in January 1982, my father suddenly died of a heart attack. It was a blow to me but more so to my mom. After my father's passing, we spent most Sundays with my mom.

In early 1983, I moved full time into the New York practice office of C&L and expanded my range of clients as an audit manager. I also began to have other assignments. Perhaps the most notable of these was doing "preacquisition reviews"—due diligence reviews of a company that a client was looking to acquire—with clients such as Citicorp Venture Capital, the private equity arm of Citicorp. The partner on these engagements was Louis (Lou) Moscarello. Lou was a legend in the firm, and deservedly so. He had been the audit partner on a number of the firm's largest clients, had written books on accounting, and had broadened the range of practice activities and clients. The most memorable thing about Lou was his personality, that included a huge capacity for work, his demanding but fair treatment of all who worked for him, and his witty and penetrating one-liners. To this day, many of us who had the opportunity and good fortune to work with Lou will recount the adventures and one-liners. As an example of his quips, one day when I was balding fast and furious, I was in the men's room combing what was left of my hair when I heard Lou's voice from behind me proclaiming, "Robert, you're combing a memory!"

Working for Lou was a rite of passage into the partnership for a number of us at C&L. Some passed, and some failed. I guess I passed because in 1985 and with the support of Lou and a number of other senior partners in the New York office, including Art Simon, Tom Fitzpatrick, Harvey Bazaar, Ken Marshall, and Sy Jones, I made partner. An even more important event that year was our daughter's birth. Nicole was born in September 1985 and by then we had moved to a larger house in South Orange.

The Roaring '80s and Bad Bob

At the ripe old age of 32, I was now a partner in one of the major accounting firms. My portfolio of clients and assignments included being an audit partner on a number of major engagements—AT&T Information Systems, D&B, Shearson Lehman Brothers (Shearson), and several other clients. On each of the big jobs, I was one of the partners. We had very large teams, which made for a great *esprit de corps*. Though most of us have since left the firm, I continue to see many of my colleagues from those days: Barry Winograd and Denis Salamone from the Shearson team; Ray Pitek, Frank Tanki, Nelson Dittmar, Dick Stolz, Jerry Kelley, and Linda Ianieri from the AT&T team; and Howard Weiser and Linda Bergen from the D&B engagement.

In addition to auditing, we were involved in helping sell and, in some cases conduct, a growing range of other services, including management consulting projects, preacquisition reviews, and other attest-related services. In particular, Barry, Denis, and I were able to extend the range and size of nonaudit projects for Shearson during the late 1980s, to the point that Shearson became one of the largest C&L clients in terms of overall billings. This was quite an accomplishment given that Shearson was a subsidiary of American Express, an Arthur Young audit client. We had some very interesting audit experiences (for example, in the wake of the stock market crash on October 19, 1987, and the sharp losses suffered by some of our Wall Street audit clients).

I was also put in charge of a small but growing practice—Corporate Finance Advisory Services. This was a band of partners and staff with particular technical expertise that provided accounting and tax advice on mergers and acquisitions (M&A) and corporate finance transactions and new financial products. In effect, we provided help in structuring transactions and financial products to maximize accounting and tax opportunities. Initially, most of our clients were from the Wall Street houses: investment bankers and corporate finance people working on deals and financial products. C&L was the leading accounting firm on Wall Street in those days, with clients such as Goldman Sachs, Shearson, Drexel Burnham Lambert, Dillon Read, Brown Brothers Harriman, L.F. Rothschild, and many other securities firms and investment banks. We had an on-call service through which the "deal people" at these firms could directly access our partners and staff. Eventually, the practice grew to include a number of major corporate clients who wanted help in evaluating the accounting and tax aspects of M&A and corporate finance transactions Wall Street firms were pitching.

The Corporate Finance Advisory Services work was interesting but also demanding. We often worked on major transactions with high-powered investment bankers and their teams. Successfully serving their needs required people who were smart, creative, and knowledgeable in corporate finance and M&A and in the technical accounting and tax rules. We needed people like Warren Wintrub and David Goodrich, who were veterans of this activity, and younger, rising stars in the firm, including Woody Wallace and John Bishop on the accounting side and Phil Clements, Jules Reich, and Ed Abahoonie from the tax practice. It was a gilded age of the leveraged buyout, junk bonds, and financial engineering. Clients expected immediate answers, around the clock accessibility to us, and a can-do attitude on our part. I could recount many experiences, but the following one epitomizes the environment in which we operated.

One evening, I received a phone call from a well-known financial product developer at a major Wall Street firm. Over five minutes, he outlined a new corporate financing technique that he and his team had begun developing. He ebulliently enumerated the potential advantages of this technique to companies in terms of cost of capital and tax advantages and told me why this could be a major homerun for his firm (and him personally). He was calling me to verify the treatment for accounting and financial reporting that his team had come up with. When I told him that a particular aspect of the accounting treatment would not be as favorable as his team had described, he erupted, saying, "What? You have just managed to potentially kill one of the most revolutionary advances in corporate finance in decades! I am going to call you back in an hour and you better have a solution to the problem you just created!"

I quickly checked and double- and triple-checked the relevant accounting rules and called one of our national office partners at home to make sure I was on the right track. Approximately five minutes before the hour had elapsed, my phone rang. It was the investment banker's executive assistant calling to remind me that her boss would be calling in five minutes and that he was expecting to hear good news. Sure enough, on the strike of the hour, he called and said, "Well, have you found a way around the accounting issue?" I told him no. I apologized and said the rule was the rule. He asked, "Are you absolutely certain?" I told him "Yes." He replied "OK, I just wanted to make sure you were certain. Thanks." I went home that night several pounds lighter knowing I had given our client the best possible advice.

In the rather sparse free time between my audit assignments and the Corporate Finance Advisory Services work, I also managed to author and coauthor several monographs and articles on M&A and corporate finance topics, explaining the ins and outs of the latest techniques and products. As the securitization market grew, I also became involved with, and eventually in charge of, our services to the major commercial and investment banks in that arena.

It was heady stuff. I did it from the mid-1980s through 1993, a period of great innovation and expansion on Wall Street. The practice grew substantially, and we were involved in advising on numerous major transactions and new financial instruments and financing techniques. I became known as "Bad Bob" internally and by some of our clients for my structuring expertise, a moniker that later would sometimes be resurrected in my standard-setting role when, in considering potential accounting alternatives, I would raise the possibility for abuse through structuring.

Moreover, my experiences in transaction structuring taught me that the areas that were most ripe for designing transactions and arrangements to achieve desired accounting outcomes were those where the accounting rules departed from basic principles of economics and finance and areas where, because of the detailed requirements and many exceptions and bright lines present in the accounting rules, minor changes in the form of a transaction or arrangement could produce a large change in the resulting accounting treatment. Some of these transactions were

- arrangements designed to boost reported earnings by triggering gain recognition on appreciated assets carried on a historical cost basis while retaining the underlying risks and rewards of those assets;
- financing techniques involving the issuance of debt-like securities that were treated as equity under the accounting rules;
- financings involving equity securities and hybrid securities that were accorded favorable treatment in computing earnings and earnings per share;
- transactions designed to obtain off-balance sheet treatment, for example under lease accounting and the rules applying to special purpose entities;
- techniques designed to minimize the dilutive effects of M&A transactions through the use of pooling of interests accounting and other structures that qualified under the accounting rules as common control mergers, joint ventures, and partial combinations; and
- transactions that arbitraged the lack of discounting of future cash flows in accounting for insurance loss reserves and deferred tax assets and liabilities.

Indeed, together with colleagues at C&L, I coauthored various articles and monographs explaining the ins and outs of a number of these transaction structuring techniques.[1]

In short, during my years in transactions structuring, I learned that there were many ways to use the accounting rules to design and employ techniques to achieve desired accounting and financial reporting outcomes. In many cases, these techniques did not require significantly altering the underlying substance of the transactions and arrangements. But they did significantly change the resulting accounting in ways that might not be readily apparent to the readers of a company's financial statements. The corollary of this is that if one views such transaction structuring as an activity that runs counter to sound and transparent reporting to investors and the capital markets, then curbing such activity would require changes in accounting standards to bring them closer to economic and finance concepts, the elimination of exceptions and bright lines, and greater disclosure requirements around structured transactions. These lessons were to later affect my thinking as an accounting standard setter.

---

[1] For example, see Robert H. Herz and Edward J. Abahoonie, "Alphabet Stocks and CPUs: Innovative but Complex," *Mergers & Acquisitions*, November/December 1986, pp. 24–29; Robert H. Herz and Edward J. Abahoonie, "Innovations to Minimize Acquisition Goodwill," *Mergers & Acquisitions*, March/April 1990, pp. 35–40; and Robert H. Herz and Raymond L. Dever, John M. Bishop, and P.G. Mikael Winkvist, *Accounting for Joint Ventures and Partial Business Combinations*, Coopers & Lybrand LLP, 1995.

Poacher Turned Gamekeeper

By 1993, I had quickly risen within the ranks of the C&L partnership. In addition to the Corporate Finance Advisory Services, I continued to be an audit partner on numerous accounts and had led or been involved in many other assignments. A few years prior, the New York-based accounting firm of Oppenheim Appel & Dixon (OAD) had collapsed. OAD had a large client base in the hedge fund industry. Herman Schneider, a senior C&L tax partner and recognized expert in the tax rules and regulations relating to securities transactions, and I aggressively marketed C&L to the former OAD hedge fund clients, and we were successful in acquiring many of them for the firm. I became the audit partner on several of these accounts.

My Spanish came in handy from time to time. For example, I traveled a number of times to Mexico City in the early 1990s in connection with the privatization and initial public offering of Telmex, the state-owned Mexican telecommunications company. We had a large team working on this major project that included people from C&L Mexico; Bill Decker, who headed the rapidly growing practice in C&L that worked on cross-border offerings; a number of other U.S. partners and managers with technical accounting and SEC expertise, including Jack Parsons, Steve Derrick, John Glynn, and myself; and Steve Heindel, a partner in on our benefits consulting practice, to help deal with the pension accounting and actuarial issues relating to the offering.

Around 1990, I participated in a U.S. business delegation to Argentina. Louise accompanied me on this trip. Our visit to Buenos Aires included an official state dinner, hosted by Argentine President Carlos Menem. At the start of the event, there was a long reception line to meet the President. Upon reaching the front of the reception line and being greeted by Menem in English, I responded in Spanish (*Castellano*). Menem, perhaps somewhat surprised, exclaimed "Oh, you speak *Castellano!*" Continuing our conversation in *Castellano*, I explained that I had spent my teenage years in Argentina. The president then turned to Louise (who, with long brown hair and dark eyes, could probably be mistaken for an Argentinian girl) and started chatting with her in *Castellano*. I quickly interjected, telling the President that Louise was from England and did not speak Spanish. The President chuckled and said in *Castellano*, "Oh, English. Notwithstanding our recent differences (probably referring to the Falklands War of 1982), I actually love the English. They invented so many wonderful sports and are not particularly good at any of them!" Louise nudged me and whispered "what did he say?" Not wishing to cause an international incident, I whispered back "he says he loves the English." Later that night back in our hotel I informed Louise of President Menem's full quip about the English.

Accounting Changes: Chronicles of Convergence, Crisis, and Complexity

In the early 1990s I was elected to the governing body of C&L, which was called Firm Council. Comprising approximately 10 percent of the total number of partners, it was sort of a group of tribal elders. At the time of my election to Firm Council, I was the youngest member. What's more, once elected, I would remain a member for the rest of my career at the firm. Within a few years, however, the partners voted to reform firm governance, and the self-perpetuating Firm Council was dissolved, and elections were held for a new, smaller U.S. Board of Partners. I was elected to that first Board of Partners and subsequently reelected again after the merger between C&L and PW. Ultimately, I also served on the Global Board of PricewaterhouseCoopers (PwC).

I had also been serving as a member the Investment Committee of the C&L Partner Investment Funds. In essence, these were a series of annual closed-end investment pools for the benefit of the active and retired partners of C&L. Each year, beginning in the mid-1980s, we raised money from our partners, partly on a mandatory basis and partly through additional voluntary contributions by partners, and invested the funds in a variety of venture capital, private equity, operating real estate, and oil and gas investments. I served as a member of the investment committee for more than a decade until we stopped taking in new money after the merger with PW. It was a labor of love for those of us on the committee, which included Herman Schneider and several other senior partners of the firm, such as Nick Moore who went on to be the CEO of C&L and the first Global Chairman of PwC. Overall, the funds did pretty well, with our fair share of winners, but also some big losers, particularly among the real estate investments.

This is all background leading up to my appointment as the senior technical partner of the firm. In late 1993, Gene Freedman, then CEO of C&L, asked me to transition into the role of technical partner. In the world of the major accounting firms, the CEOs were "the gorillas," and the senior technical partners were "the chimpanzees" or "the chimps." Ron Murray, then senior technical partner, was nearing the mandatory retirement age. I had worked with Ron while I was in the national office in the early 1980s and afterwards in addressing technical issues on my audit clients and in connection with our Corporate Finance Advisory Services work. He had been something of a mentor, and I greatly respected his technical capabilities. I had also worked very closely over the years with several of the national office partners, such as Ray Dever and Steve Lis, whom I counted as some of my closest friends in the firm.

Becoming the senior technical partner was a great honor and a great responsibility. It involved heading up the firm's functions relating to accounting and SEC matters. This included working with the FASB, the SEC, and other standards setters and regulators; developing and issuing firm policy and practice guidance on these matters; working on a daily basis with our practice partners to address and resolve often difficult accounting, auditing, and SEC issues for their clients; and visiting many clients to discuss financial reporting issues and developments. In effect, I was going from being a bit of a "poacher" in terms of the work advising investment bankers and corporate clients on accounting structuring to being the head "gamekeeper."

Before leaving the New York practice, I needed to find a successor to lead the Corporate Finance Advisory Services. I was able to entice Ray Beier, a partner at Deloitte & Touche, who headed up the practice in this area, to join C&L. It was a good move, and to this day, Ray and I remain very good friends. Ray continued to build the practice, eventually transforming it into more of a client and practice support activity on major M&A and financial transactions. Later, while I was at the FASB, he would assume a senior role for thought leadership on accounting and financial reporting in the national office of PwC.

Although Gene Freedman had been the person to ask me to take on the national office role, other senior partners, including Tom Fitzpatrick, who I worked for and with on a number of nonaudit assignments, and Harvey Bazaar, the managing partner of the New York office, were also very supportive of my undertaking the national office role. Perhaps the most important person in my coming to the national office was Pat McDonnell. He had recently been appointed to head the business assurance (BA) line of service. Starting around 1993, the firm went through a major reorganization of its operations. Until then, the U.S. firm had been largely organized on a geographical basis, in terms of regions with regional managing partners and offices with office managing partners who reported to the regional managing partners. These territorial barons were responsible for all services delivered to clients in their geography. For decades, audit had been the dominant service, followed by tax services. However, during the 1980s and early 1990s, C&L and the other major accounting firms rapidly grew other service lines, most notably management consulting but also various advisory services. Responding to this change, the firm's operations and management structure were reorganized into distinct lines of service: BA, tax, management consulting services (MCS), and financial advisory services (FAS).

When I rejoined the national office in early 1994, my good friend Barry Winograd was also there. He had been recruited from the practice to head the auditing side of the effort, with a particular focus on revamping the firm's audit methodologies and supporting systems, processes, and tools. Pat also had a right-hand man: Rich Baird. Together, the four of us (Pat, Rich, Barry, and me) spearheaded a major transformation in the firm's audit and assurance practice, increasing both the size and overall quality, efficiency, and profitability of the BA line of business. Pat had been a Marine and was a master at executing major campaigns and motivating the troops. The BA leadership team implemented the transformation of the BA business across the country. In addition to the four of us, the team included the geography heads of the BA line of service and the leaders of various nonaudit assurance services. Denis Salamone, Barry's and my compatriot from the Shearson days, was on the leadership team as the head of BA for the New York Metro area.

For our part in the accounting and SEC area, we significantly revamped a number of our national office processes; instituted enhanced outreach and communication programs to the practice, clients, and the academic community; and established a number of Centers of Excellence around the country to provide more hands-on assistance to the practice in addressing technical issues. Although many of the ideas behind these changes may have been mine, most of the credit for transforming them into reality rests with my fellow partners in the national office, including Ray Dever, Steve Lis, Randy Vitray, Ken Dakkduk, Nelson Dittmar, Mike Johns, John Gribble, Brett Cohen, and, very importantly, Jim Harrington, who served as my right-hand man on a lot of these initiatives. A number of partners around the country who led regional Centers of Excellence in accounting and SEC matters were also heavily involved with these projects. As well, our work involved frequent interaction with many other parts of the firm, including senior management and the Office of the General Counsel led by David McLean, Michael Garrett, and Walter Ricciardi.

On the family front, we made periodic visits to Manchester and took many other vacations in the United States, Europe, and the Caribbean. In 1994, we toured Israel with Louise's parents, my mom, and her first cousin from Argentina, ending in Jerusalem for Michael's Bar Mitzvah at the Western Wall. I am glad my mom and Louise's parents were able to be with us because in 1995 my mother fell ill and went through a three-year, gut wrenching process of dying, Louise's mother died in 1998, and Louise's father died in 2002.

Professional Affairs

Part of being the senior technical partner of one of the major accounting firms is getting involved with all sorts of professional committees and activities. I relished these opportunities. For a number of years, I had already been a member of the FASB's Financial Instruments Task Force that periodically met with the board and FASB staff to provide input and advice on the FASB's many projects dealing with various aspects of accounting for, and disclosures relating to, financial instruments. In 1996, I also became a member of the Emerging Issues Task Force (EITF), the body that addresses a variety of emerging and often contentious accounting and reporting issues. Members of that body included leading technical accountants from the major accounting firms and from industry. Some of those I served with during my years on the EITF were John Stewart of Arthur Andersen, Ed Trott of KPMG (later to be one of my fellow FASB board members), Norman Strauss of Ernst &Young, Bill Mooney and John Dirks of PW (soon to become my fellow partners at PwC), Phil Ameen of General Electric, David Sidwell of J.P. Morgan (who I later worked with on the 2007–08 SEC Advisory Committee on Improvements to Financial Reporting and, since June 2011, on the board of directors of Fannie Mae), John Smith of Deloitte & Touche (who later became a member of the IASB), Susan Bies of the First Tennessee National Corporation (who later served as a member of the Board of Governors of the Federal Reserve), Ed Nussbaum of Grant Thornton, Lee Graul of BDO Seidman, Ray Krause of McGladrey & Pullen, and Ernest Baugh of Joseph Decosimo. Also participating as official "observers" were the chairmen of the AICPA's Accounting Standards Executive Committee (now known as the Financial Reporting Executive Committee), who during my term on the EITF were Mike Crooch of Arthur Andersen (who was later my fellow FASB Board member) and Dave Kaplan of PW (soon to be my fellow partner at PwC), and the Chief Accountant of the SEC, who during my term on the EITF were Michael Sutton and Lynn Turner (who had been my partner at C&L and who I have known since we were both managers in the national office of C&L in the early 1980s).

I also became the Chairman of the SEC Regulations Committee of the AICPA that periodically meets with the SEC staff to discuss current SEC reporting issues, provides guidance to the profession on these matters, and holds the largest annual financial reporting conference in the United States; a member of the executive committee of the SEC Practice Section of the AICPA; and a member of the (governing) Council of the AICPA. I was also a member of the International Capital Markets Advisory Committee of the New York Stock Exchange. In addition, I became a member of the National Steering Committee, a group comprising the technical heads ("the chimps") and leaders of the governmental affairs functions of each of the major firms, that provided policy advice to the CEOs of the major accounting firms ("the gorillas") on major issues and developments affecting the profession.

In the years leading up to the year 2000 (Y2K), there were significant concerns about the potential for widespread computer systems malfunctions on January 1, 2000. Leaders of the accounting profession were concerned that companies were not taking the steps necessary to ensure continuity of their computer systems and that auditors would be blamed for not having warned the investing public of the potential for widespread problems or of the very significant costs companies were incurring or would need to incur to address the potential problem. So, we reasoned that additional disclosures by companies might both alert investors and the capital markets to these issues and pressure companies to undertake the actions necessary to avoid a shutdown of their systems.

At the urging of the National Steering Committee, at the start of the Annual AICPA Conference on Current SEC Developments in December 1997, I used my position as Chairman of the AICPA SEC Regulations Committee to briefly speak about the issue and to urge the SEC to require enhanced disclosures by companies on their preparedness and planned actions relating to Y2K. With the help of former SEC General Counsel James Doty (who at that time was with the law firm of Baker Botts and is now Chairman of the Public Company Accounting Oversight Board), we drafted potential language for an SEC release, held discussions with senior SEC staff members, and I, together with AICPA Chairman Stuart Kessler, sent a letter to SEC Chairman Arthur Levitt, Jr., and SEC Commissioner Isaac Hunt, Jr., on the need for enhanced disclosure requirements. The SEC quickly responded by issuing Staff Legal Bulletin No. 5 in January 1998 requiring additional Y2K disclosures by issuers. Readers will remember that the predicted Y2K computer problems never occurred in any great measure. Although I would like to think our effort to spur better disclosures and attendant actions by companies to avoid the potential problem had something to do with Y2K turning out to be a nonevent, I don't think that would be an honest assessment of what transpired.

At C&L, I was working internally on additional matters. My U.K. counterpart, Roger Davis, and I coheaded an international committee that established the firm's global positions on major professional matters. One of the members of that group was Bob Muter from Canada, who I would also work with on the Accounting Standards Oversight Council of Canada starting in 2011. As well, I became president of the C&L (and later the PwC) Foundation that supported university education in terms of funding curriculum development, academic research, endowed chairs, and bricks and mortar. In addition, I served on the American Accounting Association's Financial Reporting Standards Committee.

All this put me in regular contact not only with leaders of the major accounting firms but with policymakers and thought leaders, including those in Washington, D.C. I began to have a sense of storm clouds on the horizon threatening the profession and major accounting firms. Much has been written about the years leading up to the reporting scandals in 2001–02 and the demise of Arthur Andersen and about how the profession and, in particular, the major accounting firms lost their way in terms of serving the public. For me, that could be the subject of another book based on my experiences from the mid-1990s through early 2002. Suffice it to say that, in my role as the senior technical partner of C&L and then of PwC, I never felt pressured to do the wrong thing and we regularly took tough stands on client accounting and reporting matters. Pat McDonnell and then Dennis Nally, who I reported to at PwC, always supported the national office decisions, so I did not worry about the partners who called us for assistance on issues. Rather, what I worried about were those who didn't call, either because they didn't spot a big issue or because they were afraid they might anger an important client. In that regard, I believe the system for evaluating and compensating audit partners may have sent some mixed messages. On the one hand, partners were told that doing a good audit was job number one, but on the other hand, they were measured and rewarded based in part on their success in growing firm services at their audit clients and on the results of client satisfaction surveys.

I also think it was clear during those years of booming stock markets (what Alan Greenspan famously termed irrational exuberance) that the Wall Street "earnings game" had an effect on corporate behavior. Feeling constant pressure to meet or just beat Wall Street's quarterly earnings estimates for their company, some corporate managers would try to find ways, either through altering the timing of transactions or through accounting maneuvers, to get to the desired level of quarterly earnings. We experienced some of this in the national office around quarter-ends, with audit partners calling in with quarter-end reporting issues on clients looking to boost reported earnings and earnings per share to the meet consensus forecasts (what I termed "dialing for pennies per share").

So it was that during this period of a booming economy and capital markets and significant growth and change in the profession and at the major accounting firms that the merger between PW and C&L, the two firms I had worked for during my entire career, was announced.

A Merger of Equals and "the Dream Team"

The merger was publicly announced in mid-September 1997. Nick Moore had called the members of the C&L board earlier that month to bring us into the loop. Internally and externally, it was billed as a merger of equals, and indeed, in rolling out the new organizational structure, leadership of the merged functions came from both firms. From my vantage point, the premerger process went remarkably smoothly, except that I was naturally disappointed that Pat McDonnell would not continue to lead the audit and assurance line of service. In course, it was announced that I would be the Americas leader of what was to be called

Professional, Technical, Risk and Quality (R&Q). I would be reporting to two people, Dennis Nally, a U.S. PW partner who was to head the assurance line of business across the Americas, and a U.K partner, David Morris, who would be the global head of R&Q. In a twist of fate and good fortune, I had worked with David some 20 years earlier at PW in Manchester, and indeed, we had some common acquaintances and had lived on the same small street in Didsbury.

I would now have a significantly larger portfolio of responsibilities, covering not only the United States but all of the Americas and including audit policy and risk management of the audit and assurance practices. In terms of the U.S. functions, I inherited what I can only describe as a "dream team." From C&L, I had the national office group of Ray Dever, Jim Harrington, and others, plus Jim Gerson on audit policy and Rick Steinberg on corporate governance. Jim was a leader in the profession and Chairman of the Auditing Standards Board at the time of the merger. The PW side also had leaders in their fields, including Dave Kaplan and John Dirks; Jay Hartig, Rick Muir, and Wayne Carnall, leading SEC practitioners; Jan Hauser, a highly respected expert in various technical accounting areas; and Jay Brodish who had long headed PW's risk management function. Likewise, the merger brought together many experienced lawyers in the Office of the General Counsel, including Larry Keeshan and Erica Baird from the PW side and David McLean and Walter Ricciardi from C&L. My group worked closely with General Counsel on legal, SEC enforcement, and litigation matters involving the audit practice.

I will always count the quick and successful integration of the PW and C&L R&Q groups as one of the proudest accomplishments of my career. It would not have been possible without the shared sense of mission, professionalism, and enthusiasm among the two groups; the leadership of certain senior partners from each group; and a lot of very hard work. Within the first year of the merger, we had issued a complete set of PwC policies and guidance and had effectively integrated our national office processes. We then managed to move everyone from our two legacy national offices to a new office in Florham Park, NJ, without losing anyone, despite many people having to relocate their families.

I continued on in many of my firm and professional roles. For me, the merger was a good thing, perhaps in part because it brought together the two firms I had worked for and enabled me to broaden my international activities, which, based on my background, was something I enjoyed. More importantly and with the benefit of hindsight, I think it also made sense in terms of the developments that were about to impact the profession and the resulting profound effects on the major accounting firms.

Chapter 1: My First 49 Years

Could You See It Coming?

By 1999, it started to become clear that the major accounting firms (or, as they called themselves, professional service firms) were entering a challenging period in their dealings and relationship with the SEC. SEC Chairman Arthur Levitt and Chief Accountant Lynn Turner had spoken publicly about the many accounting practices that companies were using, with the apparent blessing of their auditors, to inappropriately manage reported earnings. At PwC, we were in the midst of a wrenching investigation by the SEC of apparent violations of auditor independence rules that, in the end, did not come up with many serious violations but led to a needed strengthening of our internal systems (and those at other major accounting firms and across the profession) to monitor compliance with the independence requirements, as well as some revisions in the independence rules by the SEC. It was becoming evident from the meetings of the newly created Independence Standards Board that there were major, perhaps irreconcilable, differences in view between the SEC and major accounting firms on key issues relating to scope of services by the firms. Sensing the changing landscape, Ernst & Young sold its management consulting arm to Cap Gemini, and at PwC, we negotiated a deal, which fell through, to sell our MCS business to Hewlett Packard. (PwC later sold the MCS business to IBM, albeit at a much lower price.) We sold other businesses, including our valuation practice and parts of our human resources consulting business. I was involved in these activities, both as a member of the board and in addressing some of the technical accounting issues that arose in these transactions.

All of this was a prelude to the major shocks that were coming in the wake of the reporting scandals that began to surface in late 2001 at Enron, WorldCom, Adelphia, and other companies. These shocks included the federal indictment, and rapid disintegration and demise of Arthur Andersen and the passage of the landmark Sarbanes-Oxley Act in July 2002. My role as Chairman of the FASB would be profoundly affected by all of this; but again, I'm getting ahead of myself. I must recount a few more key events in my career and life that led up to my becoming Chairman of the FASB.

International Bob

Postmerger, we had a global R&Q leadership team. In addition to David Morris and me, there were the leaders of R&Q for the EMEA (Europe, Middle East, and Africa) and the Asia-Oceania "theaters." Mary Keegan, who headed the firm's activities relating to international accounting and policy matters, was also a member of the global R&Q

team as was David Scott, a partner from Canada who headed the global risk management over our audit and other assurance services. Mary, now Dame Mary Keegan, later left PwC to chair the U.K. Accounting Standards Board and then went on to become a senior Treasury official in the United Kingdom. Mary and I, together with another London PwC partner, David Phillips, joined Professor Robert Eccles of Harvard in coauthoring the book *The ValueReporting Revolution: Moving Beyond the Earnings Game* that was published in early 2001 and attracted a fair amount of attention in accounting and public policy circles. The book was essentially an exposé of some of the deficiencies in the corporate reporting system, including the whole earnings game that pervaded quarterly reporting, and a call for reforms to enhance the content, organization, and methods of delivery of corporate financial and nonfinancial information. Certainly, it reflected my view of financial statements and financial reporting as products that need to be customer focused and properly serve the marketplace, a view and passion that has driven and continues to drive much of my thinking about accounting and financial reporting.

All this, plus serving on the Global Board of PwC, kept me crossing oceans frequently. To those international activities, I added other important ones that extended beyond PwC. In 2000, I became the first Chairman of the Transnational Auditors Committee (TAC). This committee was a joint undertaking between the International Federation of Accountants and a newly constituted group called the Forum of Firms (FOF) consisting of the major global accounting firms and approximately 25 other international networks of accounting firms. The role of TAC was and continues to be to promote the enhancement of cross-border audits around the world through the development and implementation of consistent policies and practices by FOF member firms. Serving with me on TAC were senior partners from the major accounting firms and some of the international networks. Our meetings occurred in various parts of the world.

During 2000 and 2001, I also chaired a working group of the FASB's business reporting research project (BRRP). Consistent with the theme of *The ValueReporting Revolution: Moving Beyond the Earnings Game*, the BRRP was formed to examine and assess the growing range of financial and nonfinancial information that companies were providing to investors and the means for delivering such information. A number of BRRP working groups focused on particular industries and electronic delivery of corporate information. The group I chaired examined ways to better coordinate GAAP and SEC disclosures and potential approaches to reorganize and streamline the information in SEC Form 10-K filings. Our working group issued a detailed report in March 2001 with numerous recommendations.

Perhaps of greatest significance to my future role at the FASB was my appointment at the beginning of 2001 to the newly established International Accounting Standards Board (IASB). In August 2000, I was with Jim Leisenring of the FASB at the annual meeting of the American Accounting Association in Philadelphia, Pennsylvania. Jim, a good friend, asked me to write a letter supporting his candidacy to become a member of the new IASB and suggested that I might also want to consider throwing my hat into the ring. My immediate reaction was "no way" because I was happy at PwC. When Jim informed me that there were up to 2 spots on the IASB for part-time members, I thought about it some more and eventually, with the blessing of PwC, submitted my name as a candidate, was interviewed by the selection committee, and was chosen as one of the original 14 members of the IASB. I served on the IASB as a part-time member until July 2002 when I joined the FASB.

Unforgettable Events and a Fork in the Road

The final confluence of a number of events and some difficult choices on my part led to my becoming Chairman of the FASB. In the year or so preceding my selection for that role, I, by necessity, became a master multitasker. I still had my many day jobs at PwC, I was a part-time member of the IASB, and I was Chairman of TAC. I very much enjoyed TAC and being on the IASB, probably because I believed both had important public policy missions and because of the international nature of the work. My colleagues on both groups were interesting, dedicated, and accomplished individuals. I still vividly recall the first gathering of the original IASB members in February 2001 at a small country hotel in Streatley-on-Thames outside of London. It was essentially a get-to-know each other meeting combined with some initial brainstorming about the potential agenda and priorities of the new board. There was a sense of excitement among us of being at the start of something that could potentially transform international accounting and the global capital markets. My fellow IASB Board members were Sir David Tweedie (Chairman), Thomas Jones (Vice Chairman), Mary Barth, Hans-Georg Bruns, Anthony Cope, Robert Garnett, Gilbert Gelard, James Leisenring, Warren McGregor, Patricia O'Malley, Harry Schmid, Geoffrey Whittington, and Tatsumi Yamada. We came from nine different countries and diverse backgrounds that collectively represented a wealth of experience in accounting, financial reporting, and business. More than 11 years later in August 2012, many of us were again together at a reunion of the original IASB board members and spouses/significant others in Bellagio on Lake Como in

Accounting Changes: Chronicles of Convergence, Crisis, and Complexity

Italy. In addition to enjoying the beautiful surroundings and catching up with one another, we reflected on the many changes in the world of accounting and financial reporting in the intervening years, and on the broader developments and major events that had affected virtually all aspects of life. After that first meeting in February 2001, the IASB started official monthly meetings in April 2001, mostly in its office in London, but a couple times per year, we had the meetings in other major foreign capitals.

I think most people in the world who were over the age of three remember where they were and what they were doing on September 11, 2001. I was in London at an IASB meeting. It was early afternoon there when Jim Leisenring, who had been called out of the boardroom for a phone call, returned and informed us of the attacks on the World Trade Center in New York City and on the Pentagon in Washington, D.C. Our meeting stopped. I called home, and Louise told me what she knew about the horrific events that were unfolding. Soon afterward, we were asked to evacuate the IASB's offices in the City of London because there were fears of potential terrorist attacks on the financial district of London. I remember making several phone calls that afternoon to Louise and friends and colleagues in New York and New Jersey. I also recall receiving e-mails that PwC staff members had been on the planes that crashed into the World Trade Center and Pentagon. A group of about 20 of us who now found ourselves stranded in London, got together for an impromptu dinner on the evening of September 11 at the Chancery Court Hotel. Our group included some of the IASB board members and members of other accounting standards boards from various countries who had been meeting with the IASB that morning and the prior day. Ed Jenkins and Mike Crooch were there from FASB. They had gone out to Heathrow Airport to fly back to the United States but their flight had, of course, been cancelled. Indeed, all the flights to the United States from London were cancelled for several days, and it was not until September 15 that I was able to fly home. On the one hand, I was very frustrated with not being able to return home and see my loved ones and friends at this time of tragedy for our country. On the other hand, I also recall the kindness and deep expressions of sorrow and empathy for the United States and Americans from many people in London.

Certainly, the world changed after September 11, and other events were occurring that would also change my career and life. At PwC, both Nick Moore and Jim Schiro retired. They had led the firm since the merger as the global chairman and global CEO, respectively. Sam DiPiazza, who had been the U.S. CEO, became the global CEO, and the need arose to elect a new U.S. leader in early 2002. A number of my fellow partners urged me to run for that job. Before throwing my hat into the ring, however, I consulted with both Sir David Tweedie,

Chapter 1: My First 49 Years

Chairman of the IASB, and Paul Volcker, who chaired the trustees of the foundation that had oversight of the IASB, to ensure that my becoming the U.S. CEO of PwC would not, in their view, present a problem with my continuing on the IASB in a part-time role. I received the green light from both of them and decided to go for it.

To select the U.S. CEO, a committee of partners solicited the names of potential candidates, vetted those candidates, and came up with one or more names to submit to the U.S. partners for a vote. My understanding is that the committee narrowed the field down to two candidates who seemed to have broad support and relevant experience: Dennis Nally and me. We were both interviewed by the committee. They asked me whether, if elected, I would step down from the IASB so that I could devote full-time attention to PwC. I responded that I believed I could do both roles and that, in my view, it was important for the senior partner of the firm to be directly involved in major activities affecting the profession and the firm. I harkened back to the days when in the early 1970s, the head of C&L, Phil Defliese, also chaired the AICPA and the Accounting Principles Board, which was the accounting standard setter at that time. Apparently, the committee did not agree because I was informed that unless I would agree to leave the IASB, it could not go forward with submitting my name to the vote of the partners. At the time, I did not agree with that decision or point of view, but in retrospect, I understand and respect it: it came right at the time Arthur Andersen was in free fall and the profession and C&L were facing great uncertainties and challenges. So, the committee went forward with Dennis, who became the U.S. CEO, a job that, by most accounts, he did well for many years. He is now the global CEO of PwC.

I occasionally wonder about the road not taken and what might have been, but I made my decision and have no regrets. As it turned out, it enabled me to take on another role that suited my interests and experience, that of FASB Chairman.

In late 2001 then-FASB Chairman Ed Jenkins announced he would not seek a second term. In early 2002, right around the time I was involved in the PwC U.S. CEO process, people, including Chairman of the SEC Harvey Pitt and SEC Chief Accountant Bob Herdman, asked me to consider becoming a candidate to succeed Ed Jenkins. I was flattered but informed them of the ongoing process at PwC to elect a new U.S. CEO.

When I did not go forward in that process and after consulting with both the leadership of PwC and Sir David Tweedie and Paul Volcker, I became a candidate for FASB Chairman. In April, the Appointments and Evaluations Committee of the Trustees of the Financial Accounting Foundation interviewed me and soon thereafter I was informed that I had been selected as the new Chairman of the FASB, effective July 1, 2002.

Between April and July 1, I spent some time at the FASB in Norwalk, CT, getting up to speed. Louise and I decided not to take up permanent residence in Connecticut. (Nicole was still in high school in New Jersey at the time.) Instead, we bought a townhouse in Stamford, approximately a 15-minute drive from the FASB's office. Ed Jenkins was terrific in helping me transition, including introducing me to key people in Washington, D.C. Nevertheless, right on the eve of my assuming the chairmanship, the massive WorldCom reporting fraud came to light. This triggered a renewed spotlight on corporate financial reporting and a flurry of activity in Washington, D.C., that would result in the passage of Sarbanes-Oxley within a month. In the midst of all this, my becoming the new FASB chair received a fair amount of press coverage. An article at that time in *The Economist* was headlined "Bob Herz Faces the Daunting Task of Restoring Confidence in American Accounts." The first paragraph rather dramatically stated

> "ARE you nuts?" was the response of close friends of Bob Herz when told that he was accepting the job of chairman of America's Financial Accounting Standards Board (FASB). Mr. Herz, after all, was leaving a safe position as a senior partner at PricewaterhouseCoopers, the world's largest accounting firm, to step into the heart of the current crisis of confidence in corporate America. Only last a week, Worldcom and Xerox announced the two largest profit restatements in history. This week, on July 1st, Mr. Herz took up the job of steering accounting standards in a safer direction. Nuts? Probably not. Brave? Certainly.[2]

So it was that on July 1, 2002, I became Chairman of the FASB.

Some Basics About the FASB

The chapters that follow are based on information in the public domain and chronicle the major initiatives and standard-setting activities of the FASB during the more than eight years I was Chairman. I will explain, in what I hope is an understandable and interesting way, what I viewed as key issues behind some of the more noteworthy and controversial subjects we addressed and will offer my perspectives on those issues. I will also discuss what I recall as some of the key factors affecting our work during these years, including the effects of changing economic, financial, and business environments on financial reporting and our standard-setting activities.

First, though, it's important for readers to understand some basics about the FASB, its role, and how it operates. This will give context to what I will discuss in subsequent chapters. For those readers already

---

[2] "Face Value, Called to Account," *The Economist*, July 4, 2002.

well acquainted with the FASB and accounting standard setting, feel free to skip this section.

FASB, FAF (FASB's parent organization), and the Financial Accounting Standards Advisory Council (FASAC) (FASB's main standing advisory group) were born in 1973 out of dissatisfaction with the prior U.S. accounting standard-setting body: the Accounting Principles Board (APB) of the AICPA. Criticisms of the APB included that it was dominated by the accounting profession, in particular the major accounting firms. Those criticisms reflected concerns that the APB's composition (18 part-time members), processes, and resulting pronouncements lacked due regard for the public interest and the broader constituency for financial reporting. Accordingly, the report of the Wheat Committee, a commission that examined these issues in the early 1970s, recommended the establishment of a new structure to provide greater independence and improved public due process in establishing the financial accounting standards that govern the preparation of financial reports by nongovernmental entities.

Since its founding in 1973, the FASB has been the designated organization in the private sector for establishing these standards in the United States for public companies, private companies, and not-for-profit entities. The stated mission of the FASB is "to establish and improve standards of financial accounting and reporting that foster financial reporting by non-governmental entities that provides decision-useful information to investors and other users of financial reports." That mission is viewed as critical to the proper functioning of the capital markets and the economy.

For public companies, the FASB's authority and role is delegated by the SEC. The SEC has officially designated the FASB as the recognized standard setter and the standards issued by the FASB as authoritative. For private companies and not-for-profit entities, the FASB's standards are recognized as authoritative by the AICPA and state boards of accounting. Independence and thorough public due process were guiding principles in establishing the FAF and FASB in 1973 and continue to be so. The FAF is a separate organization, independent of other business and professional organizations. The trustees appoint the members of the FASB and the FASAC (and since 2012, the members of the Private Company Council that, as further discussed in chapter 6, work with the FASB on private company reporting matters) and are responsible for protecting the independence and integrity of the standard-setting process. (The FAF trustees have similar duties with respect to the Governmental Accounting Standards Board, which establishes accounting standards for state and local governments, and the Governmental Accounting Standards Advisory Council, GASB's principal advisory group.) However, authority for the determination of the FASB's agenda and standards establishment rests with the FASB.

FASB board members are all full time and sever their prior employment connections. For most of its history, the FASB has been a seven-person board, with members drawn from the various constituencies in the financial reporting system: public accounting, corporate financial executives, investors and other users of financial information, and academia.

The mission is accomplished through a thorough and open public due process that involves and actively encourages broad participation by all stakeholders in the financial reporting system and careful consideration by the FASB of the views of stakeholders. Input is obtained through a variety of means, including through discussions with the FASAC and other advisory groups; regular meetings with many other constituents; issuing discussion documents and exposure drafts of proposed standards for public comment; and public roundtables, field visits, and field tests on proposals. The input is carefully analyzed and evaluated by the FASB and its staff of more than 60 full-time professionals. Meetings of the board are "in the sunshine," open to public observation and available via Internet and, as needed, telephone. In comparison with some other legislative and rule-setting bodies, the public meetings of the FASB often include extensive open discussion and debate among board members on the matters being addressed.

Funding of the FASB and FAF is now largely derived from a mandatory levy under Sarbanes-Oxley on all SEC registrants and registered mutual funds. Prior to Sarbanes-Oxley, much of the funding came from voluntary contributions, most notably from the accounting profession. The change under Sarbanes-Oxley was meant to bolster the independence of the FASB and the FAF. The FAF also derives revenues from the publication and licensing of FASB and GASB materials, but FASB standards are available to the public free of charge on the Internet.

Although the work of FASB is meant to be independent, objective, and unbiased, the FASB is accountable to the trustees of FAF for effectively fulfilling its mission. In regard to their impact on public companies, both the FASB and the FAF are accountable to the SEC, which maintains oversight over their activities, and, ultimately, to the U.S. Congress. Both the SEC and Congress have the power to block or overturn standards issued by the FASB, but they have rarely done so. However, the SEC and committees of Congress have often held hearings related to accounting standards and FASB proposals, and the SEC has been periodically asked to examine and report back to Congress on specific accounting and financial reporting issues.

The structure of, and approach to, accounting standard setting in the United States has served as something of a model for other countries and for the IASB and its parent foundation.

Chapter 2: Charting Course

> Clearly, the events of the past year have shaken confidence in our reporting system and in our capital markets. While it would seem that many or most of the problems stem from outright violations of rules and fraud by greedy and unscrupulous executives, apparent audit and corporate governance failures, structuring of sham transactions by investment bankers, and research analysts conflicts, I also think the problems have prompted broader questions about virtually every aspect of our corporate reporting system, including accounting standards and accounting standard setting. I think those questions are appropriate, are healthy, and, quite frankly, I think they were overdue. As with crises in other areas of business or life, this prompts reflection, introspection, a better understanding, and then rebuilding, change, and renewal. So it must be with our corporate reporting system.[1]

Like most new leaders of an organization, I arrived at the FASB with lots of ideas. Certainly, in the wake of the reporting scandals of 2001–02, it could not be business as usual for anyone involved in accounting and financial reporting. As noted by Manuel Johnson, Chairman of the FAF, in the 2002 FAF Annual Report:

> In the wake of the widely reported corporate scandals of last year, the entire U.S. financial reporting system was put under the microscope of the nation's leaders, including the President and Congress—as well as the public and media.... The public's interest in accounting issues soared in 2002 as newspaper headlines blared, almost daily, about corporate financial

---

[1] Robert H. Herz, on December 12, 2002, at the 2002 AICPA National Conference on Current SEC Developments.

misdeeds. As a result, investor confidence suffered and cries for reform were raised in many circles.

In order to get a better handle on the challenges and opportunities facing the FASB, in the period between being appointed as the new chairman and assuming that role and during my first months as chairman I spoke with many constituents: current and former FASB members and senior staff; FAF trustees; members of the Financial Accounting Standards Advisory Council (FASAC); many members of Congress; officials at the Government Accountability Office, the Department of the Treasury, the Board of Governors of the Federal Reserve System, the SEC, and other regulators; and many others familiar with the FASB and financial reporting.

Not surprisingly, there were a variety of perspectives and, in some cases, significant differences in views. For example, many in the corporate community believed that the FASB had not been sufficiently responsive to their concerns about disclosure overload, operationality, and cost-benefit and particular accounting approaches that, in their view, did not properly portray the operating realities of their business. On the other hand, users and many in Congress seemed to believe the opposite. Rightly or wrongly, they seemed to believe that the FASB and the SEC had been overly accommodative to the corporate community and had permitted too many exceptions in standards and rules and too much flexibility that had enabled off-balance financing, inadequate disclosure, and form-over-substance transactions. Implicit in these comments was a view that standard setters may have been too focused on the views and needs of preparers and auditors and should become more attune to the needs of investors and other users of financial information.

On the positive side, just about everyone I spoke with agreed that the FASB should be independent. However, members of Congress and users I spoke with seemed to emphasize independence more in terms of freedom from undue influence from the corporate and auditor communities, while the corporate and auditor communities were fearful that the FASB might effectively become an arm of the federal government and subject to all the attendant political pressures. In that regard, I think the Sarbanes-Oxley Act of 2002 struck an appropriate balance. Although providing for mandatory funding of the FASB, the legislative history behind Sarbanes-Oxley clearly emphasized that such funding was not intended to federalize the organization or put it in a position that would subject it to political pressures. As I noted at the time in major speeches, "Time will tell whether that balance is achieved in practice."

Sarbanes-Oxley significantly altered many aspects of the U.S. financial reporting system, including the creation of the new Public Company Accounting Oversight Board (PCAOB) to oversee auditors of SEC registrants and assume responsibility from the AICPA's Auditing

Standards Board for establishing auditing standards in that arena. However, it is noteworthy from a historical perspective that when it came to accounting standard setting, a principal focus of Sarbanes-Oxley was on strengthening the FASB by buttressing its independence through the establishment of a mandatory funding mechanism. This replaced the need for (and ability of) the FAF to obtain voluntary contributions from the business community and accounting profession to finance the FASB's operations. I feel that a lot of credit for this goes to my predecessor, FASB Chairman Ed Jenkins, and others at the FASB and FAF. Their proactive efforts helped ensure that key policymakers understood the importance of preserving, protecting, and enhancing the FASB's ability to operate in an independent manner in a period when all aspects of the financial reporting system were subject to intense scrutiny.

> In commenting on two bills recently introduced in Congress that include provisions concerning the Financial Accounting Standards Board ("FASB"), Edmund L. Jenkins, Chairman of the FASB stated, "The commitment to the FASB's independence and open due process that is expressed in the two bills is very important as we address issues related to the Enron matter."
>
> "The standards developed by the FASB over the past quarter century have provided the backbone for our nation's vibrant capital markets because of the transparent, credible and reliable nature of the information that results from their proper application," Mr. Jenkins stated. "Impairment of the FASB's independence by legislation could have a negative impact upon the quality of that information and, consequently, the longstanding competitive advantage of the U.S. capital markets."[2]

The importance of the FASB's ability to conduct its standard-setting activities in an independent, objective, and unconstrained manner was also specifically noted and explained in an April 2003 SEC Policy Statement redesignating the FASB as the U.S. accounting standard setter for public companies. It stated

> While effective oversight of the FASB's activities is necessary in order for the Commission to carry out its responsibilities under the securities laws, we recognize the importance of the FASB's independence. By virtue of today's Commission determination, the FASB will continue its role as the preeminent accounting standard setter in the private sector. In performing this role, the FASB must use independent judgment in setting standards and should not be constrained in its exploration and discussion of issues. This is necessary to ensure that the standards developed

---

[2] March 19, 2002, news release *FASB Chairman Comments on Proposed Legislation*. www.fasb.org/news/nr031902.shtml.

are free from bias and have the maximum credibility in the business and investing communities.[3]

This SEC Policy Statement was issued soon after William Donaldson succeeded Harvey Pitt as Chairman of the SEC in March 2003. I very much welcomed the inclusion of the preceding paragraph in the SEC Policy Statement. Moreover, the issuance of the SEC Policy Statement redesignating the FASB as the recognized accounting standard setter was necessary for us to begin obtaining funding under Sarbanes-Oxley. As previously noted, Sarbanes-Oxley ended the FAF's ability to fund FASB with voluntary contributions from the private sector and instituted a mandatory funding mechanism. However, the mandatory funding could commence only after the SEC had redesignated the FASB as an official accounting standard setter. As discussed in some press articles at the time,[4] we had encountered a bit of a challenge with Harvey Pitt over the conditions for SEC redesignation:

> An article in the *Wall Street Journal* ("FASB Recognition Stalled Amid Fight Over Control," February 21, 2003) reveals that in the weeks leading up to his departure, Harvey Pitt pushed for and failed in an attempt to establish greater SEC control over the Financial Accounting Standards Board.
>
> Mr. Pitt's plan was for the SEC to hold tighter control over FASB, the make up of the membership of the Financial Accounting Foundation, the selection of the members of the FASB, and the standard-setting agenda of the organization. His proposal would have given the SEC a greater representation at FASB meetings and would have given the SEC access to confidential FASB documents. According to the article, Mr. Pitt withheld crucial SEC recognition of the FASB pending acceptance of the greater control, essentially blocking the ability for the independent accounting standard setter to receive the critical funding it needs to survive.
>
> As part of the Sarbanes-Oxley Act, funding for the FASB is to be changed so that operating funds come from fees imposed on listed corporations, instead of the current funding model, which generates much of the revenue from public accounting firms and publication sales. Lawyers believe that the FASB cannot impose fees on public corporations unless it receives SEC recognition.
>
> In the end, FASB lobbying to assert and maintain its independence won out. "We need to be able to do our thing in an independent, objective and thorough way," FASB Chairman Robert Herz to the *Wall Street Journal*. "We don't want to be subject to constant interference or domination of our agenda."

---

[3] April 25, 2003, Securities and Exchange Commission Policy Statement *Reaffirming the Status of the FASB as a Designated Private-Sector Standard Setter*.
[4] "Pitt's Final Days Reveal Move to Assert More Control Over FASB," AccountingWeb, February 23, 2003.

According to the Journal, FASB has enough cash on hand to last through the fall. The new SEC Chairman William Donaldson is in a position to quickly recognize the FASB with no additional strings attached, allowing it to get the funding it needs to increase staffing and continue its duties.

As noted in chapters 3, "Stock Option Controversies—Take Two," and 5, "The Financial Crisis," there would be attempts during my years as Chairman of the FASB to intervene in our standard-setting activities through political means, requiring actions to defend and protect the independence of the FASB. Nonetheless, despite these episodes, overall, I believe the FASB's independence was maintained and generally respected by most constituents, the SEC, and Congress.

With regard to international convergence of accounting standards, most people I spoke with at the time seemed to support that goal, and many also supported moving toward a more principles-based accounting system, believing that U.S. standards had become too complex and too detailed with too many rules issued from too many bodies. However, many were also quite skeptical about whether a principles-based approach could work in the United States. Finally, many were critical that the FASB had been too slow in identifying and dealing with emerging problem areas, and there was a general urging of the FASB that as the independent and primary accounting standard setter in the United States, it needed to take more responsibility and control of the overall situation.

So, informed by these discussions with stakeholders from the investment, business, and government sectors and with my own ideas on potential initiatives, I assumed the role of Chairman of the FASB with no shortage of challenges and opportunities. However, although the Chairman of the FASB has a number of specific responsibilities, including developing the technical agenda, the official operating procedures of the FASB are such that the chairman cannot effectively accomplish things without the buy-in and cooperation of other Board members. For example, until 2008, all changes to the FASB technical agenda had to be officially voted on, and approved by, a voting majority of Board members. Although from 2008 and onwards I could make changes to the technical agenda, that could only be done after consultation with the rest of the Board. Moreover, any changes to the FASB's official operating procedures must be approved by a majority of the Board members. Ultimately, the issuance of exposure drafts and final standards requires a majority vote of the Board. So, obtaining input and buy-in from my fellow Board members was necessary to effecting change. It was also the wise course of action and consistent with the way I had operated in leading other groups and efforts.

At the request of the trustees of FAF, the Board and senior staff launched a series of wide-ranging reviews in July 2002 to address these issues, challenges, and opportunities. The reviews lasted into the fall of that year and covered such matters as our approach to standard setting (including agenda setting and project management); the feasibility of a more principles-based approach to standard setting in reducing the level of detail and complexity in U.S. standards; options for more actively fostering international convergence; ways to increase the level of investor and user involvement in our activities; and other internal organizational issues relating to human resources, internal processes, and constituent relations. As part of these reviews, we considered whether modifications to the existing structure of U.S. accounting standard setting, including the roles of the Emerging Issues Task Force (EITF) and the Accounting Standards Executive Committee (now known as the Financial Reporting Executive Committee [FinREC]) of the AICPA might improve the overall quality and effectiveness of U.S. accounting standard setting. Although these reviews were spearheaded by FASB board members (Mike Crooch, Neal Foster, Gary Schieneman, Katherine Schipper, Ed Trott, John Wulff, and me) and our staff directors (Sue Bielstein, Kim Petrone, and Larry Smith), we also actively sought input and advice from others inside and outside the organization.

As I have found throughout my career, when one person opens the door for new thinking, others join in with additional ideas. So it was with these meetings. Not only did I get buy-in for most of my key ideas and initiatives, but the group added new ones to the mix and carefully considered these in the context of the many points of information and stakeholder perspectives. What emerged from these reviews and discussions and with support from the FAF trustees was a set of strategic objectives and action steps that were to guide many of our activities over the coming years. Commenting on these reviews in the 2002 FAF Annual Report, FAF Chairman Manuel Johnson noted,

> the FAF asked the FASB Chairman to undertake an extensive review of the FASB's operations, process and people to determine where greater efficiencies might be gained. This covered a spectrum of technical activities the FASB has had in progress and includes the new course it is charting for accounting standards in this country. I am pleased to report, as can be noted elsewhere in this publication under the FASB Chairman's Q&A, that much of the work on that project is now complete. The FASB has embarked on a continuous improvement effort in its standard-setting work and is implementing changes, where appropriate, to enhance the overall effectiveness of the organization.

The reviews had three overarching strategic objectives: (1) improving the standards and the standard-setting process, (2) simplifying the structure of U.S. accounting standards setting and making the accounting standards more understandable, and (3) converging U.S. standards with those of the International Accounting Standards Board (IASB). I viewed these three objectives as somewhat interrelated in that, ideally, the convergence effort with the IASB might also help improve and simplify GAAP. The following sections offer more details about these objectives.

Improving Standard Setting

In the wake of the reporting scandals of 2001–02 that led to Sarbanes-Oxley, a number of specific accounting and disclosure issues required standard-setting action. FASB was already working to address some of these issues before I joined the board, specifically the rules relating to consolidation of special purpose entities and the accounting and disclosure requirements relating to guarantees. They had issued exposure drafts[5] of new standards on these subjects that would form the basis of FASB Interpretation Nos. 45[6] and 46.[7] However, the reporting scandals brought to light other accounting areas that some thought needed prompt standard-setting attention. Most notable among these was accounting for employee stock options, which I will discuss in the next chapter. Issues stemming from the reporting of large unrealized gains by Enron and others related to trading in illiquid energy derivatives were addressed in EITF Issue No. 02-3, "Issues Involved in Accounting for Derivative Contracts Held for Trading Purposes and Contracts Involved in Energy Trading and Risk Management Activities," that was finalized in early 2003.

Beyond specific technical issues, some important process improvements needed attention. Prior to my arrival at the FASB, the FAF Trustees changed FASB's decision-making voting requirement from the previous 5-2 super majority to a simple majority of 4-3 in an effort to enable the FASB to speed up the development and issuance of standards without compromising their quality. Also, just prior to my joining the FASB, the Board had reorganized the staff, splitting the role of director of technical and research activities into three director roles: one with responsibility for major projects, another with a focus on technical application and implementation activities, and the third to work on strategic, process, and staffing matters.

---

[5] May 2002 exposure draft *Guarantor's Accounting and Disclosure Requirements for Guarantees, Including Indirect Guarantees of Indebtedness of Others* and June 2002 exposure draft *Consolidation of Certain Special-Purpose Entities—an interpretation of ARB No. 51*.
[6] *Guarantor's Accounting and Disclosure Requirements for Guarantees, Including Indirect Guarantees of Indebtedness of Others—an interpretation of FASB Statements No. 5, 57, and 107 and rescission of FASB Interpretation No. 34* (now codified in FASB *Accounting Standards Codification* [ASC] 460, *Guarantees*).
[7] *Consolidation of Variable Interest Entities—an interpretation of ARB No. 51*.

I believed other process issues needed consideration, the most of important of these being the apparent lack of significant involvement of investors and other users of financial information in the FASB's standard-setting activities. Although the stated mission of the organization focused on investors and other users as the intended primary beneficiary of the accounting standards (that is, as the main customer for the FASB's product), I felt that constituency was underrepresented in the standard-setting process. One of seven Board members came from the investor community; few if any of the FASB staff had such a background; none of the EITF members were users; and although there were some users on the FASAC and other advisory groups, those groups seemed to me to be dominated by public accountants and financial executives.

Trying to focus accounting standard setting and the broader realm of financial reporting on the needs of the users of the product was certainly not a new idea. As noted, it is core to the FASB's stated mission and was, I believe, supported by many, if not most, prior FASB Board members. Also, the CFA Institute advocated for it in its 1993 white paper *Financial Reporting in the 1990s and Beyond: An Executive Summary*. In addition, this was the focus of the 1994 report *Improving Business Reporting—A Customer Focus: Meeting the Information Needs of Investors and Creditors* issued by the AICPA Special Committee on Financial Reporting (also known as the Jenkins Committee after its chairman, Ed Jenkins, who later went on to become the Chairman of the FASB); of the book *The ValueReporting Revolution: Moving Beyond the Earnings Game* that I coauthored; and of other notable works, such as the 2002 book *Quality Financial Reporting* by Paul B. W. Miller and Paul R. Bahnson.

Prior to the reporting scandals of 2001–02, most investors and users of financial information were not that interested in accounting standard setting and were reluctant to get involved in the FASB's activities. However, that seemed to change in the wake of the reporting scandals, so I and others at the FASB believed we were now in a better position to advance this important aspect of our accounting standard-setting process. Accordingly, we went about trying to systematically and proactively increase the direct involvement of investors and other users in our standard-setting activities. First, and with the leadership of Gary Schieneman, who was the FASB Board member from the investment community, we created a new FASB User Advisory Council. Comprising approximately 25 senior people from a cross-section of users representing equity and fixed income investors and analysts, buy side investors, sell side analysts, pension funds, mutual funds, individual investors, and credit rating agencies, this council provided the Board with perspectives on major reporting issues and trends. Later, based on the suggestion by Don Young and the efforts of Don and Tom

Linsmeier, we established an Investors Technical Accounting Committee to provide the Board with detailed technical input on specific standards under development. Don also led the creation of a facility through which our staff could solicit input on specific accounting and reporting issues from portfolio managers and analysts at many of the country's largest mutual fund groups. We also recruited two experienced people from the investment community to serve as full-time liaisons with investors and other users, who, together with Board member Marc Siegel further broadened and intensified the FASB's direct engagement with users on each major project and its communications with the user community on standard-setting developments.

Starting at the beginning of 2003, we reconstituted the EITF to include 2 users, which has since been increased to 3 of the 14 EITF members. As a matter of due course, users are represented on virtually all project advisory groups, including the FASB's Small Business Advisory Committee, Private Company Financial Reporting Committee (and now on the new Private Company Council), and Not-for-Profit Advisory Committee. The number of users on the FASAC has been steadily increasing in recent years. Very importantly, the 7-member FASB now includes 2 board members who were professional financial statement users. The Board also meets annually with the accounting committees of the CFA Institute and the New York Society of Securities Analysts. As a result of all these changes and activities, I believe that FASB is now better able to obtain relevant and timely input from a broad range of users on virtually all its standard-setting activities. Although that input often reflects a diversity of views among users on particular issues, I believe that it does affect the Board's standard-setting decisions. In recent years, the IASB, the SEC, and the PCAOB have also established investor advisory committees.

There have been other important process improvements. Early on in my tenure at the FASB, we thoroughly mapped all our processes in order to identify and eliminate redundant and nonvalue-adding processes. We also expanded the FASB's public due process. In the past, not all FASB documents that changed or interpreted U.S. GAAP were exposed for public comment, including consensuses of the EITF and Technical Bulletins and questions and answers issued by the FASB staff. Now, everything that changes or interprets the official literature, including consensuses reached by the EITF, are issued for public comment, so the Board is able to obtain and consider such input prior to finalizing new guidance. Prior to 2002, FASB standards were not available to the public free of charge. Since then, they have been available free of charge through the FASB website and, more recently, through the FASB *Accounting Standards Codification*. Also, public meetings of the FASB, once available only by telephone, have now, for a number of years, been webcast.

We also broadened the range of standing advisory groups providing input and counsel to the Board and FASB staff. That included establishing a number of new groups, including the Small Business Advisory Committee, the Private Company Financial Reporting Committee, the Not-for-Profit Advisory Committee, and the Valuation Resource Group. Also, very importantly, in order to better meet the new and increasing demands on the organization resulting from the heightened focus on financial reporting and from international convergence, FASB staff numbers were increased, and new positions were created and filled, including the aforementioned investor liaisons, an academic fellow, and a valuation fellow. In 2006, under the leadership of Board member Tom Linsmeier, the FASB created a Financial Accounting Standards Research Initiative to promote relevant accounting research on major issues being addressed by the Board.

So, starting in 2002 and continuing throughout my 8 years at the FASB, a number of changes came about that I believe have enhanced the overall quality of the FASB's standard-setting process. Very importantly, further process improvements continue to be made since I left, including the commencement by the FAF of a formal program for postimplementation review of major standards and, as discussed further in chapter 6, actions by the FASB and the FAF Board of Trustees relating to standard setting for private companies.

Can We Make Things Simpler?

Coming out of the strategy meetings we held in 2002, there were also some very important changes aimed at reorganizing and rationalizing the structure of accounting standard setting in the United States and at simplifying and making the U.S. GAAP literature more useable. The following excerpt from the book *The ValueReporting Revolution: Moving Beyond the Earnings Game* that I coauthored encapsulated my view of the problem in the year 2000:

> The chairman and the chief accountant of the SEC often proclaim that the United States has the best financial reporting system in the world. If quality is measured by the sheer volume of pronouncements, rules, and regulations and by their level of detail and complexity, then America certainly leads the rest of the world. The U.S. Generally Accepted Accounting Principles represents a vast array of official pronouncements made over the past 40 years by various bodies, including the FASB and its predecessors, the Accounting Principles Board (APB) and the Committee on Accounting Procedure (CAP), the FASB Emerging Issues Task Force (EITF), and the Accounting Standards Executive Committee (AcSEC) of the AICPA. These pronouncements appear in various forms: FASB statements, interpretations,

> technical bulletins, and implementation guides, EITF consensuses, AcSEC Statements of Position, and industry accounting and audit guides, just to name the principal ones.... If this weren't sufficient, for public companies, there is a whole set of rules and regulations that interpret and supplement the GAAP rules. Those interested will find them in the SEC's core rules such as Regulations S-X and S-K, as well in more than 100 specific Staff Accounting Bulletins, almost 50 Financial Reporting Releases, and hundreds of Accounting Series Releases.
>
> Had enough yet? In order to stay fully current with GAAP, it is not sufficient to know and understand just the official pronouncements; the SEC staff regularly deems it appropriate and important to proclaim their latest views on particular reporting and disclosure matters through speeches and comments at EITF and other professional meetings, which, although not official, effectively carry the same weight for anyone trying to comply with all the rules. All this effort ends up as an extraordinarily detailed set of rules about what companies can and cannot do in their external financial reporting. These rules are have become so complex that a rapidly decreasing number of CFOs and professional accountants can fully comprehend and apply all the rules and how to apply them.[8]

I wrote those words, and clearly, I felt strongly about what I viewed as a major issue. When I got to the FASB, I was in a position to try to do something about it. Through discussion with my fellow Board members, we identified the following four core issues that had contributed and were continuing to contribute to the overall problem:

1. Many different bodies were issuing U.S. GAAP.

2. The various pronouncements issued by these bodies were written in differing formats, styles, and levels of depth and only loosely interconnected.

3. Some of the pronouncements and related guidance were too complex in terms of the level of detail and number of exceptions and bright lines.

4. The style of writing and format of the pronouncements made them hard to understand by anyone not steeped in the technical accounting literature.

Attacking these issues would not be easy and would need to be done in a systematic manner. The approach would need to include rationalizing the overall structure of U.S. accounting standard setting, reorganizing and codifying the mass of pronouncements that comprise U.S. GAAP,

---

[8] Robert G. Eccles, Robert H. Herz, E. Mary Keegan, and David M. H. Phillips, *The ValueReporting Revolution: Moving Beyond the Earnings Game*. Hoboken, NJ: Wiley, 2001, pp. 110–111.

addressing the rules-based approach, and improving the understandability of the proposals and standards issued by the FASB.

Rationalizing the Structure of U.S. Accounting Standard Setting

The first step was to try to reduce the number of organizations issuing U.S. GAAP pronouncements. In effect, new U.S. GAAP was flowing out of three different organizations: the FASB, AICPA, and SEC. Further, although the EITF was, in name, a task force of the FASB, over the years, it had taken on something of a separate life of its own.

1. First, we approached the AICPA to try to stop it from issuing new U.S. GAAP requirements through AcSEC. In my view, over the years, the AICPA, through AcSEC and industry committees, had done a lot of very good work in developing and issuing Statements of Position (SOPs) and industry Audit and Accounting Guides on a variety of accounting subjects. However, the FASB, not the AICPA, was the official accounting standard setter. This position was bolstered by the SEC's redesignation of FASB as the recognized standard setter for public companies, pursuant to Sarbanes-Oxley. Initially and quite understandably, the AICPA leadership did not seem to enthusiastically embrace our point of view and request. However, after further discussions and to the AICPA's credit, we agreed that AcSEC would finish up some work in progress and would then would cease issuing SOPs or embedding new U.S. GAAP requirements in industry Audit and Accounting Guides. However, I also personally and publicly encouraged the AICPA to continue updating, developing, and publishing industry Audit and Accounting Guides because I have always viewed these as particularly valuable learning and reference tools for those involved in the accounting and auditing of companies in particular industries, and the AICPA continues to publish these guides.

2. Next, we took more ownership of the EITF by becoming more involved in the agenda and deliberations of that body. Board members are expected to attend the meetings of the EITF and, as appropriate, to express their views and concerns on particular issues being discussed. Moreover, the EITF's official procedures were revised to require that the FASB Board formally ratify (or reject) all EITF consensuses before they became U.S. GAAP. A few years later, we began requiring exposure for public comment of all proposed EITF consensuses and consideration of comments received prior to the consensuses being finalized by the EITF and ratified by the FASB.

3. Finally, we went to the SEC staff and asked them to consider, wherever possible, referring issues to the FASB that they believed required standard-setting action, instead of issuing a formal pronouncement or trying to change U.S. GAAP via other means. In this way, such matters could be addressed through the FASB's public due process. They agreed to try to do this. Although on a few occasions since then the SEC staff have felt compelled, in the interest of timeliness, to issue accounting guidance, I believe the understanding and arrangement by which they refer issues to the FASB has generally worked well.

Through these steps, we were able to rationalize the overall accounting standard-setting structure in the United States. We also believed we needed to reduce the number of types of pronouncements issued by the FASB and to ensure that all proposed changes to U.S. GAAP were exposed for public comment. We started issuing a new type of document: FASB Staff Positions. FSPs generally contained implementation and application guidance on specific matters or were issued to defer the effective date of a pronouncement. They replaced FASB Technical Bulletins, Implementation Guides, and Staff Q&As that, although not subject to formal due process, did have the force of official U.S. GAAP. Although the name Staff Position may have conveyed that they were only staff documents, they were subject to due process by the Board, including discussion and voting on by the Board at public meetings and exposure of the draft FSPs for public comment.

The Accounting Standards Codification—Reorganizing and Codifying U.S. GAAP

So, we had reduced the number of standard setters and the number of types of pronouncements that would be issued, but we still had the problem that the existing U.S. GAAP literature consisted of more than 2,000 separate, loosely connected documents. In our view, that negatively affected the overall usability of the U.S. GAAP literature, including hampering the ability to efficiently and effectively do research on accounting issues. It also complicated our efforts to identify and describe the effects new proposals and standards would have on the existing literature. In discussing these issues, the strategic review group birthed the idea of what was to become the "Codification" or, formally the FASB *Accounting Standards Codification*™ (ASC). The idea was a simple one: let's reorganize this mass of literature into a single document organized by major accounting topic. However, we also realized that translating this idea, or vision if you will, into reality would be a major undertaking. I asked Larry Smith, our new director of technical application and implementation activities, to give it some thought. We were also in for a great stroke of luck. Tom Hoey, who had led the development of Arthur Andersen's accounting research platform, was available. We hired Tom to be the project manager on the development of the Codification under the oversight of Larry Smith and the Board.

We also needed to obtain approval of the FAF trustees and buy-in from the SEC for what would likely be a multiyear, multimillion dollar undertaking. We needed to prove the business case for such a major project. Tom's first task, under Larry's and my oversight, was to develop the specifications for the project in order to size the likely costs and to conduct surveys of users of the accounting literature to better assess the potential benefits. Tom developed a comprehensive blueprint for the project and the resulting product that included estimates of the timing and costs. We conducted an extensive survey of users of the accounting literature, including accounting practitioners and financial statement preparers. The results of the survey strongly confirmed the problems with the existing structure of U.S. GAAP. For example, of the 1,400 survey respondents, 80 percent believed that the structure of U.S. GAAP was confusing, and 85 percent believed that accounting research took an excessive amount of time. There was also strong support for the development of the Codification with 95 percent of the survey respondents agreeing that the FASB should undertake the project.[9]

The Codification project was the accounting version of a national works project. In addition to involving many of us at the FASB and members of the FAF staff, we recruited scores of professionals to work on the project as mappers and authors. Consistent with their titles, the mappers mapped the existing literature into the approximately 90 Codification topics and subtopics under each topic. The authors would then develop the topics and subtopics, adhering to a set of strict guidelines to ensure they did not change existing U.S. GAAP, just reorganize it, and that there was a consistent structure and format across the Codification. The development process incorporated numerous controls to ensure completeness and accuracy. There were also processes to identify potential conflicts and redundancies in the existing literature, which then required resolution by the Board, as well as instances of literature that, although not authoritative, were nevertheless widely relied upon and should be included in the Codification. The Codification also includes, by topic, the relevant SEC guidance and requirements. The authored topics and subtopics then went through several levels of review, including by designated reviewers at the major accounting firms and in industry; by members of the FASB staff; and, ultimately, by FASB Board members. The Codification was housed on a state-of-the art database that was specifically developed for the purpose and that incorporates many different functionalities.

---

[9] For example, see the presentation by Thomas Hoey at the 8th Annual Financial Reporting Conference at Baruch College on April 30, 2009, and available at http://zicklin.baruch.cuny.edu/centers/zcci/zcci-events/downloads/2009-frc/hoey.ppt.

Chapter 2: Charting Course

The development phase was completed in late 2007. In January 2008 we launched it to the public for trial use, or "verification," at the same time conducting FASB ASC webcasts and launching online training modules to familiarize people with FASB ASC and its capabilities. People were encouraged to provide feedback on their user experience, enabling the core development team to address issues and further refine functionalities. On July 1, 2009, after formal approval by a vote of the Board, FASB ASC became the official source of U.S. GAAP, replacing the thousands of pronouncements from which it was derived. In announcing this in a FASB news release on July 1, 2009, I stated, "Today's launch of the Codification represents a milestone in U.S. accounting standards. After years of development, this much more efficient, user-friendly method of researching up-to-date solutions has become a reality. I want to thank the many people at the FAF, the FASB, and the hundreds of constituents that contributed to the successful completion of this very major endeavor." As also noted in that news release, in order to prepare constituents for the change, the FASB had provided a number of tools and training resources prior to the official launch, including an online tutorial in using FASB ASC, extensive Q&As and background materials, and various webcasts, presentations, and alerts.

FASB ASC has changed the way accounting research is done, and it has also, presumably, affected how the literature is taught. It also changed the form and format of all new standards issued by the FASB. No longer are FASB pronouncements issued as FASB Statement No. X, FASB Interpretation No. Y, or FASB Staff Position No. Z; rather, they are now issued as documents that amend, add to, or replace the relevant sections of FASB ASC. The same goes for consensuses of the EITF that have been ratified by the Board. FASB obtains ongoing feedback on the Codification, including suggestions for improving its usability, from constituents in order to continue to enhance the content, search capabilities, and overall user friendliness.

The FAF and FASB codification team performed the additional important step of linking the eXtensible Business Reporting Language (XBRL) U.S. GAAP Taxonomy to FASB ASC. This link facilitates cross-referencing between specific U.S. GAAP requirements and defined terms and the related XBRL data definitions. Starting in 2010, the FAF and FASB assumed responsibility for the ongoing development and maintenance of the XBRL U.S. GAAP Taxonomy, proposing and issuing periodic updates to the taxonomy in order to keep it up to date with changes in accounting standards and to improve the usability of the taxonomy.

Access to the FASB ASC is available free of charge through the FASB's website. A "Professional View" version of FASB ASC that incorporates more sophisticated search capabilities and functionalities is available on a subscription basis but is free of charge to accounting faculty and students at qualifying universities and colleges.[10]

Clearly, the development and launch of FASB ASC as the single source of U.S. GAAP represented a major and important milestone in the history of accounting standard setting in the United States. It was a huge undertaking, it came in largely on time and on budget, and I believe everyone involved in the project can take great pride in helping transform what was an ambitious vision into reality. My special admiration and thanks to Larry Smith and Tom Hoey and his core team who did a masterful job guiding and shepherding this large and challenging endeavor from conception and design to successful completion.

Addressing Complexity and Improving the Understandability of Standards

Thus far, in this section, I have described how we addressed the first two issues relating to the complexity of the U.S. accounting literature: the too many standard-setters issue and the mass of loosely connected pronouncements issue. What about the second two issues: the complexity of the standards themselves and improving the readability and understandability of the standards? In my view, the complexity of accounting standards (in particular, U.S. accounting standards) reflects, at least in part, broader issues in our financial reporting system that I will discuss at length in chapter 6, including the subject of principles-based, or objectives-oriented, standards. Nevertheless, in recent years, the FASB has made a number of efforts to try to reduce the complexity of its pronouncements and improve their overall understandability. These have included format changes, such as putting the objectives and principles in boldface font and having the summary at the front of the standard specifically address why the FASB is issuing the pronouncement; the scope of the document; how it will improve current accounting practices; how it will change current practice; its effect on convergence with International Financial Reporting Standards (IFRS); and the effective date of, and transition method(s) for, the new requirements. In developing standards, the Board has tried to avoid the use of exceptions, bright lines, and overly prescriptive guidance, and there were other efforts to write the documents in plain English.

Although I believe all these efforts have improved the understandability of proposed and final standards issued by the FASB, I also believe there is room for continued improvement. I believe that the joint development of major standards with the IASB has been a positive in that regard. It forces both boards to try to ensure that the joint

---

[10] Access to, and information about, Financial Accounting Standards Board *Accounting Standards Codification*™ can be found at http://asc.fasb.org.

standards are understandable both in the United States and across many other parts of the world. However, fitting the new standards into the FASB ASC format can be challenging and requires a continuing eye by the FASB staff and Board about readability and understandability. Finally and as discussed later in this book, I believe that progress on the Conceptual Framework and Disclosure Framework projects could help lead the way to enhancing the overall understandability and usefulness of financial statements.

International Convergence

The third strategic objective we agreed upon in the summer of 2002 was trying to foster convergence between U.S. GAAP and IFRS. This was not a completely new initiative because, previously, the FASB had, for many years, pursued efforts at harmonization or internationalization of accounting standards. For example, during the mid-1990s, the FASB undertook a major project to systematically catalog, describe, and explain the differences between the structure, standards, and processes of the International Accounting Standards Committee (IASC) and those in the United States. The FASB had also been an active member of the Group of Four Plus One (G4+1) accounting standard setters that met periodically and published a series of discussion documents on major accounting topics and had worked with certain other national standard setters to develop common standards (for example, with Canada on segment reporting). Both the FASB and the SEC had long supported the concept of a single set of high quality international accounting standards as a means for improving international comparability of financial information and reducing the costs to financial statement preparers, auditors, and users. However, as I will discuss in greater depth in chapter 4, "International Convergence," a larger portion of the FASB's activities since 2002 has been devoted to the convergence program with the IASB.

A driving force behind this movement has been the continuing globalization of capital markets and capital flows, including increased investment by U.S. investors in foreign securities. Looking at the world of accounting and financial reporting in 2002, there were two sets of widely accepted standards in use across the world: International Accounting Standards (formerly IAS now IFRS) and U.S. GAAP. IASs had been developed by a body called the IASC and were used by companies in a number of countries. The establishment of the IASB in 2001 to replace the IASC and the announcement by the European Commission that it planned to require the use of IASs by all listed companies in the European Union starting in 2005 provided added impetus to the IASs and their potential future use around the world. U.S. GAAP was widely used, not only in the United States, which is the largest national economy and capital market in the world, but also around the world. This was due to two things: the spread of U.S. corporations across the globe and the requirement that foreign companies seeking to raise capital in the U.S. public markets either use U.S. GAAP or reconcile key financial statement items to U.S. GAAP.

So, it made sense that achieving a truly global set of accounting standards would require the IASB and FASB to work together. Also, the reporting scandals of 2001–02 led some to question the long-held belief in this country that our standards were the best in the world. Some called for a movement to more principles-based standards along the lines of IASs, a view supported by both Paul Volcker, who chaired the trustees of the IASB's oversight body, and Harvey Pitt, the then-Chairman of the SEC. Indeed, Sarbanes-Oxley called for the SEC to study whether the United States should move to more principles-based accounting standards and specifically required the U.S. accounting standard setter to consider the potential benefits to U.S. investors and the public interest of international convergence.

For my part, I considered this a labor of love. It was in keeping with my international background, experience, and interests. I had just been a member of the IASB and chair of the Transnational Auditors Committee. I had done a lot international assignments at Price Waterhouse, Coopers & Lybrand, and PricewaterhouseCoopers and served on the Global Board and in other international roles. My training in U.K. accounting and reporting and my knowledge of both U.S. GAAP and IASs had led me to conclude that there were relative strengths and weaknesses among the various sets of accounting standards.

So, as discussed in chapter 4, starting with the Norwalk Agreement in October 2002, international convergence between the FASB and the IASB became an important part of both board's efforts. That, together with pursuing the improvement and simplification objectives, was to guide a good part of the FASB's activities during my years as chairman.

Setting Course

In this chapter, I have provided an overview of the key strategic objectives we set in 2002 and the initiatives and actions we then took in pursuit of those objectives in the ensuing years. I believe it is important for any organization to have a vision and set of strategic objectives to guide its actions and overall direction, particularly in turbulent and changing times. I was fortunate to join the organization at a moment in history that, although presenting many challenges, also provided significant opportunities for new ideas and new directions. As well, I was blessed with having terrific colleagues at both the FASB and FAF. Once charted, we set course, guided by the strategic objectives, the action steps

Chapter 2: Charting Course

we had mapped out, and the FASB's constant mission of developing and issuing high-quality standards through an independent, thorough, and open due process. As chronicled in the chapters that follow, in changing and sometimes rough seas, the sailing was not always smooth, and we were not always able to stick to the course that we had charted. Some changes in course were needed in response to changes in the broader environment in which the FASB operates. Overall, I believe the plans, initiatives, and actions we developed in my early months at the FASB and that we then subsequently implemented have had an important, lasting, and beneficial impact on accounting standard setting and financial reporting, both in the United States and internationally.

Chapter 3: Stock Option Controversies—Take Two

> An assault is underway to convince Congress that it should block the Financial Accounting Standards Board's proposed rule requiring companies to expense employee stock options ... some have responded to this pronouncement with renewed legislative efforts to undercut FASB's authority and politicize the rule-making process. These are counter to the health of our financial markets. The preservation of FASB's independence is fundamental to maintaining transparent, competitive and liquid markets. If the U.S. is to retain its credibility in the global marketplace, Congress must resist the temptation to interfere with FASB.[1]

In chapter 2, "Charting Course," I noted that two of the three strategic objectives we set after I arrived at the Financial Accounting Standards Board (FASB) were improvement of standards and international convergence. The subject of accounting for employee stock compensation and, in particular, for employee stock options represented the confluence of these two objectives. It was an area requiring improvement in the existing standards, and it was a subject of a major ongoing project by the IASB. As I discuss in this chapter, it was also a very controversial and politically charged subject that the FASB had addressed in the not too distant past.

In 1995, the FASB issued FASB Statement No. 123.[2] That statement was the result of a FASB project to reconsider the accounting for stock-based

---

[1] Senator Richard C. Shelby, "Cut It Out, Congress," *Wall Street Journal*, 6 May 2004.
[2] *Accounting for Stock-Based Compensation.*

compensation, including stock options issued to corporate executives and employees. The project lasted more than 10 years and generated an immense amount of controversy. Many, if not most, constituents opposed the FASB's proposal to require the recording of compensation based on the fair value of stock options granted to employees. As explained in the following paragraphs, under the then-existing accounting standards, companies were able to avoid recording compensation expense for so-called "fixed price" stock options. In contrast, the accounting rules required that the fair value of restricted stock granted to employees be recorded as compensation expense. Because of this and other anomalies in the accounting rules, the compensation plans of many companies included fixed-price stock options. That practice was particularly prevalent among high-tech companies and venture capital-backed companies.

The opposition to the FASB's proposal was fierce and politically charged, attracting the attention of Congress and other policymakers in Washington, D.C. The FASB had few allies. Even institutional investors, believing that the granting of stock options helped align the interests of management with those of shareholders, generally opposed the FASB's proposal. Under pressure from Congress, Arthur Levitt, the then-Chairman of the SEC, urged the FASB to withdraw the proposal, an action he would later describe in his book *Take on the Street* as his worst decision as SEC Chairman. Levitt said the following in the June 20, 2002, PBS *Frontline* episode "Congress and the Accounting Wars":

> When I came to the SEC, this new FASB rule to expense stock options had galvanized the American business community and brought literally hundreds of CEOs to my office in Washington to urge me to prevent the FASB from going ahead this proposal.... But what happened during the course of this fierce debate and dialogue was that the Congress changed, and Newt Gingrich brought to power a group of congresspeople who were determined to keep FASB from enacting this rule proposal. My concern was that if Congress put through a law that muzzled FASB, that would kill independent standards setting. So I went to the FASB at that time, and I urged them not to go ahead with the rule proposal. It was probably the single biggest mistake I made in my years at the SEC.

Ultimately, in issuing FASB Statement No. 123, five of the seven FASB Board members agreed to a compromise under which companies were encouraged but not required to adopt the fair-value-based method of accounting for employee stock options. If they chose not to adopt, they could continue to use the existing accounting and provide disclosures in the footnotes relating to the fair value of the options granted and what reported earnings and earnings per share would have been had the options been accounted for as a compensation expense under the fair-value-based method. I can imagine that this must have been a very

Chapter 3: Stock Option Controversies—Take Two

difficult decision for each of the FASB Board members. Paragraphs 60–62 of FASB Statement No. 123 address the decision not to require the fair value-based method:

> 60. The debate on accounting for stock-based compensation unfortunately became so divisive that it threatened the Board's future working relationship with some of its constituents. Eventually, the nature of the debate threatened the future of accounting standards setting in the private sector.
>
> 61. [T]he Board decided that the extent of improvement in financial reporting that was envisioned when this project was added to its technical agenda and when the Exposure Draft was issued was not attainable because the deliberate, logical consideration of issues that usually leads to improvement in financial reporting was no longer present. Therefore, the Board decided to specify as preferable and to encourage but not require recognition of compensation cost for all stock-based employee compensation, with required disclosure of the pro forma effects of such recognition by entities that continue to apply Opinion 25.
>
> 62. The Board believes that disclosure of the pro forma effects of recognizing compensation cost according to the fair value based method will provide relevant new information that will be of value to the capital markets and thus will achieve some but not all of the original objectives of the project. However, the Board also continues to believe that disclosure is not an adequate substitute for recognition ... in the financial statements.... The Board chose a disclosure-based solution for stock-based employee compensation to bring closure to the divisive debate on this issue—not because it believes that solution is the best way to improve financial accounting and reporting.

Virtually no companies chose to adopt the preferable fair-value-based approach and, as a result, were able to continue to avoid recording any compensation expense related to fixed-price employee stock options. During the bull stock market of the 1990s and into 2001, the use of such employee stock options by many companies grew significantly. Executives at many companies and employees at companies with broad-based stock option plans experienced a significant increase in their net worth. However, some began to question the soundness of this trend.

> AFL-CIO, the main American trades-union federation, points out that, thanks largely to share options, the average American chief executive now takes home 419 times the wage of the average factory worker. In 1980, he made 42 times as much.
>
> But put to one side questions of justice and inequality. Force down the thought that the chief executive's enormous share options may demoralise the deputy chief executive and make the company harder to manage. Ignore the bleating bondholder, who sees his risk rise as companies borrow to buy back shares to give to executives. The fundamental question is whether share-option

55

schemes are doing what they were designed to do: aligning the interests of managers with those of owners, motivating bosses to do their level best by shareholders.

Are share options working? Are other shareholders seeing gains from handing over so much equity to their managers? Or are bosses receiving the largest peacetime transfer of wealth in history simply for being in the right job at the right time—namely, during America's strongest equity bull market ever? Indeed, could share options be encouraging bosses to behave in ways that are contributing to a bubble in share prices which, should it pop, will leave everyone worse off? ...

First, it is hard to tell whether profits have, in fact, risen all that much, for the cost of most executive share-option schemes is not fully reflected in company profit-and-loss accounts. Attempts by the Financial Accounting Standards Board (FASB) to require firms to set the cost of options against profits were killed by corporate lobbyists in 1995. They argued that if the cost of option schemes were treated in that way, fewer of them would be awarded, fewer people would have reason to maximise shareholder value and the economy would suffer.[3]

However, as required under FASB Statement No. 123, companies now did have to calculate the value of stock options issued to employees and provide disclosures of the pro forma effects on reported earnings and earnings per share. Although I believe that was an important step forward, there is an old saying in accounting, backed by extensive academic research: "disclosure is not an adequate substitute for bad accounting." The accounting for fixed-price employee stock options was, in my view, a prime example of that saying because, as to be discussed, allowing companies to not recognize compensation cost relating to these instruments in computing earnings resulted in significant distortions in reported results, in the design of executive and employee compensation plans, and in corporate governance at many companies. In turn, such distortions can give rise to potential misallocation of capital across the economy.

What's the Problem?

The then-existing accounting rules relating to employee stock compensation were issued in 1972 as APB Opinion No. 25.[4] Those rules generally required the recognition of compensation expense for grants to employees of stock, stock options, and other forms of stock-based compensation, such as stock appreciation rights. However, stock option grants were exempted from the rule if they met certain conditions of

---

[3] See http://business.illinois.edu/doogar/303/Articles/economistoptiongrants.htm.
[4] *Accounting for Stock Issued to Employees.*

vesting and strike price. Options could have no vesting requirements other than continued employment through a certain period (so-called "time vesting"). Also, the strike price of the option (that is, the price the employee had to pay to exercise the option) could be no lower than the market price of the stock on the date the option was granted. A typical example of an employee stock option meeting these conditions is one that has a 5-year life (that is, it expires 5 years from the date of grant); vests 3 years from the date of grant, provided the employee was still with the company; and has a strike price equal to the market price of the stock at the date of grant—say $20. In this example, the option is issued "at the money" and has no intrinsic value at the grant date (that is, there is not a positive difference at the grant date between the value of the stock and the strike price that has to be paid to buy the stock).

So why does such an option have value at the date it is granted if, as in the example, the employee would have to pay $20 to get a share of stock that right now is also worth $20? The answer lies in the holder's right to exercise the option at future dates when there might be a positive pay-off. Stock prices go up and down. In our example option, if the employee continues to work for the company for the next 3 years, the option will vest, and he or she will be able to buy the stock for $20 at any time during the succeeding 2 years. During those 2 years, the stock may trade at various levels above and below $20. It might go as high as $50, in which case the option would be $30 "in the money," and the employee would have a $30 gain if he or she were to exercise the option at that point in time. Therefore, the value of the option depends on the probabilities and amounts of potential future positive pay-offs. Various option-pricing models have been developed over the last 40 years to value all sorts of options, and there are markets for many different types of options, including options on the stocks of individual companies and on indexes based on baskets of stocks, such as the S&P 500. These models provide a means of valuing an option at any point during its life.

Intuitively, one can understand some of the key factors that drive the value of an option. For example, the longer the life of an option, the higher its value. Let's take the sample option in the previous paragraph and assign a 10-year rather than a 5-year life. When that option vests in 3 years it could be exercised at any time during the next 7 years. This makes the option more valuable than an option with a 5-year life because there would be more chances in 7 years than in 2 years for positive pay-offs and potentially higher positive pay-offs during that period. Similarly, the more volatile the price of the stock, the higher the value of an option to purchase that stock because the higher the volatility, the greater the chances and amounts of potential positive pay-offs. Accountants have debated and accounting standard setters have extensively discussed whether the compensation expense related to employee stock options should be based on the value of the option at the date it is granted or the date it vests or on the ultimate pay-off to the employee if and when it is exercised. There are conceptual accounting arguments for and against using each of these. For various conceptual and practical reasons, accounting standard setters have decided that it should be measured at the date the option is granted, and that amount is then charged to compensation expense over the time period the employee works to vest in the option. So, in our example, assume the value of the option is $6 at the date it is granted. Because the employee has to work 3 years for the option to vest and become exercisable, compensation expense of $2 would be recognized in each of those 3 years. The same accounting approach is used for grants of stock to employees. For example, if the employee had been granted a share of stock worth $20 at the grant date and it vested if the employee continued to work for the company for 3 years, $6.66 of compensation expense would be recognized in each of 3 years following the date of grant.

The exception under APB Opinion No. 25 that was allowed to continue under FASB Statement No. 123 enabled companies to compensate employees at no accounting cost. As such, it created an accounting bias for using such options and against using other forms of compensation, including cash, grants of stock, stock appreciation rights, and stock options with performance requirements, all of which resulted in the recognition of compensation expense. Some of the resulting accounting seemed perverse and counterintuitive. Let's look again at our sample option for an example of this. The employee has to continue to work for the company for 3 years for the option to vest. Now let's add an additional requirement: the option vests only if the company also increases its net income by at least 50 percent over that period. In that case, the accounting rules under APB Opinion No. 25 required that compensation expense be recorded based on the intrinsic value of the option over the 3 years. Yet, because the option contained an additional condition for it to vest, it would likely be less valuable to the employee and potentially less costly to the company than the one that required only continued service by the employee. Further, the exception applied only to stock options granted to employees. The accounting rules have long required that stock options granted to suppliers or providers of debt financing to the company be valued and expense be recognized based on those values. As Warren Buffett had famously quipped, "If stock options aren't a form of compensation, what are they? If compensation isn't an expense, what is it? And, if expenses shouldn't go into the calculation of earnings, where in the world do they go?"[5]

---

[5] "Use and Abuse, the Trouble with Options," *The Economist*, 18 July 2002.

In summary, the existing accounting rules created an incentive for companies to use a particular form of compensation based on the impact on reported earnings, not underlying economic, financial, business, corporate governance, or human resource considerations. As Donald Delves, a well-known compensation consultant, put it in his book *Stock Options & the New Rules of Corporate Accountability: Measuring, Managing, and Rewarding Executive Performance*,[6]

> Executive stock options are a problem for two reasons. First companies have granted too many of them. Second they are ineffective incentives and rewards at most companies. This has been exacerbated by accounting rules that contributed directly to the untenable mess that all of us involved in executive compensation, including executives, board members, and compensation consultants must address.... Under current accounting a very narrow definition of a derivative security—specifically an at-the-money call option granted to an executive receives a very special accounting treatment. These options have no expense whatsoever associated with them.... Through this strange but very tempting little loophole, truckloads of options have been delivered to executives with no expense to the companies granting them. Because of this same loophole, hundreds of billions of dollars of shareholder value has been transferred to executives with virtually no controls or limitations.... More importantly because of this loophole, approximately 95 percent of public companies pay their executives in *exactly* the same way, using *exactly* the same specific derivative security. And they have blindly granted them in substantial and ever-increasing numbers.... There is no way that if every company in America started with a blank sheet of paper, virtually all of them would simultaneously conclude that this particular form of incentive is precisely the best one for them. That is absurd.

In addition to the favorable accounting treatment of employee stock options, there were also tax motivations to use them as a form of compensation. First, although no cost had to be recorded for accounting and financial reporting purposes, companies were able to take a deduction in computing taxable income, generally based on the spread between the value of the stock issued to the employee upon exercise of an option and the strike price paid by the employee to exercise the option. Second, stock options were generally exempt from Internal Revenue Code Section 162(m) that was enacted by Congress in 1994 and capped an employer's annual tax deduction for compensation to an employee at $1 million. Therefore, the use of stock options became a preferred method of compensating senior executives.

---

[6] Donald P. Delves, *Stock Options and the New Rules of Corporate Accountability: Measuring, Managing, and Rewarding Executive Performance.* New York: McGraw-Hill, 2004, pp. 6–7.

So, given these accounting and tax incentives, it is not surprising that there was an explosion in the use of stock options by companies. According to professors Joseph R. Blasi, Douglas L. Kruse, and Aaron Bernstein, authors of *In the Company of Owners: The Truth about Stock Options*, from 1992 to 2001, the top 5 executives of the largest 1,500 U.S. companies made $67 billion in gains from stock options. The authors also reference a study by the Board of Governors of the Federal Reserve System that found that if stock options had been expensed between 1995 and 2000, annual corporate earnings growth would have been 5 percent, not the reported 8.3 percent.[7] Merrill Lynch estimated that had options been expensed, earnings for the S&P 500 would have been 21 percent lower in 2001 and 39 percent lower in the IT sector.[8]

The use of stock options could result in reducing the reported earnings per share of a company because the stock issued by a company to satisfy stock option exercises or issuable to satisfy outstanding "in-the-money" stock options is counted in the denominator of the earnings per share calculation. However, in order to eliminate or reduce this dilution of earnings per share, some companies would engage in large-scale purchases of their stock in the market, purchases of so called "treasury stock" that reduce the number of shares counted in the earnings per share calculation. In doing so, some companies, particularly some major high-tech companies that made heavy use of stock options, were expending a significant portion of their operating cash flow to purchase treasury stock to meet stock option exercises.

Moreover, the failure to recognize compensation expense relating to fixed-price employee stock options in determining reported earnings had a number of harmful effects on investors and shareholders, in the design of executive and employee compensation arrangements, on corporate governance surrounding executive pay, and, perhaps most importantly, on the efficient allocation of capital across the capital markets and between companies and industry sectors. I summarized these in a letter to Congressman Barney Frank, "Letter to Representative Barney Frank: May 10, 2004," shown here in exhibit 3-1.

---

[7] Joseph R. Blasi, Douglas L. Kruse, and Aaron Bernstein, *In the Company of Owners: The Truth About Stock Options*, Basic Books, 2003.

[8] See Justin Lahart, "Bracing for an Earnings Hit." *CNN/Money.* July 17, 2002, http://money.cnn.com/2002/07/11/news/options/index.htm.

Exhibit 3-1: Letter to Representative Barney Frank: May 10, 2004

Via Facsimile

May 10, 2004

The Honorable Barney Frank
House of Representatives
Washington, DC 20515

Dear Representative Frank:

At the May 4, 2004, hearing before the Capital Markets, Insurance and Government Sponsored Enterprises Subcommittee of the Committee on Financial Services you asked me a very appropriate and relevant question—Who's harmed by the current situation under which certain employee stock options are not required to be expensed? The purpose of this letter is to provide you with a more complete and yet concise response to your question.

Investors and Shareholders

Many prominent investors, and financial, economic, and accounting experts agree that the fixed plan employee stock option accounting anomaly results in an absolute and relative distortion of profitability and other key financial metrics. The greater the use of those instruments the greater the distortion. The distortion may mislead investors, particularly, but not limited to, less sophisticated investors, and footnote disclosures are not an adequate remedy.

Many also agree that the anomaly and related distortion was a contributing factor to the stock market bubble, the severity of the subsequent crash, and some of the recent high profile corporate reporting scandals and subsequent bankruptcies. Those events resulted in significant investor losses and an overall loss in investor confidence.

Many also agree that the anomaly encourages some companies to issue an excessive amount of fixed plan employee stock options resulting in an opaque transfer of economic value from shareholders to employees. In order to maintain their stock price in the face of such dilution, studies have shown that companies expend large amounts of cash on stock buybacks that have absorbed much of their free cash flow. The result is that there is less cash available for other purposes, such as research and development or employee training, which may be more beneficial to the long-term value of the company and its shareholders.

Many, including prominent compensation experts, also agree that the anomaly discourages companies from utilizing other forms of equity-based compensation that may be more beneficial to the long-term value of the company and its shareholders, and that may have better incentive properties in terms of attracting, motivating, and retaining employees, than fixed plan stock options. Examples often cited include performance based-options and restricted stock.

Misallocation of Capital Across the Capital Markets and Between Companies and Industry Sectors

Many prominent investors and financial and economic experts contend that the fixed plan employee stock option accounting anomaly can result in a misallocation of capital across the capital markets and between companies and industry sectors. In effect, the biased and distorted accounting creates an unlevel playing field that inappropriately favors those companies that are the greatest users of fixed plan employee stock options over other companies that have either chosen to compensate their employees in different ways (including different forms of equity-based compensation) or use fixed plan employee stock options but have voluntarily elected to expense them. Thus, the overall effect may be a diversion of investment and capital resources away from their most efficient employment. As Federal Reserve Chairman Greenspan recently noted in commenting on this subject "we're getting a distorted view as to what the profitability of a particular operation is and you will get a distortion in the allocation of capital."

I hope this letter is responsive to your question. The attachments include excerpts from articles and other materials addressing the above points and other related points in more detail. I would be happy to discuss any of those points with you or your staff, or provide additional explanatory materials, at your request.

Sincerely,

Robert H. Herz

Attachments

Addressing the Accounting Issues in the Face of Pressure Politics

One of the initial projects undertaken by the IASB in 2001 was the accounting for stock-based compensation, or, as we called it (I was member of the IASB at the time), accounting for share-based payment. There were no existing International Accounting Standards in this area at that time. In exploring the issues, the IASB concluded that employee stock options should be accounted for as compensation and viewed the fair-value-based method previously proposed by the FASB and used in the United States for the footnote disclosures under FASB Statement No. 123 to be a reasonable approach. The heightened focus on financial reporting in the United States stemming from the reporting scandals of 2001–02 led a number of parties to question whether the existing accounting for stock options had been a factor behind some of the scandals and a causal factor in what was perceived by some as undesirable and reckless behavior by corporate executives seeking to reap a big personal payday through the exercise of their stock options at inflated prices for their company's stock. So, there were calls from investors, financial analysts, and others for changes in the accounting for employee stock options.

During the second half of 2002, a number of U.S. public companies announced they would start recognizing compensation cost for employee stock options, including many major companies in the financial services industry. Very notably, Microsoft, which had long made heavy use of employee stock options, announced on July 8, 2003, it would begin recording compensation expense relating to option grants and would be moving more to the use of restricted stock instead of options in its compensation plans. Then-Chairman of the Federal Reserve Alan Greenspan spoke publicly about why he believed compensation expense should be recorded for employee stock options, stating the following in a May 3, 2002, speech to the Financial Markets Conference of the Federal Reserve Bank of Atlanta that was entirely devoted to the subject of expensing of stock options:

> The seemingly narrow accounting matter of option expensing is, in fact, critically important for the accurate representation of corporate performance. And accurate accounting, in turn, is central to the functioning of free-market capitalism—the system that has brought such a high level of prosperity to our country.... The estimation of earnings is difficult enough without introducing biases into the calculation. I fear that the failure to expense stock option grants has introduced a significant distortion in reported earnings—and one that has grown with the increasing prevalence of this form of compensation.... To assume that option grants are not an expense is to assume that the real

resources that contributed to the creation of the value of the output were free.... The particular instrument that is used to transfer value in return for labor services is irrelevant. Its value is not.... With an accounting system that is, or should be, measuring the success or failure of corporate strategies, the evolution of accounting rules is essential as the nature of our economy changes. As the measurement needs change, rules must change with them.

I remember thinking at the time that the fact that the Chairman of the Federal Reserve had specifically chosen to make this accounting matter the focus of a major speech evidenced the broader significance of addressing this issue to the capital markets and economy.

At the same time, a number of other parties, principally from the high-tech, biotech, and venture capital industries, continued to strongly oppose a potential change in the accounting for employee stock options. In November 2002, the IASB issued an exposure draft, *Share-based Payment*, that proposed the expensing of stock options. That same month, FASB issued Invitation to Comment, *Accounting for Stock-Based Compensation: A Comparison of FASB Statement No. 123, and Its Related Interpretations, and IASB Proposed IFRS, Share-based Payment*, soliciting input from constituents on whether the FASB should undertake a project to reconsider the accounting for stock-based compensation, including employee stock options. Although a majority of companies that responded did not favor the FASB undertaking such a project, many other parties, including most users of financial information, believed that a second look was warranted and changes were needed. Accordingly, in March 2003, the Board voted unanimously to add a project to reconsider the accounting for stock-based compensation.

The Board did so expecting that the FASB would again likely face very strong opposition from members of the high-tech, biotech, and venture capital industries. Indeed, senior representatives of those industries quickly made their views known to us, the SEC, and members of Congress. They argued that the existing accounting was appropriate and that recording compensation expense for fixed-price stock options was flawed for a number of reasons, including that the real cost of employee stock options was already captured via their potentially dilutive effect on earnings per share calculations and that it was impossible to accurately value an employee stock option at the date it is granted. They also maintained that their ability to grant employee stock options without recording compensation expense was essential to the successful operation of their business model, attracting and retaining key people, and their ability to successfully innovate. As such, any changes to accounting that discouraged the use of employee stock options would have severe negative consequences on companies and industries that were vital to the growth and vibrancy of the U.S. economy and on the competiveness of the United States in global markets. In other words, it was very bad public policy. For example, the website of Cisco Systems, a leading high-tech company that actively opposed the recognition of compensation expense for employee stock options, included the following "Key Messages" on these public policy issues:

> Broad-based stock option plans give employees at all levels a chance to own a "piece of the rock" and increase productivity for the company.
>
> Options programs keep companies competitive in recruiting and retention—especially needed in time of global competition for engineering talent.
>
> As other countries are graduating many more engineers and math and science PhDs than the US—which lead to innovative new technologies and research—stock options must remain a key tool for recruitment and retention for companies.
>
> Employee stock options fuel innovation and the entrepreneurial spirit.
>
> More countries are also recognizing that the promise of company ownership motivates all workers. China, for example, has the utilization of stock options at the center of its five-year economic expansion plan.
>
> Expensing stock options could lead to elimination or curtailment of broad-based options plans.[9]

I had visited Silicon Valley many times and, while I was a member of the Coopers & Lybrand (C&L) Boston office, worked on the audits of "Route 128" technology companies. We had invested in venture capital funds and start-ups in the C&L Partner Investment Funds. This had given me an appreciation for the spirit of entrepreneurialism and innovation among the players in these industries. I also gained genuine admiration for the success of venture capital-backed companies in developing many high-tech and biotech breakthroughs that have greatly benefited our country and mankind and for their ability to grow these companies into major corporations that have contributed to overall job and wealth creation. So, I was not dismissing the public policy arguments about the importance of employee stock options to these sectors and, by extension, our economy and country. However, I was deeply committed to the role of the FASB and accounting standards in fostering financial reporting that faithfully reflects the economics of transactions, to "tell it like it is" as best we can and within cost-benefit constraints. That objective is aimed at fostering more efficient and effective allocation of capital, a public policy goal that is critical to a sound economy. Financial reporting is meant to be as unbiased as possible and not to be purposefully skewed to favor or

---

[9] See www.cisco.com/web/about/gov/archive/stock_options.html.

disfavor a particular type of arrangement, specific companies, or particular industries. Another way of stating this principle is that accounting should not be used as a way of providing either a subsidy or penalty for particular transactions, companies, or industries. So, I believe my fellow Board members and I were determined, consistent with our mission and public policy role, to continue our systematic, careful, and thorough reconsideration of the accounting and financial reporting issues relating to employee stock options and other forms of stock-based compensation. That required us to carefully examine the arguments for and against various potential accounting treatments of employee stock options, including reviewing a number of alternatives that would be presented to us by companies, academics, and others during what became a very thorough and extensive two-year examination of these matters.

Just as the Board had experienced back in the 1990s, there were virtually constant efforts to discredit, delay, and derail our project. These efforts were spearheaded under the rubric of the International Employee Stock Options Coalition, "the Coalition" as they referred to themselves. It was well-funded, included a number of industry groups comprising the high-tech and other sectors, and employed various lobbyists and public relations professionals. They walked the halls of Capitol Hill meeting with members of Congress, organized "fly-ins" of CEOs and executives to lobby legislators, and helped place numerous articles and op-ed pieces opposing our efforts.

Just prior to our public meeting in March 2003 to vote on whether to add the project, we received the letters shown in exhibit 3-2, "Letters From Senate and House of Representatives to the Financial Accounting Standards Board on Employee Stock Options." One of these letters was from 15 members of the Senate urging us to proceed with caution in undertaking a reconsideration of the accounting for employee stock options. The other letter, similar to the first, was from 40 members of the House of Representatives, and it also urged us to proceed with caution.

Exhibit 3-2: Letters From Senate and House of Representatives to the Financial Accounting Standards Board on Employee Stock Options*

March 7, 2003

Financial Accounting Standards Board
MP&T Director — File Reference 1101-001
401 Merritt 7
P.O. Box 5116
Norwalk, CT 06856

Dear Board Members:

We are writing in response to the FASB's Invitation to Comment on accounting for stock options to express our concern that the process is basically flawed because the Invitation to Comment specifically directed respondents not to comment on whether stock options granted to employees result in compensation expense for the issuing company.

As many of the comment letters that have been submitted make clear, that is precisely the threshold question about which many experts disagree. It seems quite odd to us that you would want your respondents to pass over that crucial question. We would therefore urge the FASB - consistent with the historical commitment to due process - to carefully weigh the comments of those who nonetheless chose to address it.

Investors need accurate, reliable and meaningful information to make informed investment decisions. Accounting rules should reflect accounting principles that are generally accepted within the accounting profession, especially those that promote the disclosure, transparency, comparability and reliability of financial statements.

We believe a mandatory expensing standard - such as that proposed by the International Accounting Standards Board and apparently which is under consideration by the FASB - may not meet these important tests. Indeed, the comment letters submitted to the FASB thus far, as well as other materials on the public record, strongly suggest that a mandatory expensing standard will mislead investors with inaccurate information, skew the financial picture of companies (particularly those with volatile stock prices) and eviscerate broad-based stock options plans that are vital to economic productivity and employee advancement.

...

A recently published book, *In the Company of Owners: The Truth About Stock Options (And Why Every Employee Should Have Them)* includes extensive research showing that broad-based stock option plans, over the past 20 years, enhanced productivity, spurred capital formation and enhanced shareholder value. The authors, Rutgers University Professors Joseph Blasi and Douglas Kruse and *Business Week* senior writer Aaron Bernstein, describe the extraordinary degree to which high-tech companies have "shared the wealth" with their employees, terming this "partnership capitalism." Their study of what they call the High Tech 100 - the 100 largest public companies that derive more than half their sales from the Internet - shows that employees hold a 19 percent ownership stake, which is more than the ownership stake held by senior executives.

This study and others demonstrate that the widespread employee ownership that defines broad-based stock option plans is good for workers, good for investors and good for the economy. As Staples wrote in its recent comment letter, "the role of stock options in the phenomenal growth and success of Staples cannot be overstated. From its founding, Staples has issued options as compensation for employees deep into the organization. These options, and in particular this egalitarian way of issuing them, were instrumental in providing the entrepreneurial incentive to create a $12 billion company in only 15 years." We encourage the FASB not to adopt accounting standards that are likely to destroy this valuable tool.

...

In sum, timely, accurate and meaningful disclosures, coupled with shareholder approval of all stock option plans, are the accounting and corporate governance reforms that, in our view, will best serve investors. They are far better than mandatory expensing which will effectively end the use of broad-based stock option plans and their ability to contribute to increases in productivity, the expansion of employee ownership, and to growing the economy.

Thank you for considering our views.

Sincerely,

Sen. Mike Enzi, R-Wyo.
Sen. George Allen, R-Va.
Sen. Barbara Boxer, D-Calif.
Sen. Joe Lieberman, D-Conn.
Sen. John Warner, R-Va.
Sen. Patty Murray, D-Wash.
Sen. John Ensign, R-Nev.
Sen. Harry Reid, D-Nev.
Sen. Larry Craig, R-Idaho

Chapter 3: Stock Option Controversies—Take Two

Sen. Maria Cantwell, D-Wash.
Sen. Conrad Burns, R-Mont.
Sen. Debbie Stabenow, D-Mich.
Sen. Pete Domenici, R-N.M.
Sen. Edward Kennedy, D-Mass.
Sen. Gordon Smith, R-Ore.

Congress of the United States
House of Representatives
Washington, DC 20515

January 30, 2003
Financial Accounting Standards Board
MP&T Director — File Reference 1101-001
401 Merritt 7
P.O. Box 5116
Norwalk, Connecticut 06856

Dear Sir or Madam:

In response to the Financial Accounting Standards Board's recent Invitation to Comment on accounting for employee stock options, we write to express our strong opposition to any proposal which would mandate the expensing of broad-based stock option plans. We appreciate the opportunity to provide our comments and request that FASB give its highest consideration to them.

Events of the past year have eroded investor confidence and contributed to significant concern about the adequacy of our laws, rules and policies governing corporate oversight, financial reporting, and accounting practices. Restoring investor trust, revitalizing our capital markets, eliminating corporate fraud and abuse, and growing America's economy are objectives each of us shares.

We do not wish to set accounting standards. However, in light of the proposed International Accounting Standards Board (IASB) standard that would mandate the expensing of employee stock options, and FASB's close coordination with IASB, we believe it is important to express our strong concerns about an approach that would limit transparency, truthfulness and accuracy in financial reporting, precisely at a time when America and its investors need these qualities the most. The public interest will not be served by an accounting standard that results in the disclosure of inaccurate corporate financial information and a flawed picture of company performance.

It is apparent to us that a mandatory expensing standard lacks a clear and widely accepted accounting rationale. Accounting experts have vastly divergent views as to whether employee stock options should be accounted for as a cost to be deducted from earnings. Many respected, independent experts find that the "cost" of employee stock options is already accounted for and disclosed to investors through diluted earnings per share. Investors would be better served by full and complete disclosure of this diluted earnings per share number.

Additionally, pricing models currently available, such as Black-Scholes or slight variations on it, were designed for entirely different kinds of options that have little in common with employee stock options. The same model can produce widely differing results depending on the particular guesstimates a company decides to use. Highly subjective numbers that are not reliable or meaningful are of no use to investors, and in fact, hurt their ability to make informed decisions. We concur with the view recently expressed by one expert that "[i]f anything, expensing options may lead to an even more distorted picture of a company's economic position and cash flows than financial statements currently paint." (William Sahlman, Professor of Business Administration, Harvard Business School, "Expensing Options Solves Nothing," *Harvard Business Review*, December 2002.)

Moreover, mandatory expensing would effectively destroy broad-based stock option plans, which enhance financial opportunities for workers at all levels, stimulating economic growth and productivity. Broad-based employee stock options plans play a vital role in America's economy, helping employees, shareholders, and companies alike. A recent study found that broad-based plans - which grant options to most, if not all, employees - have bestowed significant economic benefit on tens of thousands of "rank and file" workers over the past two decades, enhanced productivity, spurred capital formation, and fueled the growth of some of our nation's most innovative companies. The Rutgers University researchers make a compelling case that such plans are a form of "partnership capitalism," that "makes most companies more competitive and creates more wealth for shareholders." (Blasi, Kruse, and Bernstein, *In the Company of Owners*)

Commendably, FASB has just recently required more timely and extensive disclosure of information about employee stock options. In light of the serious negative consequences and dislocation likely to arise from mandated expensing, it seems more prudent to allow the new disclosures to work and perhaps, supplement them further with additional and more investor-friendly information. Accurate, timely and rigorous investor-friendly disclosures would do more to inform investor decision-making than new overlapping mandates hastily applied.

Accounting principles that foster transparency, truthful and accurate financial reporting, and meaningful disclosure are critically important to help investors make informed investment decisions, and to foster efficient and growing capital markets. We support accounting principles

Chapter 3: Stock Option Controversies—Take Two

that serve the public interest in this way, and we do not think a mandatory expensing standard meets this test.

At a time when our government is searching for new ways to stimulate the economy, we need a clear vision about the importance of broad-based stock option plans to the nation's entrepreneurial soul and the workers and investors who are part of it. We should adopt policies that encourage and expand the availability of broad-based stock option plans, not destroy them.

Sincerely,

Reps. David Dreier, Anna G. Eshoo, Darrell Issa, Jay Inslee, Joseph Crowley, Adam Smith, Dennis Moore, Zoe Lofgren, Carolyn McCarthy, Gary Miller, Cal Dooley, Jerry Weller, Pete Sessions, Ron Kind, Jennifer Dunn, Mike Honda, Rick Boucher, Bob Goodlatte, Lamar Smith, Tom Davis, J.D. Hayworth, Jane Harman, Doug Ose, David Wu, Joe Barton, Rick Larsen, Amo Houghton, Dennis Cardoza, Steve Israel, George Nethercutt, Darlene Hooley, John Boehner, Mike Simpson, Greg Walden, C.L. "Butch" Otter, Jeff Flake, Chris Cannon, John Carter, Heather Wilson, Bob Etheridge

*http://www.enzi.senate.gov/public/index.cfm/2003/3/enzi----fasb-stock-options-process-is-flawed; Office of Rep. Anna Eshoo (D-CA).

Soon after we began our deliberations on the issues, I was asked to participate in a roundtable discussion in Washington, D.C., on May 8, 2003. Although not an official Congressional hearing, the event was sponsored by Senators Michael Enzi, George Allen, and Barbara Boxer and was titled "Partnership Capitalism Through Stock Options for America's Workforce." I recall Senators Enzi and Allen and Representative Anna Eshoo being at the event and making strong statements against any expensing of stock options. I was accompanied by my fellow Board member Mike Crooch, and apart from us and Acting SEC Chief Accountant Jack Day, most of the other participants were from the Coalition or parties that opposed stock option expensing: John Doerr, a well-known venture capitalist from Kleiner Perkins, senior executives from technology companies, a NASDAQ official, and some lobbyists. At one point, Tom Stemberg, the CEO of Staples, made a cameo appearance, extolling the virtues of stock options. In short, the event seemed to have been carefully staged to try to attack and embarrass FASB. Mike and I, with the help of Jack Day, attempted to explain the reasons behind the project and our planned thorough due process and to respond to some of the inaccurate assertions made about our process and motives. For example, in response to Senator Allen's contention that nobody knew how to value employee stock options, I pointed out that for many years, they had been required to be valued and those values reported in the audited footnotes to the financial statements of public companies.

The May 9, 2003, article "Lawmakers, CEOs Criticize FASB for Options Move" in *Accountancy* reported, "It was billed as a roundtable, but seemed more like a boxing ring Thursday as lawmakers and CEOs rained verbal blows on America's accounting rulemaker for moving towards a requirement to expense stock options. Robert Herz, Chairman of the Financial Accounting Standards Board, left the Capitol Hill hearing room bloody but unbowed, saying he would proceed with the effort to develop new rules on stock option expensing."

Many Congressional hearings[10] by various committees in the House and Senate were to follow, and we continued to receive letters regarding the stock compensation project from individual members of the House and Senate and from groups of Representatives and Senators. A list of all open letters about this project can be found on the FASB website.[11]

During the course of our project, various bills drafted by the Coalition were introduced into the House and Senate that were aimed at blocking or delaying us in issuing a requirement to record compensation expense for employee stock options. One of the first of these bills, the Broad-Based Stock Option Plan Transparency Act of 2003, was introduced into the House of Representatives in March 2003. Although this bill would have required a number of new disclosures in SEC filings relating to employee stock options, it would also have prohibited the SEC from recognizing as generally accepted accounting principles any new accounting standards regarding the treatment of stock options for a period of more than three years. This would give the Department of

---

[10] 5/8/03: "Preserving Partnership Capitalism through Stock Options for America's Workforce." Senate Roundtable (Enzi, Allen, Boxer).

6/3/03: "Accounting Treatment of Employee Stock Options." House. Financial Services Committee. Capital Markets, Insurance and Government Sponsored Enterprises Subcommittee (Baker).

11/12/03: "The Financial Accounting Standards Board and Small Business Growth." Senate. Banking, Housing, and Urban Affairs Committee. Securities and Investment Subcommittee (Enzi).

4/20/04: "Oversight Hearing on Expensing Stock Options: Supporting and Strengthening the Independence of the FASB." Senate. Governmental Affairs Committee. Financial Management, the Budget and International Security Subcommittee.

4/28/04: "The Impact of Stock Option Expensing on Small Business." Senate. Small Business and Entrepreneurship Committee (Snowe/Enzi).

5/4/04: "The FASB Stock Options Proposal: Its Effect on the U.S. Economy and Jobs." House. Financial Services Committee. Capital Markets, Insurance and Government Sponsored Enterprises Subcommittee (Baker).

7/8/04: "FASB Proposals on Stock Options Expensing and HR 3574, the Stock Option Accounting Reform Act" House. Energy and Commerce Committee. Commerce, Trade and Consumer Protection Subcommittee.

[11] See www.fasb.org/jsp/FASB/CommentLetter_C/CommentLetterPage&cid=1218220137090&project_id=1101-001.

Commerce time to conduct a study on the economic impacts of the new standard, particularly on the high-tech and other high-growth industries, of broad-based employee stock option plans on job creation and employee retention, innovation, and U.S. competiveness. In other words, the bill would have imposed a lengthy moratorium on any changes in accounting for employee stock options. In my testimony on June 3, 2003, before the Subcommittee on Capital Markets, Insurance and Government Sponsored Enterprises of the House Committee on Financial Services, I explained why we strongly opposed the Broad-Based Stock Option Plan Transparency Act of 2003:

> First, the moratorium would unduly intervene in the Board's independent, objective, and open process to make unbiased decisions on the substance and timing of improvements to the accounting for stock-based compensation. Such intervention would be in direct conflict with the expressed needs and demands of many investors and other users of financial reports.... Second, the moratorium would have an adverse impact on the FASB's efforts to achieve timely convergence of high-quality international accounting standards on stock-based compensation. The FASB is actively working with the International Accounting Standards Board and other national standard setters to achieve convergence in this important area and in other areas.... Finally, and perhaps most importantly, the moratorium would establish a potentially dangerous precedent in that it would send a clear and unmistakable signal that Congress is willing to intervene in accounting standard setting. That signal would likely prompt others to seek political intervention in the future activities of the FASB. We have all witnessed the devastating effects and loss of investor confidence in financial reporting that have resulted from companies intentionally violating or manipulating accounting requirements. What impact then on the system, and on investors' trust in financial reports, might there be if it were perceived that accounting standard setting was being biased toward the pursuit of objectives other those relating to the fair financial reporting or that the FASB was being blocked from pursuing improvements in financial reporting?

This was one of many bills introduced into Congress designed to stop our efforts on improving the accounting for stock-based compensation and one of the many Congressional hearings that would be held on this subject. Notwithstanding all these ongoing pressure tactics, we carried on with our thorough, public due process on the project. Between March 2003 and March 2004, when we issued the exposure draft of the proposed standard for public comment, we systematically discussed the issues relating to accounting for stock-based compensation arrangements at a total of 39 public Board meetings and met with many companies, industry organizations, employee benefit plan consultants, auditors, investors, and other interested parties to discuss the issues.

We issued the exposure draft *Share-Based Payment* on March 31, 2004, with a comment period ending June 30, 2004. It provided an overall set of principles in accounting for share-based payments and included a significant amount of specific guidance covering a variety of arrangements, including employee stock options. As the Board had done back in the 1990s (and consistent with the IASB's new standard issued in February 2004), the March 2004 FASB exposure draft proposed eliminating the no compensation expense exception for the fixed-price employee stock options. We received more than 14,000 comment letters, the vast majority of them form letters. There were thousands of form letters from employees of companies opposed to the expensing of stock options and also thousands of form letters from trade union members supporting our proposal. Exhibit 3-3, "March 2004 Financial Accounting Standards Board Exposure Draft Comment Letter Samples," shows a sample form letter in support of our efforts and a sample form letter opposed to the project. The business press abounded with articles and commentaries on the subject. The FASB website has a list of all letters concerning this project.[12]

---

[12] See www.fasb.org/jsp/FASB/CommentLetter_C/CommentLetterPage&cid=1218220137090&project_id=1102-100&page_number=1.

Exhibit 3-3: March 2004 Financial Accounting Standards Board Exposure Draft Comment Letter Samples

Form Letter: Make Companies Put Stock Options on the Books.
Letter of Comment No: *5903*
File Reference: 1102·100

June 27, 2004 2:51 PM
Director, Major Projects and Technical Activities Financial Accounting Standards Board
File Reference No. 1102-100
Share-Based Payment; an amendment of FASB Statements No. 123 and 95
Norwalk, CT 06856-5116

Subject: Make Companies Put Stock Options on Books

Dear Director, Major Projects and Technical Activities Standards Board:

I strongly support your proposal to require companies to expense stock options. Not expensing stock options has promoted their overuse in CEO pay against the long-term interests of shareholders. For example, I believe stock options provided a financial incentive for Enron executives to cook the books.

The retirement savings of America's working families depend in part on all companies, including small businesses and start-ups, having honest accounting practices. Companies that do not expense stock options are hiding their true cost from investors, creditors and other consumers of financial reports. In my opinion, stock option compensation should not receive preferential accounting treatment.

In conclusion, I urge you to require stock option expensing as soon as possible. Independent experts, such as the Financial Accounting Standards Board, should set the standards on stock option expensing, not the politicians in Washington. Stock options are a compensation expense, and this cost can be reliably estimated using your proposed accounting method. I believe corporate executives should be ashamed for trying to hide the cost of stock options from their investors.

cc:
Senator Richard Shelby

Form Letter: Silicon Valley Bank

Letter of Comment No: 5599
File Reference: 1102-100

Dear Mr. Director,

I'm writing today to request that you reject the expensing of Stock Options as a FASB policy.

75% of my colleagues at Silicon Valley Bank participate in either our employee stock option program or our Employee Stock Purchase Plan (ESPP). It's no wonder why we often refer to ourselves not merely as employees, but as the "employee-owners" of Silicon Valley Bank[.]

Like many innovative companies in Silicon Valley and across the country, SVB has long embraced the ideal of employee ownership—via options or an ESPP—as a way for individuals to benefit directly from their contributions to the company's success.

Having said that, today the future of such broad-based employee ownership stands in jeopardy. It's for that reason that I'm writing today.

In response to the March 31, 2004 Financial Accounting Standards Board's Exposure Draft, the Share-Based Payment and Amendment of FASB Statements No. 123 and 95, I respectfully request the FASB to reconsider its position.

Employee stock options and Employee Stock Purchase Plans make me feel like I have a stake in the success of Silicon Valley Bank, and they motivate me to work harder. I believe that if SVB is forced to expense all employee stock options and ESPPs, my company might no longer offer such programs to the majority of employees. This would negatively impact morale, productivity, and innovation.

In addition, expensing stock options and ESPPs is bad accounting. The potential dilution of each investor's share of company ownership is the real cost of employee stock options. It's a cost that is already reflected in "diluted earnings per share" estimates in company financial statements.

In fact, there is no accurate, reliable, and consistent way to value employee stock options. Many leading economists believe that investors will not be well served by the misleading "guesstimates" produced by current option valuation formulas.

In closing, I'd like to once again urge the FASB to reconsider its position on this important issue. Broad-based stock option plans and ESPPs enhance productivity, increase shareholder value and benefit employees. Broad-based plans should be encouraged, not eliminated.

Respectfully,
[Names omitted]

Chapter 3: Stock Option Controversies—Take Two

Congress held four separate hearings related to the proposal between April 2004 and July 2004. I testified at each of these hearings, in some cases together with a fellow board member. In July 2004, the House of Representatives took up consideration of the Stock Option Accounting Reform Act. It proposed that compensation expense be recorded only for stock options granted to the company's CEO and the four other most highly compensated employees and then only to the extent of the intrinsic value of the options granted to those five people. I testified at a hearing on July 8, 2004, of the Commerce, Trade and Consumer Protection Subcommittee of the House Committee on Energy and Commerce, explaining the many reasons we opposed the Stock Option Accounting Reform Act. Rick White, a former member of Congress, Chairman of the International Employee Stock Options Coalition, and then president and CEO of TechNet, a group of executives from technology companies, testified in support of the Stock Option Accounting Reform Act, stating the following in his testimony:

> One issue that has come up and several members have mentioned it, and I also think Chairman Herz mentioned it several times in his testimony, is whether it is appropriate for the Congress even to be involved in this effort. I want to make sure that people understand how important it is that Congress should be involved. There are some things that we let experts decide in our society, but there are some things we don't let them decide. There are some good reasons for that. We let engineers decide how to get a spaceship to the Moon, we let lawyers decide how a contract should be written, but we don't let them decide whether we go to the Moon, we don't let them decide whether a contact should be formed. Those are decisions that we reserve to others. The reason is that experts are great in their specific area of expertise but sometimes that high expertise may prevent them from focusing on the bigger picture. I would submit that is really the problem we have here ... and I think it reveals a flaw at least in the way that Chairman Herz looks at our system.... The point of accounting standards are to accomplish things that this committee thinks is important, not just to further accounting theory. I would submit to you that if the FASB came up with an accounting theory that made sense to accounting professors but has a really negative impact on the economy, that is something the committee would want to look at.

In other words, because of the broader economic significance of this issue, Congress should intervene and ensure that the accounting for stock options continues to be distorted to favor companies in particular industries. This kind of public policy argument is often raised by opponents of proposed changes in accounting standards. They argue that their industry is vital to the U.S. economy and that the proposed accounting change will negatively affect the ability of the companies in their industry to successfully grow and employ more people—

arguments that understandably find support in Congress. As I previously explained, sound, "neutral" accounting standards that are not purposefully skewed to favor particular arrangements or specific companies and industries are also a very important public policy objective, one that I and others involved in accounting standard-setting work hard to articulate, protect, and defend.

Shortly before the Stock Option Accounting Reform Act was to be voted on by the House, Warren Buffett wrote an op-ed piece ridiculing the bill and pointing out the absurdity of its provisions, stating

> Until now the record for mathematical lunacy by a legislative body has been held by the Indiana House of Representatives, which in 1897 decreed by vote of 67 to 0 that pi—the ratio of the circumference of a circle to its diameter—would no longer be 3.14159 but instead be 3.2 .... What brings this episode to mind is that the U.S. House of Representatives is about to consider a bill that, if passed, could cause the mathematical lunacy record to move east from Indiana. First the bill decrees that a coveted form of corporate pay—stock options—be counted as an expense when these go to the chief executive and the other four highest-paid officers in a company, but be disregarded as an expense when they are issued to other employees in the company. Second the bill says that when a company is calculating the expense of options issued to the mighty five, it shall assume that stock prices never fluctuate. Give the bill's proponents an A for imagination ... and a flat-out F for logic.... The House's anointment of itself as the ultimate scorekeeper for investors, it should be noted, comes from an institution that in its own affairs favors Enronesque accounting.... If the House should ignore this logic and legislate that what is an expense for five is not an expense for thousands, there is reason to believe the Senate—like the Indiana Senate 107 years ago—will prevent this folly from becoming law. Sen. Richard Shelby (R-Ala.), chairman of the Senate Banking Committee, has firmly declared that accounting rules should be set by accountants, not by legislators. Even so, House members who wish to escape the scorn of historians should render the Senate's task moot by killing the bill themselves.[13]

Nevertheless and notwithstanding an April 2004 report by the Congressional Budget Office supporting our proposal, on July 20, 2004, the bill passed the House of Representatives by a 312-111 vote. I was disappointed but not surprised. It was an election year, and by all accounts, the lobbyists for the Coalition had mounted a full-court press on members of the House of Representatives.

---

[13] Warren Buffett, "Fuzzy Math and Stock Options," *Washington Post*, 6 July 2004.

The Coalition then focused on the Senate. In early September 2004, the Stock Option Accounting Reform Act was referred to the Senate Committee on Banking, Housing, and Urban Affairs (the Banking Committee), but the Banking Committee never took any action on that bill or on other bills designed to block our efforts. I believe that was due in large measure to the strong support we received from Chairman of the Banking Committee, Senator Richard Shelby, and Ranking Member of the Banking Committee, Senator Paul Sarbanes. Both were quite clear in their support, not only for our project but, most importantly, on the importance of our being able to conduct our due process in an independent and unbiased way. I recall going to see Senator Shelby to discuss our work, and I recall his saying in his rich Southern accent words to the effect, "I agree with you, and I will not budge in my support." Indeed, he did not budge in his support. For example, in an op-ed piece, Chairman Shelby stated the following:

> An assault is underway to convince Congress that it should block the Financial Accounting Standards Board's proposed rule requiring companies to expense employee stock options.... On Capitol Hill, some have responded to this pronouncement with renewed legislative efforts to undercut FASB's authority and politicize the rule-making process. These are counter to the health of our financial markets. The preservation of FASB's independence is fundamental to maintaining transparent, competitive and liquid markets.... The success of FASB depends on its ability to remain insulated from the political process. If attempts are made to negate the long-term benefit of its rules by focusing on short-term consideration, then investors and our markets will suffer. Our markets are the envy of the world in large part because investors trust the financial information they receive. Congress should preserve this trust, stay out of FASB's rulemaking, and let the experts do their job.[14]

We also received strong support from others in the Senate, including Senators McCain, Durbin, Levin, and Fitzgerald. Throughout the course of the project and the attacks on us and our due process, Bob Denham, Chairman of the Financial Accounting Foundation trustees; SEC Chairman Bill Donaldson; SEC Chief Accountant Don Nicolaisen; and SEC Deputy Chief Accountant Scott Taub stood shoulder to shoulder with us. We also received public support from much of the accounting profession and from a number of prominent figures—including Alan Greenspan, Paul Volcker, Warren Buffett, and then-U.S. Comptroller General David Walker—from many organizations, including the Council of Institutional Investors, the CFA Institute, the Investment Company Institute, Financial Executives International, the AFL-CIO and many trade unions, and AICPA. Along with that support, several other factors were crucial in our ability to conduct the project in a thorough,

---

[14] See footnote 1.

systematic, and objective manner. For one, the IASB had been able to issue a standard[15] requiring the recognition of expense relating to grants of employee stock options without the same type of opposition we faced in the United States. Also, very importantly, was the determination of all my Board members to properly fulfill our mission and the excellent work of our staff, including Michael Tovey, the FASB manager on this project, and Sue Bielstein, FASB director of major projects. As well, Jeff Mahoney, our Washington, D.C., representative, was tireless in his efforts to keep policymakers informed about the project and our due process. That included holding 4 public roundtables on the exposure draft, including 2 in Silicon Valley, and 21 public Board meetings and meetings with our advisory groups and with groups of constituents to discuss the exposure draft and other input on the project, resulting in the issuance of FASB Statement No. 123 (revised 2004).[16] It required the recording of compensation expense relating to all forms of stock-based compensation and became effective starting in 2005. As part of the process, we spent a considerable amount of time and effort examining potential alternatives for nonpublic entities and developing a simplified method that they could use to estimate the value and resulting compensation cost for equity instruments granted to their employees. For public companies, our standard was supplemented by guidance issued by the SEC staff in Staff Accounting Bulletin No. 107 based on some very good work done by the Office of the Chief Accountant with the Office of Economic Analysis.[17]

I devoted an entire chapter to this subject for a couple of reasons. First, at the technical accounting level, the subject of accounting for stock options is an interesting and important one. Second and more importantly, because I believe that in order to preserve the integrity of accounting standard setting and public confidence in it and in reported financial information, it was very important that we saw the project through to issuing a new standard requiring that compensation cost be recognized for all forms of employee stock awards, including stock options, and that we were able to maintain our thorough and open due process, even in the face of what were very strong attempts to achieve a different outcome through political means. Those results were important ones for the U.S. financial reporting system, for investors and the capital markets, and for the FASB being able to sustain the convergence effort with the IASB. As Professor J. Edward Ketz observed in the "Accounting Cycle" column on SmartPros.com in January 2005 about the importance of FASB prevailing in this matter,

---

[15] International Financial Reporting Standard 2, *Share-based Payment*.

[16] *Share-Based Payment*, in December 2004 (now codified in FASB ASC 718, *Compensation—Stock Compensation*).

[17] See also Office of Economic Analysis Memorandum, *Economic Perspective on Employee Option Expensing: Valuation and Implementation of FAS 123(R)*.

Chapter 3: Stock Option Controversies—Take Two

> If Congress does indeed pass the bill [referring to the Stock Option Accounting Reform Act] and the president signs it into law, then one wonders about the future of FASB. Other managers and directors and their professional advisers might rise up on other subjects, those that are disconcerting to them. Congress might pass even more legislation.... FASB might as well close its doors. On the other hand, the Congress might not overturn Statement 123. FASB might then grow a bit bolder and begin to think about some other issues that need attention. The investment community would be well served with improvements dealing with pensions, leases and special purpose entities, to name a few. While the disclosures of off-balance sheet items have improved of late, good disclosures do not substitute for bad accounting.

I also believe that some other good things came out of this episode, including the establishment of a Small Business Advisory Committee. The idea of creating such a group was posed to me by Senator Enzi at a Senate hearing in November 2003. It was a good suggestion that we quickly implemented, establishing a Small Business Advisory Committee that I believe has provided and continues to provide excellent input and advice to the FASB on reporting issues and concerns relating to small and privately held businesses. So, although I disagreed with Senator Enzi's views on accounting for employee stock options, I very much admire his passion for the small businesses of this country.

Perhaps most importantly, I think the intense debate surrounding this controversial topic and our ability to withstand the strong attempts at political intervention into our standard-setting process helped create a greater awareness and appreciation of the importance of sound accounting and financial reporting and broader support for independent accounting standard setting. So, when we tackled other important and controversial issues, such as requiring in FASB Statement No. 158[18] that the unfunded status of defined pension and retiree medical plans be shown squarely on the sponsoring company's balance sheet, although there were parties that strongly opposed the change, they did not seek to try to block it through political means. Nonetheless, as discussed in chapter 5, "The Financial Crisis," the independence of accounting standard setting was again to be tested during the financial crisis of 2008–09.

---

[18] *Employers' Accounting for Defined Benefit Pension and Other Postretirement Plans—an amendment of FASB Statements No. 87, 88, 106, and 132(R)*, issued in 2006 and now codified in FASB ASC 715, *Compensation—Retirement Benefits*.

Chapter 4: International Convergence

The Urge to Converge and Wherefore IFRS?

> Clearly, the growth of cross-border investing and capital flows and a growing endorsement of international standards in many parts of the world mean that, on the one hand, the U.S. cannot go it alone in terms of development of accounting standards, and, on the other hand, the development of international accounting standards across the major capital markets of the world requires that the U.S. be a very active participant in the process, for there can be no truly international accounting standards if the largest capital market in the world, the U.S., is not part of their development.[1]

As I briefly discussed in chapter 2, "Charting Course," international convergence between U.S. GAAP and IFRS was one of the three strategic objectives we pursued following my joining the FASB in 2002. However, the question was, "How should we pursue this objective?" There were many possibilities. For example, should it be a unilateral effort on the part of the FASB to try to move U.S. standards toward the existing international standards? Should we try to get the IASB to consider moving its standards toward U.S. GAAP? Should we try to agree on some sort of bilateral program of convergence between the two boards? If so, should it mainly involve trying to converge our existing standards, or should it look more to developing new joint standards?

---

[1] Robert H. Herz in a November 5, 2002, speech at the Financial Executive International's annual conference on Current Financial Reporting Issues.

What Does the Law Require?

Here, I believe the wording in Section 108 of Sarbanes-Oxley provided some guidance in addressing these questions. That section of Sarbanes-Oxley stipulates that, among other activities, the designated U.S. standard setter "considers, in adopting accounting principles, ... the extent to which international convergence on high quality accounting standards is necessary or appropriate in the public interest and for the protection of investors." There are a number of important words and phrases in this clause, including "considers," "extent to which," "high quality accounting standards," and "in the public interest and for the protection of investors." Clearly, although the language in Section 108 requires the U.S. accounting standard setter to consider international convergence as part of its standard-setting activities, it does not require the achievement of international convergence. Rather, it requires the U.S. standard setter to consider the merits of convergence. In doing so, it places that consideration in the context of the standards being of high quality and necessary or appropriate to the public interest and for the protection of investors. Because this is U.S. law that applies to the SEC and any standard setter the SEC designates as a source of authoritative U.S. GAAP for SEC registrants, it seems that the words "in the public interest and for the protection of investors" should be considered in the U.S. context (that is, in the context of the U.S. public interest and for the protection of U.S. investors). Of course, that does not mean that international convergence and the resulting converged standards could not also be a good thing for global investors and international capital markets. They could be good both for the United States and the international community.

Views of Standard Setters on International Convergence

Beyond that, the words in Sarbanes-Oxley do not appear to specify how the U.S. standard setter should go about its consideration of the merits of international convergence. The legislation appears to leave that to the standard setter, with oversight from the SEC. In that regard, the SEC, FASB, and FAF had publicly supported the goal of developing a single set of high-quality international accounting standards. In 1999, the FASB and FAF had issued *International Accounting Standard Setting: A Vision for the Future*. Although clearly supporting the objective of a single set of high-quality accounting standards, it also conveyed the FASB's and FAF's intention to maintain a leadership role in standard setting to ensure that the standards used in the U.S. capital markets, whether developed by the FASB or an international body, would be of the highest possible quality. That document also identified what the FASB and the FAF viewed as essential functions and characteristics of a high-quality global accounting standard-setting organization. The document identified a set of eight essential functions that the FASB and FAF believed should be embodied by a high-quality international accounting standard setter:

1. Leadership
2. Innovation
3. Relevance
4. Responsiveness
5. Objectivity
6. Acceptability
7. Understandability
8. Accountability

It also identified a set of minimum characteristics needed for an international accounting standard setter to achieve the eight essential functions, including having an independent decision-making body, adequate due process, adequate staff, independent fund-raising, and independent oversight. As noted in the introduction,

> Financial reporting and accounting standard setting are not immune to the changing times. We are beginning to see the emergence of a truly international accounting system—the emergence of international-level organizations and cooperative ventures among national organizations in the areas of accounting standard setting and financial statement preparation, auditing, regulation, and analysis—to deal effectively with the merging of national and international financial reporting issues.

The FASB-FAF document was issued at a time when the future structure of international accounting standard setting was under broader discussion. IASC—which since its establishment in 1973 had developed and promulgated a set of international accounting standards—had formed a Strategy Working Party in 1997 to develop recommendations on potential changes and reforms to the existing IASC structure and process. In December 1998, that group issued a discussion paper, *Shaping IASC for the Future*, proposing a number of reforms to the IASC structure and process. There was also ongoing discussion between major capital markets securities regulators, most notably the SEC and the European Commission, about the structure and process for international accounting standard setting. All of this ultimately led to the establishment in 2000 of the new IASB and its oversight body of independent trustees that reflected a number of the ideas set forth in the 1999 FASB-FAF document on the future of international accounting standard setting.

I was one of the members of the IASB when it commenced operations in 2001. A key element of our strategy was to promote and facilitate international convergence of accounting standards by working with the national accounting standard-setting bodies of major countries. In appointing the initial members of the IASB, the IASC trustees designated seven of the new Board members to act as official liaisons to the national standard-setting bodies of Australia and New Zealand, Canada, France, Germany, Japan, the United States, and the United Kingdom. The role of each of these liaison members was to enhance cooperation between the IASB and the national standard setter. Jim Leisenring, who had been a long-time FASB staff and Board member, was appointed as the IASB liaison with the FASB.

Consistent with the 1999 FASB-FAF vision document, the FASB recognized that as the accounting standard setter for the world's largest capital market and national economy, its support of, and participation in international convergence efforts were important to and made sense for both the United States and the goal of achieving common, high-quality accounting standards around the world. Following the establishment of the IASB (and before I arrived at the FASB), the FASB formed an internal strategic planning group to evaluate how best the Board and staff could work with the new IASB. One result of that effort was that in 2001, the FASB revised its operating procedures to require, in addition to the existing criteria for evaluating potential agenda projects, assessment of the extent to which a potential new project would provide opportunities for convergence with the IASB and other national standard setters.

Very importantly, the strategic planning group also concluded that the best way to maximize the FASB's ability to simultaneously meet its U.S. responsibilities and participate in international convergence in a meaningful way would be through coordinating the agendas of the FASB and the IASB as much as possible and, as appropriate, to undertake joint projects with the IASB. By doing so, the FASB might be able to both improve U.S. standards and achieve convergence between U.S. GAAP and internationals standards. In cases when it was not possible to undertake a project jointly, the FASB would decide on a case-by-case basis whether other methods of international cooperation might be feasible and desirable. For example, in the case of projects on the FASB agenda but not on the IASB agenda, the FASB could specifically seek input from the IASB, and vice versa.

As part of the cooperative arrangements between the IASB and its partner standard setters, including the FASB, a framework for monitoring IASB projects was established. From the FASB's perspective, monitoring IASB projects could help the FASB better consider international perspectives in its projects. Additionally, this monitoring would facilitate earlier identification of possible areas of convergence and divergence with international standards and could enhance FASB staff knowledge of international standards and help strengthen relationships between the staffs of the two boards. Accordingly, when the initial monitoring assignments were made, FASB staff were assigned to monitor a number of the IASB's projects.

The various partner standard setters also agreed to monitor the activities of the IASB's International Financial Reporting Interpretations Committee (IFRIC) to try to promote convergence between the guidance promulgated by IFRIC and interpretative guidance issued by national interpretive bodies, such as the Emerging Issues Task Force (EITF) in the United States, through cross-monitoring by IFRIC and the national interpretative bodies. That would be particularly important in the case of converged standards in order to avoid divergence in application of such standards. However, it was also recognized that there might well be differences in interpretations and application guidance in cases where the national standard and IFRS were not converged.

The Norwalk Agreement

All these matters had been discussed and agreed upon between the FASB, IASB, and major national standard setters by the time I joined the FASB in July 2002 and before the passage of Sarbanes-Oxley. However, I believe my arrival at the FASB and our strategic planning discussions that summer lent extra momentum to the cooperative efforts between the FASB and the IASB. In September 2002, the two boards held their first joint meeting in the FASB's office in Norwalk, Connecticut. At that meeting, the FASB and the IASB both publicly affirmed their commitment to developing high-quality, "compatible" accounting standards that could be used for both domestic and cross-border financial reporting. Both boards also committed to using their best efforts to make their standards compatible as soon as practicable and, once achieved, to work to maintain the compatibility of those standards. Following the meeting, in October 2002, the FASB and the IASB issued a Memorandum of Understanding (MoU), referred to as the Norwalk Agreement (exhibit 4-1), formally documenting their mutual commitments to work together in developing high-quality compatible accounting standards.[2] The Norwalk Agreement focused on four key points: (1) eliminating a number of targeted differences between existing U.S. GAAP and IFRS, (2)

---

[2] Financial Accounting Standards Board and International Accounting Standards Board Memorandum of Understanding at www.fasb.org/cs/BlobServer?blobkey=id&blobwhere=1175819018817&blobheader=application%2Fpdf&blobcol=urldata&blobtable=MungoBlobs and reprinted as exhibit 4-1, "The Norwalk Agreement," of this chapter.

coordinating the future agendas of the two boards, (3) continuing the existing joint projects and undertaking new ones on substantive topics, and (4) encouraging coordination of activities between the EITF and IFRIC. In a joint FASB and IASB news release, we commented on the need for such a partnership:

> Robert H. Herz, Chairman of the FASB, commented, "The FASB is committed to working toward the goal of producing high-quality reporting standards worldwide to support healthy global capital markets. By working with the IASB on the short-term convergence project—as well as on longer-term issues—the chances of success are greatly improved. Our agreement provides a clear path forward for working together to achieve our common goal."
>
> Hailing the agreement, Sir David Tweedie, Chairman of the IASB, remarked, "This underscores another significant step in our partnership with national standard setters to reach a truly global set of accounting standards. While we recognize that there are many challenges ahead, I am extremely confident now that we can eliminate major differences between national and international standards, and by drawing on the best of U.S. GAAP, IFRS and other national standards, the world's capital markets will have a set of global accounting standards that investors can trust."[3]

---

[3] October 29, 2002, news release, *FASB and IASB Agree to Work Together toward Convergence of Global Accounting Standards.* www.fasb.org/news/nr102902.shtml.

Exhibit 4-1: The Norwalk Agreement

Memorandum of Understanding

"The Norwalk Agreement"

At their joint meeting in Norwalk, Connecticut, USA on September 18, 2002, the Financial Accounting Standards Board (FASB) and the International Accounting Standards Board (IASB) each acknowledged their commitment to the development of high-quality, compatible accounting standards that could be used for both domestic and cross-border financial reporting. At that meeting, both the FASB and IASB pledged to use their best efforts to (a) make their existing financial reporting standards fully compatible as soon as is practicable and (b) to coordinate their future work programs to ensure that once achieved, compatibility is maintained.

To achieve compatibility, the FASB and IASB (together, the "Boards") agree, as a matter of high priority, to:

   a) undertake a short-term project aimed at removing a variety of individual differences between U.S. GAAP and International Financial Reporting Standards (IFRS, which include International Accounting Standards, IASs);

   b) remove other differences between IFRS and U.S. GAAP that will remain at January 1, 2005, through coordination of their future work programs; that is, through the mutual undertaking of discrete, substantial projects which both Boards would address concurrently;

   c) continue progress on the joint projects that they are currently undertaking; and,

   d) encourage their respective interpretative bodies to coordinate their activities.

The Boards agree to commit the necessary resources to complete such a major undertaking.

The Boards agree to quickly commence deliberating differences identified for resolution in the short-term project with the objective of achieving compatibility by identifying common, high-quality solutions. Both Boards also agree to use their best efforts to issue an exposure draft of proposed changes to U.S. GAAP or IFRS that reflect common solutions to some, and perhaps all, of the differences identified for inclusion in the short-term project during 2003.

As part of the process, the IASB will actively consult with and seek the support of other national standard setters and will present proposals to standard setters with an official liaison relationship with the IASB, as soon as is practical.

The Boards note that the intended implementation of IASB's IFRS in several jurisdictions on or before January 1, 2005 require that attention be paid to the timing of the effective dates of new or amended reporting requirements. The Boards' proposed strategies will be implemented with that timing in mind.

The September 2002 meeting was the first of what would be many joint public meetings between the two boards. At first, the meetings were held twice per year for two or three days at a time. Then, in 2006, that was expanded to three times per year. Since October 2009, the boards have been meeting jointly most months and sometimes multiple times during a month, either in person or via teleconference. The boards also have held numerous joint public roundtables and other meetings, and there are frequent meetings between groups of board members and staff on joint projects.

My recollection about the particular wording of the Norwalk Agreement is that the word *compatible* accounting standards, instead of *joint*, *converged*, or *common* accounting standards, was used in recognition that what mattered most was that the standards should result in the same or similar financial reporting outcomes. It also recognized the practical challenges in producing identical standards. Nevertheless, the objective was refined at our joint meeting in April 2004 when the boards agreed that, ideally, the FASB and IASB would work together to develop any major future accounting standards, with both boards issuing the same standard or very similar ones.

Short-Term Convergence Projects

The first aspect of the Norwalk Agreement involved the boards undertaking a number of projects aimed at removing a variety of specific, more narrow differences between U.S. GAAP and IFRS. They were dubbed short-term convergence projects, reflecting the belief at the time that they could be completed relatively rapidly. Although the areas included in the these projects did not represent major areas for potential joint projects between the two boards, they nevertheless presented challenges to those using, preparing, auditing, or regulating cross-border financial reporting.

Chapter 4: International Convergence

The approach to removing the differences in each area generally involved selecting between the existing U.S. GAAP and IFRS treatments of the item in question to decide which provided the higher-quality accounting. Thus, for example, if it was decided that the IFRS treatment was superior, then the FASB would propose changing U.S. GAAP to adopt the IFRS approach, and vice versa.

So, toward the end of 2002, the FASB and the IASB began deliberating a number of narrow differences. Initially, the FASB focused on potential changes to U.S. GAAP in the following areas: balance sheet classification, exchanges of nonmonetary assets, inventory costs, earnings per share, and voluntary changes in accounting policies. The IASB started looking at potential changes to IFRS in the areas of discontinued operations, restructuring costs and termination benefits, and postemployment benefits. The boards decided to jointly address a number of specific differences between their income tax accounting standards.

As a result of this effort, the FASB issued standards changing U.S. GAAP for certain aspects of inventory costs;[4] exchanges of nonmonetary assets;[5] and changes in accounting principles and error corrections.[6] In 2007, FASB issued Statement No. 159,[7] allowing a fair value option in accounting for financial assets and financial liabilities, similar to that in IFRS. With regard to balance sheet classification, consideration of those issues was moved into the major project on financial statement presentation. As the Board deliberated the issues relating to earnings per share, it became apparent they were more complex and numerous than had been expected when the short-term project was added to the FASB agenda. As a result, FASB issued exposure drafts with proposed changes in 2003, 2005, and 2008. Further consideration of these issues has been put on hold pending completion of major joint convergence projects.

For its part, in 2004, the IASB issued IFRS 5, *Non-current Assets Held for Sale and Discontinued Operations*, amending its requirements relating to discontinued operations, and amendments to International Accounting Standard (IAS) 19, *Employee Benefits*, that brought IFRS closer to U.S. GAAP in certain areas relating to the accounting for pensions and other postretirement benefits. The IASB also made significant changes to its standard on segment reporting by issuing IFRS 8, *Operating Segments*, in 2006. With these changes, the IASB essentially adopted the U.S.

---

[4] FASB Statement No. 151, *Inventory Costs—an amendment of ARB No. 43, Chapter 4*, issued in 2004, which is now codified in FASB *Accounting Standards Codification* [ASC] 330).
[5] FASB Statement No. 153, *Exchanges of Nonmonetary Assets—an amendment of APB Opinion No. 29*, issued in 2005, which is now codified in FASB ASC 845.
[6] FASB Statement No. 154, *Accounting Changes and Error Corrections—a replacement of APB Opinion No. 20 and FASB Statement No. 3*, issued in 2005, which is now codified in FASB ASC 250, *Accounting Changes and Error Corrections*.
[7] *The Fair Value Option for Financial Assets and Financial Liabilities—Including an amendment of FASB Statement No. 15*, which is now codified in FASB ASC 825, *Financial Instruments*.

approach to segment reporting. The IASB also amended IAS 23, *Borrowing Costs*, its standard relating to capitalization of borrowing costs, and in May 2011, it issued IFRS 11, *Joint Arrangements*, that aligns the accounting for joint ventures under IFRS with that under corresponding U.S. GAAP.

Achieving convergence between U.S. GAAP and IFRS on accounting for income taxes proved to be quite challenging. Although the basic approach to accounting for income taxes is the same under both sets of standards (that is, comprehensive deferred tax accounting for all temporary differences between reported amounts in the financial statements and in tax returns), both the U.S. standard (FASB Statement No. 109[8]) and IFRS standard (IAS 12, *Income Taxes*) contain a number of exceptions to the basic approach, but the exceptions are not the same. The boards deliberated these differences for several years, tentatively agreeing on a common approach to dealing with some, but not all, of them. The effort to converge was further complicated by the FASB needing to address, at the request of the SEC staff, issues relating to accounting for uncertain tax positions. That FASB project resulted in the issuance of FASB Interpretation No. 48.[9] Although FASB Interpretation No. 48 resulted in greater clarity and consistency in accounting under U.S. GAAP for uncertain tax positions, the approach is quite different than that under IFRS. Accordingly, in 2009, both boards put this project on hold and have discussed whether a better course of action might be to undertake a major joint project to more comprehensively reconsider the accounting for income taxes. However, no action has been taken yet on this matter by either board or as a new joint project.

In summary, although the short-term convergence projects resulted in eliminating or narrowing differences between U.S. GAAP in a number of areas, several of them proved to be more complicated and a lot less short-term than originally envisioned. Moreover, constituents of both boards, particularly preparers of financial statements, very understandably questioned the cost and benefit of making such changes to accounting standards that, although seemingly narrow, required companies to make potentially costly changes to their financial data systems and processes. As I will discuss further in connection with the 2006 FASB-IASB MoU, we concluded that a better approach would be to focus on achieving convergence through the boards working together to develop common standards on broader areas of accounting.

---

[8] *Accounting for Income Taxes*, which is now codified in FASB ASC 740, *Income Taxes*.
[9] *Accounting for Uncertainty in Incomes Taxes—an interpretation of FASB Statement No. 109*, in December 2006, which is now codified in FASB ASC 740.

Undertaking Major Joint Projects

In that regard, at the April 2004 joint meeting, the boards agreed to undertake three major joint projects: business combinations, revenue recognition, and financial performance reporting by business enterprises (later renamed financial statement presentation).

Both boards viewed achieving common accounting for business combinations as a priority, given the increasing importance of cross-border merger and acquisition activity. Differences between U.S. GAAP and IFRS in this area were also the most frequent cause of reconciling items reported in SEC Form 20-F filings by foreign registrants. The boards had already begun coordinating their work in this area. In 2001, the FASB had issued major standards on accounting for business combinations and accounting for goodwill and other intangible assets[10] that eliminated the pooling-of-interests method and generally required all business combinations to be accounted for under the purchase method. Similarly, in 2001, the IASB started work on a project that would eliminate use of the pooling method in favor of the acquisition (purchase) method and amend its standards on accounting for intangible assets. (The IASB completed that project in 2004 by issuing IFRS 3, *Business Combinations*, and amendments to its standards on intangible assets and impairment of long-lived assets.) At the April 2004 joint board meeting, the boards agreed to try to develop common standards on purchase method procedures (that is, on how to apply purchase accounting) and the related area of accounting for noncontrolling interests (what were generally called minority interests in the United States). That joint project resulted in the issuance of new standards in December 2007 by the FASB (Statement No. 141 [revised 2007][11] and No. 160),[12] and similar standards by the IASB. Although not fully converged, the accounting for business combinations under U.S. GAAP and IFRS is now much more closely aligned on a major subject of great importance to companies all around the world and to cross-border investing and capital flows.

Revenue recognition was another natural candidate for a joint project. Revenue is arguably the most important line item in the financial statements of most companies, so it made sense to try to converge standards in this area. Additionally, the existing revenue recognition standards in both U.S. GAAP and IFRS needed improvement. U.S. GAAP has extensive and very detailed revenue recognition guidance covering specific industries and particular transactions and arrangements, but

---

[10] FASB Statement No. 141, *Business Combinations*, and No. 142, *Goodwill and Other Intangible Assets*, which is now codified in FASB ASC 350, *Intangibles—Goodwill and Other*.
[11] *Business Combinations*, which is now codified in FASB ASC 805, *Business Combinations*.
[12] *Noncontrolling Interests in Consolidated Financial Statements—an amendment of ARB No. 51*, which is now codified in FASB ASC 810.

the guidance was developed piecemeal over many decades and can result in inconsistent reporting for economically similar transactions. In contrast, IFRS contain only high-level guidance on revenue recognition that can also result in inconsistent reporting. Accordingly, the boards have been working together since 2005 to develop a joint standard aimed at improving the consistency and comparability of reporting across a broad variety of revenue transactions. To that end, the boards issued a joint discussion paper, *Preliminary Views on Revenue Recognition in Contracts with Customers*, on revenue recognition in December 2008 and a joint exposure draft, *Revenue from Contracts with Customers*, of a comprehensive standard on revenue recognition in June 2010 and a revised exposure draft with the same title in November 2011.

Both boards had also been working on projects on financial performance reporting prior to 2004, in the IASB's case in conjunction with the U.K. Accounting Standards Board. The April 2004 decision to conduct a joint project in this area reflected a recognition that it would be important to try to achieve both improvement and international convergence in the form, format, and content of the primary financial statements. Differing formats across the world in, for example, the income statement, hampered international comparability. Perceived deficiencies in the organization and level of aggregation in the financial statements were viewed as contributing to the growing use of pro forma presentations by companies and requests for different reporting formats and more disaggregated information by professional users of financial statements. Accordingly, the boards decided to rename this project Financial Statement Presentation. This project resulted in the issuance of a joint discussion paper, *Preliminary Views on Financial Statement Presentation*, in October 2008.

The boards had been working toward publishing a comprehensive exposure draft of a proposed standard on financial statement presentation, but that has been put on hold as the boards work toward completing other major joint projects. In the meantime, they have been working to improve and converge their respective financial statement presentation requirements relating to reporting of discontinued operations and to reporting of comprehensive income, issuing, in June 2011, converged standards on the second of these in FASB ASC No. 2011-05, *Comprehensive Income (Topic 220) Presentation of Comprehensive Income.*

In addition to full joint projects, the boards undertook what we termed "modified joint projects." Under this approach, one board took the lead in a project, developing and issuing a discussion paper for public comment describing that board's preliminary views on the subject. Then, based on the work to date and constituent input, the other board would decide whether to join the project such that it would then become a full joint project through the development of a common exposure draft and, ultimately, a common final standard. Two projects were designated as modified joint projects: accounting for insurance contracts, which the IASB was already working on, and distinguishing liabilities from equity, which FASB was already working on. Both of these projects would later become full joint projects. The project on accounting for insurance contracts became an ongoing joint project. The project on distinguishing liabilities from equity, which was renamed as the project on accounting for financial instruments with characteristics of equity, is currently in inactive status as the boards focus on completing other major joint projects.

The 2005 SEC Staff "Roadmap" and the 2006 FASB-IASB MoU

Starting in 2005, listed companies in the European Union and in several other countries began having to prepare their consolidated financial statements using IFRS. The fact that IFRS were now being used by thousands of companies around the world, many of them major publicly traded multinationals, enhanced the credibility of IFRS as an international standard and added impetus to calls for its adoption in other countries. The European laws adopting IFRS allowed for continued use of U.S. GAAP through 2009 by U.S. companies and their European subsidiaries raising capital in the European capital markets. However, the reverse was not true in the United States because the SEC required all foreign registrants in their Form 20-F filings either to use U.S. GAAP or, if they used another set of accounting standards in preparing their financial statements, to reconcile the net income and stockholders' equity reported in those financial statements to U.S. GAAP.

Those requirements were aimed at, among other considerations, providing U.S. investors with more comparable financial information relating to companies whose securities are traded in U.S. capital markets. However, it was also perceived as creating an uneven playing field by some in Europe who began to question this nonreciprocal treatment whereby U.S. GAAP was allowed to be used in Europe, at least for the time being, but IFRS, Europe's new standard, was not allowed in the United States. A near-term leveling of the playing field might be accomplished by the European authorities requiring U.S. companies and their subsidiaries to use IFRS or reconcile their U.S. GAAP financial statements to IFRS or by the SEC eliminating the Form 20-F requirements to use U.S. GAAP or reconcile to it for foreign registrants that prepared their financial statements using IFRS.

The expanding use of IFRS, both by foreign registrants filing with the SEC and other major corporations around the world, coupled with the uneven playing field issue being asserted in Europe, provided both a challenge and an opportunity for the SEC in fulfilling its mandate in terms of U.S. investors and capital markets and its long-stated support for the development of a single set of high-quality international accounting standards. Those challenges and opportunities and the changing international landscape of financial reporting were addressed by SEC Chief Accountant Don Nicolaisen in an April 2005 article in the *Northwestern University Journal of International Law and Business*.[13] The article laid out what became referred to as the SEC staff "roadmap" (see figure 4-1). It was not a roadmap for adoption of IFRS in the United States or for complete convergence between U.S. GAAP and IFRS. Rather, it laid out a process and set of conditions and related activities for the SEC staff to consider whether to recommend that the SEC eliminate the reconciliation requirements for foreign registrants using IFRS. These conditions included the continued progress by the FASB and the IASB in their convergence efforts, review by the SEC staff of the quality and consistency of implementation of IFRS by foreign registrants, and continued education and sharing of IFRS implementation experiences among investors, practitioners, standard setters, regulators, and others. The roadmap also contained a possible timeline for these activities, noting that the decision by the SEC staff about whether to recommend to the SEC that it eliminate the U.S. GAAP reconciliation requirement for foreign filers using IFRS could come in 2009 or possibly sooner.

Don Nicolaisen and I had been partners at PricewaterhouseCoopers. Our working relationship continued through his tenure at the SEC from 2003 to 2005 and on the 2007–08 Treasury Department's Advisory Committee on the Auditing Profession, which Don cochaired. Now, we are fellow members of the board of directors of Morgan Stanley, and our friendship and mutual respect continues today. We were, I believe, likeminded on a number of important issues related to financial reporting. For example, we had similar opinions on the stock option controversy discussed in chapter 3, "Stock Option Controversies—Take Two." And, as discussed in chapter 6, "Complexity," we agreed that the U.S. reporting system needs to be made less complex. Finally, we were both strong proponents of the important benefits of international convergence of accounting standards. The publishing of the roadmap and the thinking it forwarded, although not representing official SEC policy, was important in guiding both the SEC's actions in this area and our convergence efforts in the period following its publication.

---

[13] Donald T. Nicolaisen, "Statement of the SEC Staff: A Securities Regulator Looks at Convergence," *Northwestern University Journal of International Law and Business*, 25, no. 3 (2005).

Chapter 4: International Convergence

Figure 4-1: SEC Staff Recommendation Roadmap

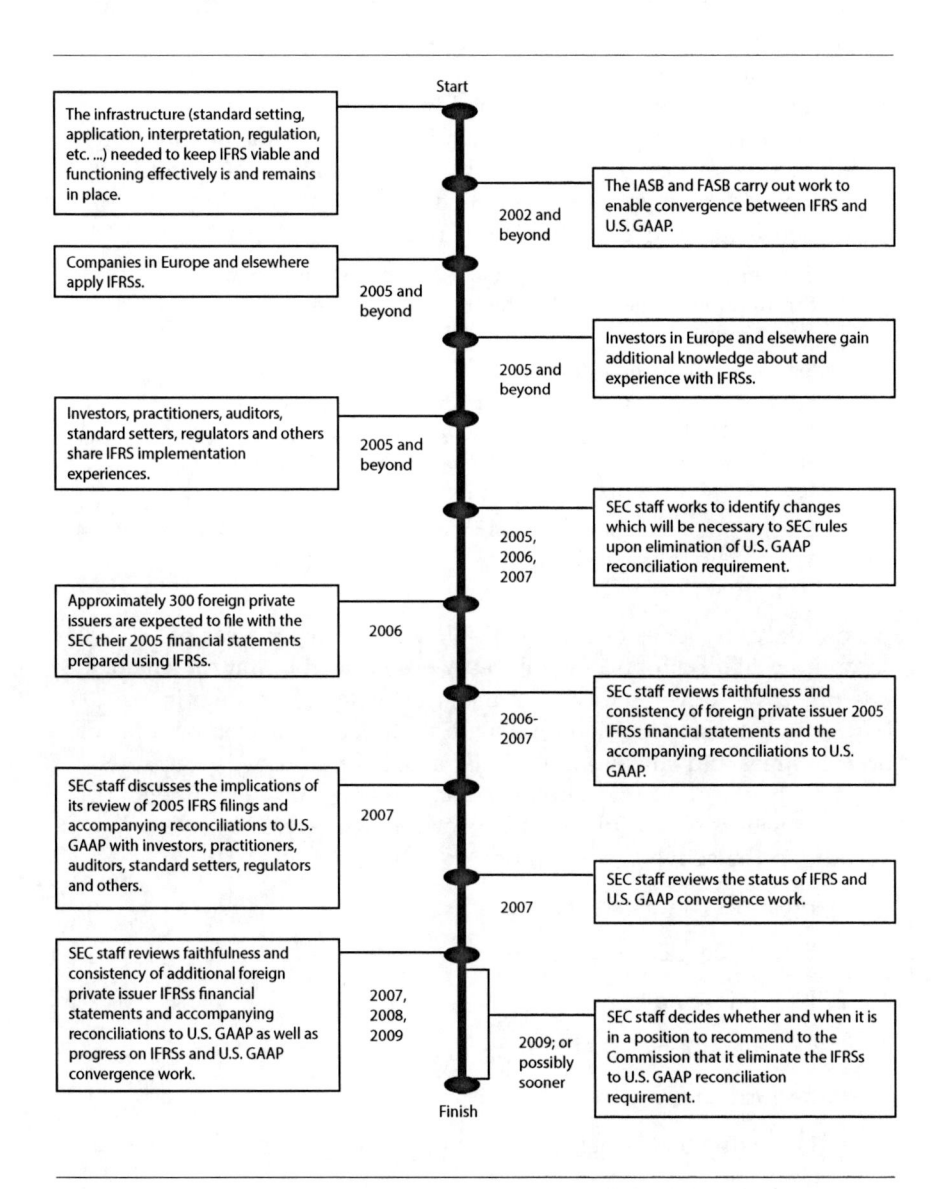

Start

- The infrastructure (standard setting, application, interpretation, regulation, etc. ...) needed to keep IFRS viable and functioning effectively is and remains in place.
- **2002 and beyond** — The IASB and FASB carry out work to enable convergence between IFRS and U.S. GAAP.
- **2005 and beyond** — Companies in Europe and elsewhere apply IFRSs.
- **2005 and beyond** — Investors in Europe and elsewhere gain additional knowledge about and experience with IFRSs.
- **2005 and beyond** — Investors, practitioners, auditors, standard setters, regulators and others share IFRS implementation experiences.
- **2005, 2006, 2007** — SEC staff works to identify changes which will be necessary to SEC rules upon elimination of U.S. GAAP reconciliation requirement.
- **2006** — Approximately 300 foreign private issuers are expected to file with the SEC their 2005 financial statements prepared using IFRSs.
- **2006-2007** — SEC staff reviews faithfulness and consistency of foreign private issuer 2005 IFRSs financial statements and the accompanying reconciliations to U.S. GAAP.
- **2007** — SEC staff discusses the implications of its review of 2005 IFRS filings and accompanying reconciliations to U.S. GAAP with investors, practitioners, auditors, standard setters, regulators and others.
- **2007** — SEC staff reviews the status of IFRS and U.S. GAAP convergence work.
- **2007, 2008, 2009** — SEC staff reviews faithfulness and consistency of additional foreign private issuer IFRSs financial statements and accompanying reconciliations to U.S. GAAP as well as progress on IFRSs and U.S. GAAP convergence work.
- **2009; or possibly sooner** — SEC staff decides whether and when it is in a position to recommend to the Commission that it eliminate the IFRSs to U.S. GAAP reconciliation requirement.

Finish

In the article, Don discussed the convergence of IFRS and U.S. GAAP as the enabler in ultimately achieving a single set of globally accepted accounting standards. The article also discussed continued progress in the convergence effort as one of the factors the SEC staff would consider in deciding whether to recommend elimination of the reconciliation requirement. The lifting of the SEC reconciliation requirement was viewed as important by the European Commission in continuing to allow U.S. companies to use U.S. GAAP in their filings in Europe.

In support of these objectives, the FASB and IASB went about developing a work plan for their continuing convergence activities. That work plan, which was published in February 2006 as the 2006 MoU, sets forth a number of specific milestones that the boards were looking to achieve by the end of 2008.[14] Perhaps more importantly, it laid out the following three interrelated principles regarding convergence between U.S. GAAP and IFRS:

> Convergence of accounting standards can best be achieved through the development of high quality, common standards over time.
>
> Trying to eliminate differences between two standards that are in need of significant improvement is not the best use of the FASB's and the IASB's resources—instead, a new common standard should be developed that improves the financial information reported to investors.
>
> Serving the needs of investors means that the boards should seek convergence by replacing standards in need of improvement with stronger standards.

Accordingly, the focus of the 2006 MoU was on major areas of accounting that both boards believed were in need of improvement. The process to develop the list of major areas to be included in the 2006 MoU was extensive and iterative, with each board developing a list of priority areas and consulting with its respective advisory groups, the staffs of the SEC and the European Commission, and other national standard setters. The MoU included seven major areas that were already on the active agenda of one or both boards:

1. Business combinations
2. Fair value measurement
3. Liabilities and equity
4. Consolidations
5. Performance reporting
6. Postretirement benefits, including pensions
7. Revenue recognition

Four other major areas not yet on the active agenda of either board were also addressed—derecognition, accounting for financial instruments,

---

[14] FASB and IASB document, *A Roadmap for Convergence between IFRS and US GAAP—2006-2008 Memorandum of Understanding between the FASB and the IASB,* 27 February 2006.

intangibles, and leases—with a description of the progress expected to be achieved in each area during 2006–08. It is important to note that the 2006 MoU did not envisage completion of any of the major projects by the end of 2008, except for business combinations and fair value measurement. The boards did issue common standards on accounting for business combinations in late 2007 and early 2008. With regard to fair value measurement guidance, the FASB issued Statement No. 157, *Fair Value Measurements*, in September 2006, which is now codified in FASB ASC 820, *Fair Value Measurement*. That FASB standard was later exposed by the IASB for public comment. The two boards then jointly redeliberated the issues and issued converged standards in May 2011 based largely on FASB Statement No. 157 and additional implementation guidance that the boards issued during the financial crisis.

The 2006 MoU also listed a number of areas for potential short-term convergence, including the aforementioned topics of the fair value option, segment reporting, borrowing costs, and joint ventures.

The 2006 MoU, as updated periodically since 2006, has served as the boards' joint work plan for convergence between IFRS and U.S. GAAP and has also been a very important part of each board's efforts to improve its respective standards. As mentioned in the key principles in the 2006 MoU, the convergence program between the FASB and IASB was undertaken not just for the sake of convergence but also as means of jointly developing improved, high-quality accounting standards. Because of the importance of the MoU to the development of global accounting standards, national accounting standard setters and others from around the world wanted to meet with the IASB and also the FASB to exchange views on international convergence and the major projects included in the 2006 MoU. Accordingly, we started meeting biannually with representatives of the Accounting Standards Board of Japan and with members of the Accounting Regulatory Department of the Chinese Ministry of Finance who establish the accounting standards used in the People's Republic of China. We also had various meetings with representatives of other national standard setters and participated in (*a*) the periodic meetings of the National Accounting Standard Setters group (now called the International Forum of Accounting Standard Setters) that provides input into the development of international standards and (*b*) the IASB's annual World Standard Setters meeting. I found those meetings to be interesting, enjoyable, and valuable to our efforts.

The meetings provided me with a sense of the commonality of many issues across the globe and of the perspectives, environments, and challenges faced by standard setters in different parts of the world. On the one hand, standard setters in different parts of the world often face similar challenges and issues when dealing with the reactions and impacts on their constituents of the changes resulting from new accounting standards and can they can often learn from one another's experiences. On the other hand, because of the differing economic, business, governmental, regulatory, and legal environments in which different national standard setters operate, different subjects may be of greater importance to some national standard setters than to others. For example, the subject of accounting in highly inflationary environments, a priority for standard setters in countries experiencing high rates of inflation, is of less relevance currently to the United States and most of the developed world. The accounting for mining operations, although highly relevant to countries such as Canada, Australia, and South Africa, is of less significance to many other countries. An important challenge for the IASB as an international standard setter is how to balance these competing priorities among the many countries that now use its standards. Conversely, a challenge arises for each national standard setter in countries that use IFRS in trying to ensure that its needs and priorities are properly considered in the formulation of the IASB's agenda of standard-setting projects and in the IASB's process for developing new standards.

Conceptual Framework

The boards also decided that they should work together to develop a single conceptual framework. The FASB's Conceptual Framework was developed principally in the 1970s and 1980s. Intended to help guide the FASB in developing standards on particular topics, it consists of a series of documents that address key concepts relating to the objectives of financial reporting, qualitative characteristics of financial reporting, the elements of financial statements (for example, assets, liabilities, revenues, and expenses), and recognition and measurement of items in financial statements. The IASB has a similar, but much shorter document, *Framework for the Preparation and Presentation of Financial Statements*, that it inherited from its predecessor body, the IASC.

Although these documents have been helpful in guiding standard-setting decisions, experience has shown that they need further work and improvement to address gaps in certain areas and to refine some of the core thinking on other key conceptual matters. Accordingly, and consistent with the boards' commitment to convergence, it made sense to develop a single, improved conceptual framework. So, near the end of 2004, the boards began that effort. The initial areas of focus for improving and converging the conceptual guidance were the objectives and qualitative characteristics of financial reporting by business enterprises, the elements of financial statements of business enterprises, and on what is termed the *reporting entity* (that is, what are the boundaries of the entity that is the subject of the financial statements). In addition to having a joint team comprising FASB and IASB staff

Chapter 4: International Convergence

members, certain national standard setters, most notably Canada and New Zealand, contributed staff to this project.

Progress on the conceptual framework project was slow and did not come easily. In September 2010, the boards issued a new converged conceptual framework chapter on the objective and qualitative characteristics of financial reporting by business enterprises. An exposure draft addressing the reporting entity was issued in 2010, but further work on this phase of the conceptual framework project has been put on hold for now as the boards focus on completing major 2006 MoU projects. Although considerable work was performed for several years on trying to improve the current definitions of *assets* and *liabilities*, that work has also been put on hold for now as the boards focus on completing major joint standards. The boards also began work on the very key area of measurement, a subject that was not fully developed in the existing framework of either board and that continues to be a subject that generates differing views among board members on specific standard-setting projects as well as disagreement and controversy among various constituents. Substantive progress has not yet been achieved on a measurement framework. Perhaps this is a result of fundamental differences in perspectives among board members at both FASB and the IASB, the need to address reporting issues from the global financial crisis, as discussed in chapter 5, and the current focus on completing the major MoU projects.

In September 2012 the IASB decided to restart work on the Conceptual Framework project. The decision reflected the very strong support the IASB received from constituents for the project in response to the IASB's 2011 public consultation on its agenda. However, it is not clear whether the FASB will participate in this work, for example, through membership in the new Accounting Standards Advisory Forum that the IFRS Foundation Trustees have established, or whether the FASB will at some point separately resume work on the Conceptual Framework.

Another phase of the planned joint framework project is to develop guidance that would assist the boards in establishing disclosure requirements. In 2009, the FASB began work on a disclosure framework project that, among other objectives, would include developing such conceptual guidance. The FASB issued the Invitation to Comment *Disclosure Framework* in July 2012.

As I discuss further in chapter 7, "Looking Back and Moving Forward," reflecting back on my years chairing the FASB, one of my greatest disappointments is not making more progress on improving the conceptual framework.

The SEC Eliminates the Reconciliation Requirement and Explores Potential Adoption of IFRS in the United States

The 2005 SEC staff roadmap for considering elimination of the reconciliation requirement for foreign registrants using IFRS contemplated a decision by 2009 or earlier. It turned out to be earlier: November 2007 to be exact.[15] In July 2007, the SEC issued a release that proposed lifting the reconciliation requirement and a concept release exploring the potential use of IFRS by U.S. public companies.[16]

Conrad Hewitt, the chief accountant at the time the reconciliation requirement was eliminated, was a strong supporter of that action and of expeditious movement toward a single set of high-quality international accounting standards. In speeches, he would say words to the effect that when he got to the SEC in 2006, he carefully reviewed the roadmap that Don Nicolaisen had developed, that he liked it, and that removing the reconciliation requirement was an important step in the journey toward a single set of high-quality international standards. Then-SEC Chairman Christopher Cox also seemed to share these views. The November 2007 SEC release that eliminated the reconciliation requirement for foreign registrants using "full" IFRS as published by the IASB states

> The Commission has long viewed reducing the disparity between the accounting and disclosure practices of the United States and other countries as an important objective both for the protection of investors and the efficiency of capital markets.... Towards this end, the Commission has undertaken several measures to foster the use of International Financial Reporting Standards ("IFRS") as issued by the International Accounting Standards Board ("IASB") and fully supports the efforts of the IASB and the Financial Accounting Standards Board ("FASB") to converge their accounting standards.... As part of our efforts to foster a single set of globally accepted accounting standards, we are now adopting amendments to accept from foreign private issuers financial statements prepared in accordance with IFRS as issued by the IASB in filing with the Commission without reconciliation to U.S. GAAP.[17]

---

[15] Securities and Exchange Commission (SEC) release, *Acceptance From Foreign Private Issuers of Financial Statements Prepared in Accordance With International Financial Reporting Standards Without Reconciliation to U.S. GAAP.*

[16] July 2007 SEC proposed release, *Acceptance From Foreign Private Issuers of Financial Statements Prepared in Accordance With International Financial Reporting Standards Without Reconciliation to U.S. GAAP*, and August 2007 SEC concept release, *Allowing U.S. Issuers to Prepare Financial Statements in Accordance With International Financial Reporting Standards.*

[17] SEC release, *Acceptance From Foreign Private Issuers of Financial Statements Prepared in Accordance With International Financial Reporting Standards Without Reconciliation to U.S. GAAP.*

This was a very important action by the SEC, one that many parties supported as a necessary step on the road to a single set of standards and as a goodwill gesture by the United States to avoid Europe and other jurisdictions imposing a counter-reconciliation requirement for U.S. companies raising capital in their financial markets. Indeed, reacting to the SEC's action, then-EU Commissioner Charlie McCreevy stated, "Now it will be Europe's turn to accept accounts in U.S. GAAP. This decision will have to be taken next year. And it is certainly my intention to propose that no reconciliation to IFRS will be needed for companies filing their accounts under U.S. GAAP. This is the only sensible way forward."[18]

I also recall that other U.S. parties, including our major stock exchanges, supported the SEC's lifting the reconciliation requirement because they believed it would help ensure that our capital markets remained competitive by making it easier for foreign companies to obtain listings on U.S. stock exchanges. They also believed that the SEC should allow U.S. issuers to use IFRS. For example, at an SEC roundtable in March 2007, Catherine Kinney, president of the NYSE Group, said "a number of large global issuers" had told the New York Stock Exchange that they would "welcome having a choice" of reporting standards and were considering moving to IFRS if the SEC were to allow that. Many of the other panelists at that roundtable also supported allowing U.S. issuers to switch to IFRS.[19]

However, others, including some institutional investors and financial analysts, believed it was important to maintain the reconciliation requirement until greater convergence between U.S. GAAP and IFRS had been achieved, such that there would be sufficient comparability without a reconciliation and that it would be premature to allow U.S. issuers to adopt IFRS. Concerns were also raised over a number of perceived structural weaknesses with the IASB, including issues relating to governance arrangements and the adequacy and stability of funding. Some of the comment letters to the SEC expressed concerns that eliminating the reconciliation requirement might prompt European companies and the European Commission, satisfied with a mutual recognition regime, to call for a halt to any further convergence between IFRS and U.S. GAAP. Exhibit 4-2, "Differing Views on International Financial Reporting Standards Adoption," shows an article and excerpts from two comment letters to the SEC covering various views on IFRS convergence at the time.

---

[18] Press release from European Federation of Accountants' Conference on Audit Regulations. Brussels, November 27, 2007.
[19] Lawrence M. Gill, "IFRS: Coming to America," *Journal of Accountancy*, June 2007.

Exhibit 4-2: Differing Views on International Financial Reporting Standards Adoption

Cheryl Rosen, "SEC, Users Voice Support for IFRS at Roundtable" in Lawrence M. Gill, "IFRS: Coming to America." *Journal of Accountancy*. June 2007. http://www.journalofaccountancy.com/Issues/2007/Jun/IfrsComingToAmerica.htm

Never mind convergence—why not just report in IFRS and forget about U.S. GAAP altogether?

It didn't take long for the question to come up in March at an SEC roundtable on its International Financial Reporting Standards Roadmap, where the very first panel raised the issue—and the panelists seemed to applaud the idea.

Chairman Christopher Cox opened the door in his opening remarks, noting that "virtually everyone—issuers, investors and stakeholders alike—agrees that the world's capital markets would benefit from the widespread acceptance and use of high-quality global accounting standards." Replacing the "Babel of competing and often contradictory standards" would improve investor confidence, allow investors to draw better conclusions, and simplify the process and cut costs for issuers, Cox said.

Soon enough, Ken Pott, head of Morgan Stanley's capital markets execution group, followed that argument to its logical conclusion, noting that "the dramatically increasing acceptability of IFRS may move U.S. companies to decide they're better off reporting in IFRS if that's allowable by the SEC."

Catherine Kinney, president of the NYSE Group, said "a number of large global issuers" already have told the stock exchange that they would "welcome having a choice" of reporting standards and are considering moving to IFRS. If U.S.-based issuers listed abroad continue to report in U.S. GAAP, she noted, European regulators "will have the opportunity—and maybe even the obligation" to question their financials, just as the SEC asks questions of companies that report in IFRS.

"Every change in regulations has unexpected side effects," she said. "And I think regulators will have to allow U.S. companies to report in IFRS. That will be a further spur to convergence, and a positive development."

It also would be in keeping with two SEC aims: a more transparent global financial reporting environment and more principles-based accounting standards.

Panelist David B. Kaplan, who leads the international accounting group of PricewaterhouseCoopers LLP, said he hoped the question of allowing U.S. companies to report in IFRS would not delay the road map's timetable but otherwise did not object to the idea. Converting U.S. companies to IFRS would mean large-scale educational efforts, knowledge transfer and system changes for the accounting profession, but CPA firms already have begun the process. "At the end of the day, we wouldn't be asking people here to do any more than what Europe has just done in changing to IFRS," he said.

KPMG's partner in charge of professional practice, Samuel Ranzilla, also on the panel, noted that "this complexity discussion is absolutely the right place to put this issue on the table" and that he "supports the elimination of U.S. GAAP reconciliation in accordance with the road map and would ask the SEC to take on front and center the issue of whether international standards are something we ought to be moving toward here in the United States."

With that discussion on the table, any question about whether IFRS was going to happen seemed moot. Summing up the first panel, Morgan Stanley's Ken Pott called IFRS "a terrific idea that can't come fast enough," and Brooklyn Law School professor and former SEC Commissioner Roberta Karmel said it "can't come soon enough." In fact, she advised the commission not to wait until it has solved every little question, but rather to "take the plunge."

In the end, Citigroup Global Markets' Managing Director J. Richard Blackett noted that allowing foreign issuers filing in IFRS to come into U.S. markets will "at the margin and perhaps theoretically" raise the cost of capital for U.S. issuers—but "certainly U.S. companies having the option to adopt IFRS will help."

The SEC announced in April it is planning to publish a concept release about providing U.S. issuers the alternative to use IFRS. Comments would be due this fall.

Gaylen R. Hansen, CPA, http://www.sec.gov/comments/s7-13-07/ s71307-108.pdf

The core concern is the underpinnings of the international standard-setting structure and its relative lack of independence vis-à-vis the Financial Accounting Standards Board (FASB). The observations below are relevant to the Commission's publicly stated goals that Release No. 33-8818 implicitly re-articulates.

The International Accounting Standards Board (IASB) is a private sector creation, meaning that it answers primarily to a non-regulatory constituency. That constituency includes much closer ties to accounting membership trade associations, international accounting firms, and large corporate, institutional and governmental organizations than does its FASB counterpart. These alliances are manifest in IASB participation and funding, which raises questions about its actual independence.

In the shadows of the Enron and WorldCom collapses, passage of the Sarbanes-Oxley Act (SOX) by Congress in 2002 was a cornerstone event enhancing independence of both accounting firms and also the private sector standard-setters that the SEC looks to for leadership within the accounting profession. Given the long and well documented history that ultimately led to an independently financed FASB, it is remarkable that the Commission would so quickly conclude that shifting this critical role to a foreign-controlled body is in our national interest without public analysis and discussion of the pros and cons. Such a dialogue should be unfettered by one-off questions—e.g. "Should IFRS to U.S. GAAP reconciliation be discontinued?" or, "Should domestic issuers have the option of electing IFRS versus U.S. GAAP?" Those questions have leap-frogged a more relevant question: "Does the IASB stand up to public scrutiny particularly when it may be subject to external pressures from its funding sources?"

The subtle focus on peripheral issues is particularly troubling since the SEC is solemnly charged by Congress with the final responsibility to establish national accounting principles and practices. *

...

Aside from autonomy and structural concerns, there is also the practical aspect of IFRS implementation. It is highly likely that if the SEC were to agree to adopt IASB standards that U.S. practitioners would need significantly more time to become get up to speed on IFRS. ...

There may be a subconscious tendency to regard IFRS as an easy fix for the many shortcomings of U.S. GAAP. A more realistic expectation would be that the IASB may solve only a few of those problems in exchange for accepting other risks. Even if the structural and practical problems noted above are satisfactorily addressed, there are a myriad of others, such as the impact of reconciling IASB standards to the U.S. federal income tax system. Also, there are serious differences and gaps between U.S. GAAP and IFRS—e.g. accounting for leases, derivatives, insurance and income taxes.

Chapter 4: International Convergence

U.S. GAAP has been discussed, debated and interpreted for decades and has stood the test of time. By contrast, for all practical purposes— IFRS financial statements have been issued in any large number only for the past three years.

* See, e.g., Securities Act of 1933, 15 U.S.C §§ 77g, 77s(a), 77aa(25) and (26)

Lee S. Ainslie, III, Managing Partner, and Jane B. Adams, Managing Director, Maverick Capital, http://www.sec.gov/comments/s7-13-07/s71307-73.pdf

While we are supportive of the SEC's goal ultimately to eliminate the reconciliation requirement for foreign private issuers who prepare financial statements in accordance with IFRS and to progress to one set of global standards, we believe the current proposal is premature. The reconciliation provides incremental information to investors that would be lost if the reconciliation requirement were eliminated. Many of these reconciling items arise because IFRS is not yet comprehensive and because it is not uniformly applied across regions. As auditors and preparers become more expert in applying IFRS, as IFRS becomes a more comprehensive set of standards, and as companies comply with recently issued standards whose implementation was delayed by IASB's moratorium, we would hope that the incremental information provided by the reconciliation diminishes significantly. Until then, we believe that the removal of the reconciliation harms investors and removes relevant information not available through other sources.

In addition, the multiple versions of "endorsed" IFRS pose real hazards to the investor. The current poor disclosure as to which IFRS requirements have been selectively excluded imperils all investors. Consequently, we support the proposal's requirement that issuers be required to state in a prominent footnote to the financial statements unreservedly and explicitly that its financial statements are in compliance with IFRS as published by IASB (excluding the IASB's proposed IFRS for Small and Medium-sized Entities).

For our part, the FAF-FASB comment letter dated November 11, 2007, to the SEC on the proposing and concept releases expressed qualified support for lifting the reconciliation requirement, stating, "The removal of the requirement that foreign private issuers reconcile their reported results to U.S. GAAP is a difficult and sensitive issue that could have important implications for the continued development of a truly international financial reporting system."[20] It went on to suggest that before the SEC removed the requirement it should ensure two things:

1. The development of a detailed "blueprint" setting forth the key issues, necessary actions to address those issues, and target dates for a transition by U.S. public companies to IFRS and commitment by key parties in the United States to the blueprint

2. A commitment by international parties to undertake the steps necessary to strengthen the IASB as the independent international accounting standard setter

The letter included an appendix that provided a detailed discussion of the many issues we believed would need to be included in the blueprint for U.S. transition to IFRS, our views on the importance of improving IFRS through the continued convergence program between FASB and the IASB, and our views on actions needed to strengthen the IASB as a global standard setter.

The SEC concept release also raised the possibility of allowing U.S. registrants to choose between using U.S. GAAP and IFRS. In our comment letter, we expressed our strong opposition to creating a two-GAAP system for U.S. public company reporting for any prolonged period of time because we believed it would decrease comparability and could increase overall costs in the reporting system.

In my opinion, and based on subsequent developments, the elimination of the reconciliation requirement gave significant additional impetus for the adoption of IFRS by many countries around the world. IFRS now became something of a passport for companies to raise capital in the major world capital markets. It was already the standard recognized in Europe and many other parts of the world, and no longer would a non-U.S. company need to either use U.S. GAAP or reconcile to it in raising capital in the U.S. markets. Although U.S. GAAP also continues to be allowed in many capital markets, I believe it is generally viewed by non-U.S. companies as more difficult and costly to implement and as providing management with fewer options and room for judgment than IFRS. Further, many outside our country view U.S. GAAP as an overly detailed and prescriptive set of standards developed in the highly litigious U.S. environment, a view that is also shared by some in the United States. So, it is not surprising that soon after the SEC lifted the reconciliation requirement, a number of countries that may have been on the fence about whether to adopt IFRS announced plans to do. Those included the major economies of Brazil, India, South Korea, and Mexico.

---

[20] See www.fasb.org/cs/BlobServer?blobkey=id&blobwhere=1175818772343&blobheader=application%2Fpdf&blobcol=urldata&blobtable=MungoBlobs.

Improve and Adopt IFRS

The FAF-FASB November 2007 comment letter reflected our view at that time that IFRS could and would likely become the globally accepted international standard. However, we also believed it was not yet a comprehensive set of standards and that, like U.S. GAAP, a number of existing standards needed improvement. We also shared the concerns of others about some of the perceived structural weaknesses in the IASB and its oversight body, including the need for the organization to obtain adequate, stable, and secure sources of funding to ensure its long-term viability and ability to operate independently. Additional concerns included ensuring that the IASB was adequately staffed and the need to eliminate national and jurisdictional endorsement approaches that could result in variations of IFRS being adopted in different parts of the world. We also advocated what became known as the "improve and adopt" approach to achieving a single set of high-quality international standards that could be adopted in the United States. Under the improve and adopt approach, the FASB would continue working with the IASB to develop major standards that improved both U.S. GAAP and IFRS and that filled in major gaps in IFRS, such as in the accounting for insurance contracts, to the point where IFRS represented a comprehensive, high-quality set of accounting standards. At that point, provided that appropriate actions had also been taken to address the structural issues around the IASB, we believed it would be appropriate to begin an orderly and well-planned transition in the United States from U.S. GAAP to IFRS. The blueprint would provide a detailed plan of the many issues that would need to be addressed in a successful transition.

My speeches and press interviews at the time and my testimony in an October 2007 U.S. Senate hearing reflected that view.[21] My fellow Board members and I also believed it would take a number of years of further work between the two boards, pursuant to the MoU and potentially in other areas, to get to the point where adoption of IFRS in the United States would be cost beneficial. In my testimony before the Subcommittee on Securities, Insurance, and Investment of the Senate Committee on Banking, Housing, & Urban Affairs on October 24, 2007, I stated

> We expect that the myriad of changes to the U.S. financial reporting infrastructure would take a number of years to complete. During that time, the FASB and the IASB should continue our cooperative efforts to develop common, high-quality standards in key areas where neither existing U.S. GAAP or IFRS provides relevant information for investors. Those common

---

[21] For example, see interview of Robert Herz in the article "FASB Chairman Advocates 'Improving and Adopting' IFRS for U.S. Companies" in the September 2008 issue of *Financial Executive* magazine.

standards, issued by both the FASB and IASB, would be adopted by companies in the U.S. and internationally when issued. In other areas that are not the subject of those joint improvement projects, we envision that that U.S. public companies would adopt the IFRS standards "as is" over a period of years. The adoption of those IFRS standards by U.S. companies would complete the migration to an improved version of IFRS.... Under this approach, new standards or existing IFRS will be gradually adopted over a period of several years, smoothing the transition process and avoiding the capacity constraints that might develop in an abrupt mandated switch to IFRS.

Indeed, in October 2007, I also stated that it would probably take at least five more years to complete the convergence program.[22] I recall that I used the words *at least* because I believed it would take a minimum of five years, assuming there were no other events and pressing areas requiring the attention of either or both boards. Although that was not intended as a prediction of the financial crisis that was soon to engulf much of the world and the impact it would have on our standard-setting activities, experience had taught me to expect the unexpected. Accounting standard setting, like many other fields of human endeavor, rarely progresses in a straight line.

I also believe the decision by the FAF trustees in early 2008 to reduce the size of the FASB Board from seven to five members reflected, along with other considerations, a view at that time that the United States might well be moving to IFRS in the foreseeable future and that the efficiency and effectiveness of the FASB's work on convergence might be enhanced though having a smaller Board. Although the FASB had always had a seven-person Board, other rule-setting bodies and agencies, including the SEC, the PCAOB, and many other U.S. agencies and commissions, have five-member boards.[23]

The SEC Proposes a New Roadmap for IFRS Adoption; the FASB and IASB Update the MoU

Not surprisingly, lifting the reconciliation requirement in November 2007 led to some major U.S. corporations and other parties to call for the SEC to also allow the use of IFRS by domestic registrants. The major U.S. accounting firms were also urging clients to start planning for the change to IFRS. There were also international calls for the United States to move

---

[22] Sarah Johnson, "The Divergence of Convergence," *CFO*, 26 October 2007. www.cfo.com/article.cfm/10046246.
[23] Marie Leone, "FASB Parent; Five Is More than Seven," *CFO*, 26 February 2008. www.cfo.com/article.cfm/10756502?f=search.

Chapter 4: International Convergence

more quickly to adopt IFRS. In August 2008, the SEC approved proposing a release regarding potential adoption of IFRS by U.S. issuers[24] This proposal was then issued for public comment in November 2008. In the press release on this, then-SEC Chairman Cox stated

> An international language of disclosure and transparency is a goal worth pursuing on behalf of investors who seek comparable financial information to make well-informed investment decisions. The increasing worldwide acceptance of financial reporting using IFRS, and U.S. investors' increasing ownership of securities issued by foreign companies that report financial information using IFRS, have led the Commission to propose this cautious and careful plan. Clearly setting out the SEC's direction well in advance, as well as the conditions that must be met, will help fulfill our mission of protecting investors and facilitating capital formation.[25]

The press release stated that the SEC would make a decision in 2011 on adoption of IFRS by U.S. issuers. It set out a number of milestones that would factor in the decision, including the degree of convergence that had been achieved and resolution of the issues relating to the funding and governance of the IASB and the IASC Foundation. Assuming a positive decision to require mandatory use of IFRS by U.S. issuers, the release proposed mandatory use starting in 2014. It also proposed permitting a limited group of major U.S. multinationals to adopt IFRS early, starting with 2009 calendar year-end filings. In order to qualify for early adoption of IFRS, a U.S. issuer would have to be among the largest companies worldwide in its industry, and within that industry, IFRS would have to be used as the basis of financial reporting more than any other set of accounting standards. The thinking behind allowing a limited early adoption of this sort was that it could increase the comparability of reporting by major U.S. corporations with major non-U.S. companies in the same industry.

In September 2008, following extensive discussion within and between the two boards and consultation with advisory groups and others, the FASB and the IASB issued an updated MoU,[26] that provided a status report on each of the projects included in the 2006 MoU, an explanation for changes in the joint work program, and estimates of forward milestones and targeted completion dates. At that point, most, but not all, of the projects were targeted for completion in or before 2011.

Why had the year 2011 become an important one in our thinking? Was it based on the writings of Nostradamus or something divined from the Mayan calendar? No, 2011 was viewed as a potentially pivotal year for a

---

[24] *Roadmap for the Potential Use of Financial Statements Prepared in Accordance With International Financial Reporting Standards by U.S. Issuers.*
[25] SEC press release 2008-184, *SEC Proposes Roadmap Toward Global Accounting Standards to Help Investors Compare Financial Information More Easily.*
[26] *Completing the February 2006 Memorandum of Understanding: A progress report and timetable for completion.*

number of reasons. First, the SEC had committed to make a decision in that year on IFRS adoption in the United States. Also, a number of major countries had announced plans to adopt IFRS in 2011 or 2012, so the IASB's intent, if possible, was to have issued major new standards in time for companies in these countries to adopt them to avoid having to first adopt the old IASB standards in these areas and soon thereafter make a second change to the new standards. Also, at the IASB, there was a concern that the required board turnover in the 2009–11 period could complicate and delay completion of projects. When the IASB was created, the initial 14 Board members had staggered terms ending in 2009–11. For example, the terms of 3 board members ended on June 30, 2010, and 3 others, including Chairman David Tweedie, ended on June 30, 2011. These board members had been heavily involved over the years with the various MoU projects, and that, coupled with the IASB's super-majority voting requirement to approve documents, was often cited by the IASB as another reason to try to expeditiously complete the projects.

A number of events were soon to affect our work plan and the environment surrounding our convergence efforts. The most significant of these was the global financial crisis that I discuss at length in chapter 5. In addition, support for the November 2008 SEC roadmap was mixed, at best, with many commentators citing a host of issues in transitioning U.S. issuers to IFRS. Leadership of the SEC changed in early 2009, with Mary Schapiro becoming the new chairman and James (Jim) Kroeker becoming the acting chief accountant (and then chief accountant in August 2009). Also, the composition of the IASB and FASB and their trustee oversight groups were changing because members' terms ended, and new people joined, including John (Jack) Brennan, who succeeded Bob Denham as Chairman of the FAF in early 2009.

Mixed Responses to the SEC Roadmap

Also very important were comment letters on the SEC's November 2008 proposing release. The SEC received more than 200 comment letters on the proposing release from a variety of market participants and stakeholders. Although certainly not an inconsequential number of comment letters, it was, in my opinion, a somewhat surprisingly low number of comment letters given the potential significance of what the SEC was proposing. The FASB often receives more than 500 comment letters on particular proposals and has received thousands of comment letters in the case of very major or highly controversial proposals. In any event, I believe the letters did enable the SEC and the SEC staff to better understand the wide range of views on the subject.

Although commenters on the proposal generally expressed support for the goal of a single set of high-quality globally accepted accounting standards, many expressed concerns with various aspects of the proposed roadmap. These concerns included questions regarding the readiness of IFRS to serve as the standards in the United States, the need for continued convergence between U.S. GAAP and IFRS, and inadequate lead time to implement what many perceived would be a difficult and costly transition to IFRS. Some commenters questioned whether the use of IFRS was actually achieving a sufficient level of comparability in financial reporting across the world in light of the existence of jurisdictional variations in IFRS and perceived inconsistencies in application, auditing, and enforcement of the standards internationally. Some commenters supported the proposed early adoption option and believed it should be broadened to include a wider group of U.S. issuers. However, many other comment letters expressed concerns with the proposed option, believing it would reduce comparability of reporting within the United States and that few companies would elect early adoption until they were certain that the use of IFRS would become mandatory.

In developing the FAF-FASB comment letter to the SEC on the November 2008 roadmap proposal, we carefully considered the extensive input we had received on the subject, including from our various advisory committees and the diverse group of stakeholders that participated in our June 2008 roundtable on the potential adoption of IFRS in the United States.[27] We had also specifically engaged two sets of independent researchers to examine the potential economic and public policy implications of the United States moving to IFRS, and their reports were attached to our comment letter. The reports of the independent researchers raised questions about the overall level of macroeconomic benefit to the United States of adopting IFRS and also raised the possibility of potential alternative paths to achieving a single set of high-quality global accounting standards, including continuing for a longer period the process of convergence between IFRS and U.S. GAAP. Our letter expressed continued support for the goal of a single set of global accounting standards but urged the SEC to conduct a thorough study on the implications for investors and other market participants of implementing IFRS for U.S. issuers. The letter also urged the SEC to consider potential alternative paths to a single set of global accounting standards before making a decision in 2011 about whether to mandate IFRS adoption. We recommended that the SEC establish a broad-based advisory committee to provide input into the study and, if a decision was made to mandate IFRS for U.S. issuers, to help develop and implement a transition plan, or "blueprint," to minimize the cost

---

[27] See www.fasb.org/cs/BlobServer?blobkey=id&blobwhere=1175818992147&blobheader=application%2Fpdf&blobcol=urldata&blobtable=MungoBlobs.

and disruptions to investors, companies, and other market participants. We also reiterated our opposition to the SEC permitting an early adoption option prior to deciding whether to mandate the use of IFRS by U.S. issuers.

Some Begin to Question America's Commitment to Global Accounting Standards

We tried to make it clear in our letter that our recommendation that the issues be further studied did not, in any way, reflect a withdrawal of support for the goal of worldwide use of a single set of high-quality accounting standards or of our commitment to continue to work collaboratively with the IASB on converging and improving IFRS and U.S. GAAP. However, I believe our letter was perceived by some parties outside the United States as a softening of our support for the IASB and for IFRS as the global set of accounting standards. Moreover, the fact that many commenters on the SEC's November 2008 roadmap proposal had raised numerous issues and concerns over potential IFRS adoption in the United States, inevitably led many parties to question whether the United States would ever truly embrace the goal of global accounting standards.

In January 2009, Mary Schapiro became the new Chairman of the SEC. At that point, the SEC roadmap proposal was still out for public comment. In commenting on it in her Senate confirmation hearing, she stated "I will tell you that I will take a deep breath and look at this entire area again carefully and will not be bound by the existing roadmap that is out for comment."[28] In the United States, I believe most interested observers viewed this as a measured and very understandable statement by an incoming SEC Chairman on a proposal she had not participated in issuing. In the wake of the financial crisis and Madoff scandal, the SEC was facing numerous challenges and many pressing issues it needed to address. However, in other parts of the world, particularly Europe, I believe Mary's statement was viewed by some with alarm as an indication of waning support by the SEC for IFRS. That, in turn, led to some calls for the IASB to halt the convergence program with FASB.

However, I think it is interesting to note that in January 2009, a new Monitoring Board was established to provide enhanced oversight and accountability over the trustees of the IASC Foundation.[29] The

---

[28] See www.gpo.gov/fdsys/pkg/CHRG-111shrg50221/html/CHRG-111shrg50221.htm.
[29] SEC press release 2007-226, *Authorities Responsible for Capital Market Regulation Work to Enhance the Governance of the IASC Foundation.*

Monitoring Board was created to establish a formal link in terms of oversight and accountability between the IASC Foundation and the IASB to public authorities, akin to the relationship in the United States between the FAF and FASB and the SEC. The Monitoring Board comprises leading officials from the Emerging Markets and Technical Committees of the International Organization of Securities Commissions, the European Commission, the Japan Financial Services Authority, and the SEC. So, Mary Schapiro, as Chairman of the SEC, became a member of the new Monitoring Board over the IASC Foundation (soon to be renamed the IFRS Foundation).

The G20 Leaders Push for Rapid International Convergence of Accounting Standards

It is also noteworthy that the official declarations coming out of meetings of the G20 that were held in response to the global financial crisis included comments urging expeditious international convergence of accounting standards and exhortations to international standard setters to work together and with regulators and supervisors to quickly develop common responses to financial reporting issues emanating from the financial crisis. For example, the communiqué issued following the April 2009 G20 meeting in London called on accounting standard setters "to work urgently with supervisors and regulators to improve standards on valuation and provisioning and achieve a single set of high-quality global accounting standards."[30] That communiqué also included a number of recommendations on specific accounting standard-setting actions, calling for them to be achieved by the end of 2009. These recommendations seemed to largely mirror those made by the Financial Stability Forum (which then became the Financial Stability Board of the G20).[31] Although these recommendations were very important, it was not, in my view, realistic to expect resolution of these complex and controversial matters within the nine-month timeframe contemplated in that communiqué.

In contrast, the communiqué issued following the September 2009 G20 meeting in Pittsburgh, PA, called upon "international accounting bodies to redouble their efforts to achieve a single set of high-quality, global accounting standards within the context of their independent standard

---

[30] Paragraph 15 of the April 2009 G20 Leaders Statement, *The Global Plan for Recovery and Reform.*
[31] See the "Accounting Standards" section of the April 2, 2009, G20 *Declaration on Strengthening the Financial System.*

setting process, and complete their convergence project by June 2011."[32] We took the words "convergence project" to mean our work plan under the MoU. For the reasons previously noted, the June 2011 target for completion was viewed as important, particularly by the IASB. I believe it is fair to say that the IASB and its trustees viewed June 2011 as a deadline for completing all the major projects on the MoU, but we viewed it as providing an important target, not an absolute deadline. Issuing sound standards that would improve financial reporting was the overriding objective. Further, although successful completion of the MoU projects would bring U.S. GAAP and IFRS into convergence in a number of major areas, there would still be many remaining differences between the two sets of standards. So, any notion that completion of the MoU would achieve complete convergence between U.S. GAAP and IFRS was not, in my view, consistent with the facts.

The FASB and IASB Respond to the G20 Call by More Than Redoubling the Convergence Effort

Prior to the G20 call to redouble our convergence efforts, the FASB and the IASB had been meeting three times per year in multiday, full board-to-board meetings. More frequent meetings had been occurring between small groups of board members, and our staffs had been working closely together for several years on major joint projects. In this way, by September 2009, we had been successful in jointly issuing a number of important documents on major projects, including discussion documents on accounting for financial instruments, revenue recognition, lease accounting, and financial statement presentation.

Responding to the call from the G20 would require us to meet more frequently. Additionally, differences in approach and project timelines between the IASB and FASB on the major project on accounting for financial instruments and SEC Chairman Mary Schapiro's perceived ambivalence toward use adoption of IFRS had led some observers to question the commitment of both boards to the overall convergence program. For example, an article in *Accountancy Age*[33] reported

> the Fédération des Experts Comptables Européens, which represents more than 500,000 accountants across Europe, said that International Accounting Standards Board should cut its losses and walk away from its US-GAAP convergence strategy.... FEE

---

[32] Paragraph 14 of the "Strengthening the International Financial Regulatory System" section of the September 25, 2009, G20 *Leaders' Statement: The Pittsburgh Summit.*
[33] Mario Christodoulou, "FEE Calls for a Halt on Convergence Talks," *Accountancy Age*, 23 July 2009.

Chapter 4: International Convergence

believes the IASB should change direction and instead "concentrate exclusively on major improvements and simplifications in International Financial Reporting Standards over the medium term."

The article called this "the latest blow to the IASB's convergence strategy," noting that "[i]n January, comments by SEC Chairman Mary Schapiro stoked concerns surrounding America's commitment to global standards."

The boards discussed these and other matters related to the joint efforts at length at our joint meeting in October 2009. We came to a number of agreements regarding the path forward that were described in a joint communiqué issued November 5, 2009.[34] That document provided a status report on the MoU projects and forward plans for completing them by June 2011. It noted that in order to expedite the process, the boards had agreed to begin meeting together each month. Very importantly, it described a number of shared goals, values, and priorities, among these that convergence for the sake of convergence was not our goal and that the standards under development needed to result in improvements to our respective existing standards. The trustees of the IASC Foundation and FAF also issued a joint statement on November 5, 2009, in support of the joint communiqué by the FASB and IASB, noting "both Trustee groups continue to support unequivocally the joint work of the IASB and FASB aimed at achieving the objectives and convergence milestones outlined in the February 2006 Memorandum of Understanding, as updated in September 2008."[35] Supportive public statements were also issued by SEC Chairman Mary Schapiro (November 5, 2009) and the IASC Monitoring Board (November 11, 2009).

So, beginning with the November 2009 meeting, the boards began meeting monthly for several days each month. A good bit of this was accomplished by the 5 FASB Board members and key staff flying to London for multiday joint meetings with the 15 members of the IASB and its staff. We also held numerous joint board meetings via teleconference. In embarking on this intensified effort, both David Tweedie and I (and, I believe, other members of our boards) believed it would enable us to make more rapid progress toward completing the major MoU projects within the 2011 timeframe set out by the G20. For example, in the IASC Foundation *Annual Report 2009*, David stated

> Our work programme is focused on substantially completing the MoU projects, and insurance, by 30 June 2011. Some commentators have suggested that the scale of the programme and the timetable are too ambitious. While I agree that the programme is

---

[34] FASB news release, *IASB and FASB and IASB Reaffirm Commitment to Memorandum of Understanding*.
[35] International Accounting Standards Committee and Financial Accounting Foundation statement, *Joint Statement of the International Accounting Standards Committee Foundation and the Financial Accounting Foundation*.

> ambitious, it is certainly achievable. The G20 have urged us to complete our work by that date and many major economies have selected 2011 or 2012 as the year to adopt IFRS on the basis of a completed programme. I want to emphasize that our primary focus remains on making significant improvements to financial reporting. The Board will not issue a new standard unless it is an improvement over its current requirements .... I believe that defined targets and deadlines impose discipline and enable us to deliver needed improvements sooner rather than later.

This undertaking was intense and amounted to far more than a doubling of our efforts. Although I believe that enabled us to make significant forward progress on many of the major joint projects, our deliberations also revealed a number of areas of disagreement among board members, both within each board and, in some cases, between the boards, and also identified additional issues requiring further exploration. For example, differences in views among board members surfaced about various aspects of the projects on lease accounting, consolidation, and insurance contracts. The inevitable result was slippage in certain projects. That slippage and revised timetables on certain projects were reflected in the joint progress report we issued in mid-April 2010 covering the first quarter.[36] At that point, we were expecting to issue joint exposure drafts by June 30, 2010, on a number of the major projects. At the FASB, we were also planning to issue a major exposure draft on accounting for financial instruments in the second quarter of 2010. Recognizing the importance of proactively informing constituents about these important exposure drafts and of obtaining broad-based input on these proposals, we had developed programs for enhanced outreach to stakeholders.

A Necessary Change in Plans

However, quite understandably, a number of concerns were voiced at our advisory council meetings and from others, perhaps more so in the United States than abroad, over the very significant challenges that constituents would face in responding to numerous proposals on major projects if simultaneously released. They very rightly, in my view, expressed concerns over their ability to properly review, evaluate, and provide well-developed comment letters on the numerous exposure drafts that were scheduled to be issued in the second quarter of 2010.

The boards recognized these very valid concerns and the importance to the development of sound accounting standards of enabling all parties to properly review, evaluate, and provide well-developed input on exposure drafts. Accordingly, at our joint meeting in late May 2010 and

---

[36] *IASB and FASB Commitment to Memorandum of Understanding: Quarterly Progress Report.*

as detailed in a joint communiqué in June 2010, we agreed on a number of significant revisions to the MoU work plan.[37] These involved changes in the timing, scope of, and approach to certain projects to prioritize our joint efforts in order to better enable the boards to complete high-priority projects by June 2011 while also maintaining proper due process, including allowing constituents sufficient time and ability to properly review, evaluate, and provide input on exposure drafts. Four major projects were designated as priority projects, with a targeted completion by June 30, 2011:

1. Accounting for financial instruments
2. Fair value measurement
3. Leases
4. Revenue recognition

For the IASB, completion of its project on insurance contracts by June 30, 2011, was also a priority. The boards also agreed to try to issue converged standards on the presentation of other comprehensive income by June 30, 2011. Issuance of final standards on other major joint projects, including financial statement presentation and financial instruments with characteristics of equity, were now targeted for dates beyond June 30, 2011, and there were revisions to the approach to be taken on other projects, such as derecognition and consolidation. SEC Chairman Mary Schapiro again issued a public statement on June 2, 2010, supporting the modified plan, emphasizing the importance of the boards issuing quality standards, and providing reassurance that the SEC continued to be on schedule to make a determination in 2011 about whether to incorporate IFRS into the financial reporting system for U.S. issuers.

The reworking of the timelines and approach to certain MoU projects was an important and, in my view, necessary action by the boards. We had worked very hard to advance the many MoU projects toward completion by June 30, 2011, but it was proving to be a very challenging and, at times, downright exhausting effort. As I observed in a speech on June 3, 2010, at the Annual SEC and Financial Reporting Institute Conference of the Leventhal School of Accounting of the University of Southern California, about the intensified convergence effort,

> I am proud to say that so far my fellow Board members and our staff (both FASB and IASB) have risen to the occasion. But I do fear potential burnout, as it's not easy to be running a marathon at sprint speed. [O]n our side, the FASB side, expeditiously completing the projects is important and we have been working hard to achieve this. But our emphasis also has been and will continue to be on seeking not only

---

[37] *FASB-IASB Progress Report on Commitment to Convergence of Accounting Standards and a Single Set of High Quality Global Accounting Standards.*

> expeditious completion and convergence but also genuine improvement in the standards.... We're also stressing the importance of maintaining full and proper due process, including extensive constituent outreach and engagement.

In looking back at the period from November 2009 when we announced the highly intensified convergence effort to May 2010 when we reworked the timetable and approach, I think it is clear that I, along with others, had underestimated the amount of time it would take to properly and fully examine, discuss, and come to decisions on the many key issues in each of the projects and had overestimated the potential effect of significantly increasing our joint meetings on our ability to expedite progress on so many projects. It was an effort that had never been tried before, and as we progressed with the many joint meetings, it became increasingly clear that despite all the hard work and good intentions, more time would be needed to properly complete projects. Making sure that constituents would be able to properly review and comment on major proposals was essential to ultimately issuing sound standards.

As planned, and by the time I retired on September 30, 2010, we had issued joint exposure drafts on revenue recognition, accounting for leases, and presenting comprehensive income.[38] At the FASB, we had issued a major exposure draft on accounting for financial instruments,[39] received very extensive input on that proposal from a wide group of stakeholders, and begun discussions with the IASB on a plan for jointly redeliberating the key issues. The IASB had also issued a major exposure draft on accounting for insurance contracts that was significantly different from the existing U.S. accounting standards on insurance.[40] We decided to solicit input from U.S. constituents on the IASB's proposal and alternative ways of improving U.S. GAAP in this area and, therefore, issued an Invitation to Comment in September 2010.[41]

Post-September 30, 2010, both the FASB and IASB made some further changes to their technical agendas, so they could focus their efforts through June 30, 2011, on the priority projects. Toward that goal, the monthly meetings between the boards continued, with the boards focusing on those projects. However, in April 2011, the boards announced further revisions to the convergence timetable that included extending the timeline for completing the projects on accounting for

---

[38] Proposed Accounting Standards Update (ASU) *Revenue Recognition (Topic 605): Revenue from Contracts with Customers* issued June 24, 2010; proposed ASU *Leases (Topic 840)* issued August 17, 2010; and proposed ASU *Comprehensive Income (Topic 220): Statement of Comprehensive Income* issued May 26, 2010.

[39] Proposed ASU *Accounting for Financial Instruments and Revisions to the Accounting for Derivative Instruments and Hedging Activities—Financial Instruments (Topic 825) and Derivatives and Hedging (Topic 815)* issued May 26, 2010.

[40] IASB exposure draft, *Insurance Contracts*, issued July 2010.

[41] FASB discussion paper, *Preliminary Views on Insurance Contracts*, issued September 17, 2010.

Chapter 4: International Convergence

financial instruments, leasing, and revenue recognition beyond June 30, 2011, in order to permit further work and consultation with stakeholders on these very major subjects.[42] The boards also decided to issue second exposure drafts on revenue recognition and lease accounting for public comment, reflecting the importance of these subjects and the fact that in redeliberating issues relating to the 2010 exposure drafts, the boards had agreed on a number of changes to those proposals. The boards were able, however, to finalize and issue common standards on fair value measurement in May 2011 and presentation of comprehensive income in June 2011.

Clearly, and very appropriately in my opinion, the boards are proceeding in a deliberate and thorough manner on the major projects, ensuring that there is proper consultation with stakeholders, careful consideration of all the input that is received, and redeliberation of issues. Also, the boards are issuing revised proposals for public comment in order to try to ensure that the final standards, when issued, are high quality, understandable, operational, and cost effective. The G20 continues to issue periodic calls urging the boards to complete the key convergence projects in support of the goal of establishing a single set of high-quality global accounting standards.

At this point, it seems likely that the boards will finalize and issue converged standards on revenue recognition in 2013. They are also working toward issuing a second exposure draft on lease accounting and, at this point, hope to issue a final standard in 2013. However, the prospects for convergence on accounting for financial instruments and insurance contracts seem less likely. In regard to financial instruments, the FASB and IASB have taken somewhat different paths to try to improve the accounting standards in this important area. At times they have been jointly working on certain aspects relating to accounting for financial instruments, including on accounting for impairments of loans and debt securities and, more recently, on the overall approach to classification and measurement. However, in 2011, they were unable to agree on the criteria for balance sheet netting of financial instruments. Each board essentially decided to stick with its existing standards and also require footnote disclosures to help financial statement users bridge what, for some major financial institutions, can be very major differences in the size of the balance sheets under IFRS versus under U.S. GAAP. The boards have also been separately considering potential changes in the accounting for hedging transactions. The FASB has been developing new disclosures on liquidity risks and interest rate risks. And recently, the FASB has also been developing an approach to impairment of loans and debt securities that is different than the one they had been previously discussing jointly with the IASB.

---

[42] April 21, 2011, FASB news release, *IASB and FASB Report Substantial Progress Towards Completion of Convergence Program.*

As of November 2012, it seems that the two boards have largely agreed on the overall approach to classifying and measuring financial instruments and will soon issue exposure drafts on this important topic. For the impairment of loans and debt securities, the boards will issue exposure drafts with their different proposed models, highlighting the differences between the two proposals, in order to obtain constituent input on both models on the differences. In addition, the IASB is finalizing a new standard on accounting for hedging transactions that the FASB plans to consider once it seems closer to finalizing the model for classification and measurement of financial instruments.

Progress on the joint project on insurance contracts has also been challenging, both because of the complexity of the issues and also because there are very understandable differences in perspective between the two boards regarding the urgency of developing a converged standard in this area. For the IASB, this has been and continues to represent a major gap in the body of IFRS, one requiring that it develops and issues a standard as soon as possible. However, we already have well-established standards under U.S. GAAP on insurance, and although there may be room for improvement, the perceived urgency to do so is not as great, and the cost-benefit considerations of requiring a major change are important. So, after several years of joint deliberations on this project and continuing differences of opinion among board members and between the boards on certain key issues, it is not surprising that FASB Chairman Leslie Seidman indicated at the June 2012 meeting of the FASB's Financial Standards Advisory Council that, in her opinion, it is not likely that the boards will achieve convergence on the accounting for insurance contracts and that the FASB is planning to step back to rethink its approach to this project.[43] As of November 2012, it seems that each board is planning to issue an exposure draft in 2013 on accounting for insurance contracts, highlighting the areas of difference between the two proposals, in order to obtain stakeholder input as a means for then deciding how best they might proceed either jointly or separately.

Moreover, beyond the current convergence projects there is uncertainty at this point about how the FASB and IASB will work together in the future. In July 2011, the IASB issued for public comment a major consultation document seeking input on its agenda for the next three years. With a growing list of potential projects requested by constituents in countries that have or plan to adopt IFRS and continuing uncertainty over where the United States stands on IFRS, joint projects with the FASB may become less of a perceived strategic imperative for the IASB and its trustees. Other countries want a seat at

---

[43] "In brief: FASB Chairman provides status update on insurance contracts project," PwC CFO Network, 7 June 2012. http://cfodirect.pwc.com/CFODirectWeb/Controller.jpf?ContentCode=THUG-8V2L4G&rss=true.

Chapter 4: International Convergence

the IASB standard-setting table and so it seems that the unique bilateral partnership between the IASB and the FASB will give way to a more multilateral standard-setting environment internationally. Additionally, from reading press accounts and talking with members of the FASB, IASB, and observers of the accounting standard-setting scene, it seems that some convergence fatigue has set in on both sides. For example, as reported on WSJ.com:

> In a speech in Australia on Friday, he [referring to IASB Chairman Hans Hoogervorst] said it's not in the best interest of U.S. or global investors for the IASB and the U.S. Financial Accounting Standards Board to spend another ten years making minor tweaks to accounting rules to get them exactly the same.... Gradual convergence between the standards "has served its purpose, but now it is time to move on," Hoogervorst told the IFRS Foundation conference in Melbourne, Australia. [M]any other international stakeholders won't support a longer, indefinite period of convergence between U.S. and international rules.[44]

As reported in the December 6, 2011, article "FASB, IASB Chiefs Agree New Convergence Model Is Needed" in the *Journal of Accountancy*, FASB Chair Leslie Seidman said the FASB would like to work with the IASB to complete the current priority convergence projects but that indefinite convergence is not a viable option practically or politically.

I had made similar observations (for example, as reported in the CFO.com article "Herz: No Convergence for 10–15 Years") at a 2009 public meeting of the Financial Crisis Advisory Group [FCAG] in response to a question from FCAG cochair Harvey Goldschmid, "In a perfect world, with full resources and free from outside influence, when could we get convergence?" I responded, "Ten to fifteen years."[45] Although my response may have surprised some, that was my assessment at the time of how long it would take the boards, working together, to achieve full convergence between IFRS and U.S. GAAP. I knew, as did other knowledgeable parties, that beyond the joint projects under the MoU, there were many other differences between the two sets of standards and that ironing those out through a continued convergence effort would likely take a long time. That's one reason I favored the "improve and adopt" approach under which we sought to work jointly with the IASB to develop new, improved, and converged standards in a finite number of major areas, at which point I believed IFRS would be a high-quality set of standards suitable for adoption in the United States. Such a process was clearly challenging and would take a number of years to complete. However, I reasoned that it would

---

[44] Emily Chasan, "IASB Chairman: "Let's Move Past Convergence," WSJ.com, 25 November 2011. http://mobile.blogs.wsj.com/cfo/2011/11/25/iasb-chairman-lets-move-past-convergence/.
[45] "Accounting Body Defends Changes on G20 Goal, Banks Fret," Alibaba.com, 16 September 2009. http://news.alibaba.com/article/detail/markets/100172967-1-accounting-body-defends-changes-g20.html.

be a more expeditious path to achieving common standards than a continued process of convergence between the boards that would need to deal with the many remaining differences between the two sets of standards beyond the completion of the MoU.

The decision on whether and how the United States moves to or toward IFRS rests with the SEC. Many paths have been suggested and are possible. Some support a gradual approach that, although not achieving full convergence between U.S. GAAP and IFRS, would be directionally consistent with continuing, over time, to move the two sets of standards closer together. That seems to be the view expressed in the November 15, 2011, letter of the FAF trustees to the SEC. This letter proposes a U.S. incorporation commitment "premised on the belief that although the pursuit of a single set of global accounting standards is a worthy objective, a more practical goal for the foreseeable future is to achieve highly comparable (but not necessarily identical) financial reporting standards among the most developed capital markets that are *based on* a common set of international standards." The FAF letter described this approach as

> a model for incorporating into U.S. GAAP independently developed and investor-focused international standards that improve financial reporting in the U.S. or that maintain the quality of financial reporting under U.S. GAAP but also advance global comparability of standards. Under this recommended approach, the U.S. would retain sovereign authority over financial reporting and standard setting for U.S. capital markets, with influential roles for the SEC and FASB that recognize the benefit of the global harmonization of financial reporting standards based on the common platform of IFRS.[46]

In contrast, the February 2012 report by the trustees of the IFRS Foundation argues for full adoption of IFRS, stating

> Convergence may be an appropriate short-term strategy for a particular jurisdiction and may facilitate adoption over a transitional period. Convergence, however, is not a substitute for adoption.... There is a natural temptation for countries (and stakeholders within those countries) to argue against full adoption of IFRS, to call for convergence of national standards and IFRS rather than adoption, or to introduce national exceptions to IFRS rules. The temptation to pursue convergence rather than adoption should be resisted. Full adoption must be the goal.[47]

To me, this difference in views between the FAF trustees and the trustees of the IFRS Foundation is not surprising given the different mission and roles of the two groups and the accounting standard-setting bodies they oversee. The mission and responsibility of FAF

---

[46] See www.sec.gov/comments/4-600/4600-158.pdf.
[47] *IFRS as the Global Standards: Setting a Strategy for the Foundation's Second Decade.*

Chapter 4: International Convergence

relates to accounting standards used in the U.S. capital markets, but the clearly stated mission of the IFRS Foundation since its establishment is to promote the achievement of a single set of high-quality global accounting standards.

Some parties on both sides believe the time has come for each board to go its own way and that each board should instead focus on making its own standards as good as possible for its stakeholders without deliberately seeking to bring the two sets of standards closer together. For example, in an article in *Accounting Today*, professors Paul Miller and Paul Bahnson, commenting on the announcement in December 2011 by SEC Chief Accountant James Kroeker that the SEC would not be making a decision by the end of 2011 on the future of IFRS in the United States, on what Miller and Bahnson see as mounting areas of disagreement between the FASB and the IASB on key issues in major projects, and on the IASB's tilt toward continental European interests, state

> The quixotic quest to create uniform international standards is dead and done.... We ask, then, who could think it makes sense to subjugate U.S. standard-setting to Europe with its perennial political and economic problems? The present disarray shows that attaining uniform global standards is an ephemeral fantasy.... Going forward, incorporation means FASB will treat both old and new IFRS as potential helpful input to its deliberations. Instead of bending over backward to find common ground with the IASB, FASB will resolve its issues as it sees fit without pressure to go along to get along.[48]

Indeed, I have heard some in the United States analogize a potential move to IFRS to the likelihood and merits of the United States adopting the metric system—in other words, the goal of getting to a single set of global accounting standards is not achievable and that we are doing just fine with our own U.S. standards. Although all these views are interesting and help inform the debate, ultimately, the decision on whether and how reporting by U.S. public companies moves to or towards IFRS rests with the SEC and could also involve Congress.

In the Meantime, Back at the SEC

In the wake of the Madoff scandal and due to ongoing events relating to the financial crisis, the SEC certainly had its hands full during 2009. So, it is not surprising that it would take until February 2010 for the SEC to issue another release relating to the potential move to IFRS for U.S. issuers. In the release *Commission Statement in Support of*

---

[48] Paul W. B. Miller and Paul Bahnson, "The Demise of the Drive to Bring International Standard-Setting to the U.S.," *AccountingToday*, 1 February 2012.

Convergence and Global Accounting Standards, the SEC reiterated its long-standing support for the development of a single set of high-quality global accounting standards. It also stated that it planned to make a decision in 2011 on whether, when, and how to incorporate IFRS into the U.S. financial reporting system. In recognition of the concerns raised by commenters on the November 2008 "roadmap" proposal, the SEC directed its staff to conduct an extensive work plan to address many of the issues raised in the comment letters, including whether IFRS is sufficiently developed and consistent in application for use in the United States; whether the IASB is an independent standard setter that sets standards for the benefit of investors; the degree of U.S. investor understanding of IFRS and the readiness of preparers and auditors to make the conversion to IFRS; and assessing the impact of moving to IFRS on U.S. laws and regulations and on companies in terms of accounting systems, contractual arrangements, corporate governance, and litigation contingencies.

The release also indicated that if the SEC were to decide in 2011 to incorporate IFRS into the U.S. reporting system, the first time U.S. companies would report under such a system would be no earlier than 2015.

The use of the word *incorporation* versus *adoption* of IFRS was interesting and suggested the possibility of a partial or piecemeal movement to IFRS by U.S. issuers (for example, by allowing but not requiring all or some issuers to use IFRS or by requiring or allowing the use of some but not all existing IFRS). Incorporation could also be achieved by continuing to have U.S. GAAP as the legal name of the standards in the United States but with all or some of those of those standards being the same as, or based on, IFRS. In that regard, in December 2010, SEC Deputy Chief Accountant Paul Beswick, floated a possible approach called "condorsement." This approach involves continued convergence through an endorsement mechanism, under which U.S. GAAP would continue to exist and the FASB would decide on a standard-by-standard basis whether the particular IFRS pronouncement is suitable for use in the United States.[49] Such an approach was further detailed in the SEC staff paper[50] issued in May 2011. The approach has some similarities to the improve and adopt path we outlined in 2007.[51]

---

[49] Remarks by Paul A. Beswick, Deputy Chief Accountant of the SEC, at the 2010 AICPA National Conference on Current SEC and PCAOB Developments on December 6, 2010.
[50] *Work Plan for the Consideration of Incorporating International Financial Reporting Standards into the Financial Reporting System for U.S. Issuers: Exploring a Possible Method of Incorporation.*
[51] Edith Orenstein, "Beswick's 'Condorsement' and Herz' 'Improve and Adopt'." FEI Financial Reporting Blog, May 31, 2011. The author compares the two approaches and concludes, "Although Herz' 'improve and adopt' model circa 2007 is not precisely the same as Beswick's 2010-2011 'condorsement,' ... I believe at the very least that Herz, through his 'improve and adopt' model can be viewed as the uncle, if not the father of condorsement."

Chapter 4: International Convergence

However, in other important respects, this approach would be similar to the endorsement processes followed in certain parts of the world for IFRS. Although aimed at ensuring the suitability and acceptability of IFRS in those jurisdictions, these can result, and have resulted, in variations of IFRS across the world. That would seem to run counter to the avowed and often reiterated and reaffirmed goal of a single set of global standards. So, U.S. adoption of such a process could not only create a U.S. version of international standards but might also encourage other countries and jurisdictions to maintain or put into place IFRS endorsement mechanisms, thereby potentially further undermining the goal of achieving a single set of international standards. For U.S. companies and other stakeholders in the U.S. reporting system, a condorsement approach could result in a lengthy period of serial changes in U.S. GAAP that could increase the overall cost and effort involved in moving to international standards.

On the other hand, incorporation of IFRS into U.S. GAAP could avoid or significantly mitigate a number of legal and regulatory issues that might arise if IFRS supplanted U.S. GAAP as the legally recognized accounting standards in this country. Because the terms "U.S. generally accepted accounting principles" and "U.S. GAAP" are embedded in many places in our federal and state laws, in U.S. tax rules and regulations, in the rules and regulations of the SEC, U.S. banking regulators, and those of other regulatory agencies, and in many contracts entered into by companies, providers of capital, and other parties, changing the legal name of the standards in use in United States could raise widespread legal and regulatory issues. In effect, incorporation would allow IFRS to be embedded in the legal wrapper of U.S. GAAP such that the actual standards would be IFRS but would, for legal purposes in the United States, still be called U.S. GAAP.

Incorporating IFRS into U.S. GAAP over time could also mitigate the challenges to the U.S. reporting system associated with a one-time complete, or "big bang," conversion to IFRS. Despite the very significant progress that has been and continues to be made in narrowing the differences between IFRS and U.S. GAAP, even with successful completion of major MoU projects, there will still be numerous remaining differences between the two sets of standards, some of which can have significant effects on the reported results and financial condition of companies. Further differences are created as the FASB and IASB issue new standards that are not the subject of joint projects between the two boards. Ironing out these differences could be challenging and could take many years. An endorsement approach would enable the FASB to continue to be involved in determining the standards used in the United States and might also facilitate the United States, through the FASB, to continue to play a significant role in the development of international standards. Finally and importantly, an endorsement approach would seem to be consistent with the previously discussed requirements of Section 108 of Sarbanes-Oxley that require the designated U.S. standard setter to consider "the extent to which international convergence on high quality accounting standards is necessary or appropriate in the public interest and for protection of investors."

The SEC staff continued its execution of the February 2010 work plan on IFRS through 2010 and 2011, and into 2012. During that period, the staff accomplished several things. They issued two requests for comment in August 2010, one soliciting input from issuers on incorporating IFRS into financial reporting by U.S. issuers and the other soliciting input from investors on this subject.[52] They also issued an interim progress report in October 2010 on their work plan activities[53] and three staff papers (the aforementioned one in May 2011 on the condorsement approach,[54] one comparing U.S. GAAP and IFRS,[55] and the third analyzing the application of IFRS in practice).[56] As well, they received comment letters, held public roundtables, and did an extensive amount of fact gathering and analysis on the wide range of issues relating to the potential use of IFRS by U.S. issuers.

Although the SEC had said it intended to make a decision on this important matter in 2011, in December 2011, Chief Accountant Jim Kroeker announced the staff would need some more time to finalize and draft its final report on the work plan. That report[57] was issued on July 13, 2012, which was also Jim Kroeker's last day at the SEC. Although it provides a comprehensive summary of the SEC staff's work, findings, and observations, it does not contain any recommendations to the SEC on whether, when, and how to incorporate IFRS into the financial reporting system for U.S. issuers. Moreover, the introductory note to the report states

> The Commission believes it is important to make clear that publication of the Staff Report at this time does not imply—and should not be construed to imply—that the Commission has made any policy decision as to whether International Financial Reporting Standards should be incorporated into the financial reporting system for U.S. issuers, or how any such incorporation, if it were to occur, should be implemented.... Additional analysis

---

[52] Both releases were titled *Notice of Solicitation of Public Comment on Consideration of Incorporating IFRS into the Financial Reporting System for U.S. Issuers.*
[53] *Work Plan for the Consideration of Incorporating Financial Reporting Standards into the Financial Reporting System for U.S. Issuers: Progress Report.*
[54] *Work Plan for the Consideration of Incorporating Financial Reporting Standards into the Financial Reporting System for U.S. Issuers: Exploring a Possible Method of Incorporation.*
[55] *Work Plan for the Consideration of Incorporating Financial Reporting Standards into the Financial Reporting System for U.S. Issuers: A Comparison of U.S. GAAP and IFRS.*
[56] *Work Plan for the Consideration of Incorporating Financial Reporting Standards into the Financial Reporting System for U.S. Issuers: An Analysis of IFRS in Practice.*
[57] *Work Plan for the Consideration of Incorporating International Financial Reporting Standards into the Financial Reporting System for U.S. Issuers: Final Staff Report.*

Chapter 4: International Convergence

and consideration of this threshold policy question is necessary before any decision by the Commission concerning the incorporation of IFRS into the financial reporting system for U.S. issuers can occur.

I will not go over in detail the many findings and observations of the SEC staff in the July 2012 final report, but will refer interested readers to the report itself. However, I thought the report did a good job explaining the many issues associated with direct and full adoption of IFRS and why some sort of endorsement approach might eliminate or at least alleviate many of these issues. These include the legal, regulatory, and contractual issues associated with replacing U.S. GAAP, the cost and effort to U.S. companies that would accompany a one-time "big bang" approach to the switch, and concerns about ensuring a proper vetting of IFRS' suitability for broad use in the United States. The report also contains some observations on areas in IFRS that are underdeveloped relative to U.S. GAAP, such as the accounting for extractive industries, insurance, and rate-regulated activities; the many areas of continuing difference between IFRS and U.S. GAAP; the need for the IASB to have a more active and effective interpretive process and to make greater use of national accounting standard setters; the need for continued improvement in the global application and enforcement of IFRS and for broader and more stable funding of the IASB and IFRS Foundation that does not include obtaining funds from public accounting firms; a recommendation that postimplementation reviews of IASB standards be conducted by the IFRS Foundation rather than the IASB itself; and the need for greater investor education and engagement relating to the development and use of accounting standards.

None of these findings and observations, in my view, is particularly surprising from a U.S. perspective. However, to some, if not many, at the IASB, the IFRS Foundation, and its broader constituencies around the world, the SEC staff report may have been disappointing and frustrating. First, because it did not contain any recommendations on a path forward for IFRS in the United States and seemed to leave that in limbo for the time being. Also, some seemed to view it as representing an overly U.S. centric view of financial reporting in increasingly globalized capital markets. For example, Michel Prada, the Chairman of the IFRS Foundation trustees, was quoted in the July 16, 2012, article "IASB Takes Swipe at SEC Delay over IFRS" in *Accountancy Age* as follows:

> While recognising the right of the SEC to determine the method and timing for incorporation of IFRS in the US, we regret that the staff report in not accompanied by a recommended action plan for the SEC. Given the achievements for the convergence programme inspired by repeated calls of the G20 for global accounting standards, a clear action plan would be welcome.

European Commission spokesman Stefan De Rynck, in the July 18, 2012, article "EU Queries U.S. Seat on Global Accounting Body" on Reuters.com, stated that discussions concerning whether the United States will adopt the IFRS have been going on for a

> very long time and, despite repeatedly expressed commitments from the U.S., things are advancing very slowly.... The lack of a clear vision from the U.S. creates uncertainty and hampers the IFRS from becoming a truly global accounting language.... It is also becoming more difficult to justify the representation of jurisdictions not applying IFRS in the IASB governance framework.

In October 2012, the staff of the IFRS Foundation issued a report to the Trustees of the IFRS Foundation analyzing the findings in the July 2012 SEC staff report on IFRS.[58] This report provides a status on the findings and issues in the SEC staff report, discusses actions that have already been undertaken in regard to a number of the findings in the SEC staff report, tactfully takes issue with certain findings and observations in the SEC staff report (for example, in regard to funding of the IASB) by providing additional information and perspectives on these matters, questions the sustainability and viability of a gradual approach to moving towards IFRS on a standard-by-standard basis, and contains an appendix discussing arguments and evidence in support of the case for global accounting standards. Overall, the IFRS Foundation staff conclude

> While the size of the US economy relative to other jurisdictions presents significant challenges in transition that are unique to the US, the experience of other countries suggests that many of the challenges can be overcome with the appropriate political will to make a commitment to the mission of a single set of global standards. Moreover, in many areas the US is better prepared than other jurisdictions to consider the adoption of IFRS.[59]

Over the past decade, I have traveled to many parts of the world, including many countries that have adopted IFRS. These countries have devoted a lot of time, effort, and cost carefully planning and implementing the adoption and have done so successfully. In some countries and jurisdictions, the move from their existing accounting standards to IFRS has also required the exercise of considerable political will by the relevant authorities. So, I think it is understandable that some in the IFRS world have expressed disappointment, frustration, and criticism over what they seem to view as continued "foot dragging" by the United States. However, I believe it is also clear that the United States is different from any other country in the world, including in the size and breadth of our capital markets and in our

---

[58] Report to the Trustees of the IFRS Foundation, *IFRS Foundation Staff Analysis of the SEC Final Staff Report—Work Plan for the Consideration of Incorporating IFRS Into the Financial Reporting System for U.S. Issuers.* October 22, 2012.
[59] *Ibid*, p. 19.

financial reporting, regulatory, and legal systems. So, rightly or wrongly, the perceived benefits of moving to global standards are viewed by many in the United States as less clear than for most, if not all, other countries.

In summary, there continues to be considerable uncertainty over when and even whether the SEC will come to any decisions on this important matter.

So, Bob, What Do You Really Think About Convergence and IFRS?

Okay, after reading a lengthy chronicle of the convergence efforts between FASB and IASB from 2002–12 and of the various twists and turns in the SEC's considerations relating to IFRS, readers are probably wondering about my opinions on the subject. Indeed, I often get asked, "How was it working with the IASB? Do you think we will ever achieve complete convergence? Will the SEC really ever approve IFRS for use by U.S. companies?"

First and foremost, for me and, I believe, for many of my fellow FASB Board members, despite the many challenges, working with the IASB on pursuing the goal of developing common high-quality international accounting standards in support of global financial reporting was a labor of love. If I did not believe in that goal, I would not have devoted a chunk of my career and life to it through chairing the Transnational Auditors Committee, serving on the IASB, and through the joint efforts between the FASB and IASB. I very much enjoyed working with and getting to know our counterparts at the IASB and other standard setters around the world, including those in Canada, Europe, Japan, and China, with whom we met periodically. For me, it reaffirmed the growing importance of global connections and served as a reminder that not all accounting knowledge (or issues) reside in the United States.

I won't reiterate all the many arguments for and against creating a single set of high-quality international financial accounting standards. The real goal is having common, high-quality, and comparable financial information for listed companies and other publicly accountable entities across the global capital markets. Achieving such a goal would, in the opinion of many commentators, prove beneficial to both investors and companies around the world and could provide significant economic benefits both globally and in the United States. Developing a single set of, or at least common, accounting and reporting standards is a necessary (but not sufficient) condition for achieving this goal. So, although we may never fully attain the goal of having a single set of high-quality global accounting standards, I have believed and continue to believe it is a goal worth pursuing. The goal helps drive standard setters toward continuing to narrow differences between national standards and IFRS, thereby resulting in increasing convergence over time. As stated in the SEC's November 2008 proposal *Roadmap for the Potential Use of Financial Statements Prepared in Accordance With International Financial Reporting Standards by U.S. Issuers,*

> The Commission recognizes that the use of a single widely accepted set of high-quality accounting standards would benefit both the global capital markets and U.S. investors by providing a common basis for investors, issuers and others to evaluate investment opportunities and prospects in different jurisdictions.... Capital formation and investor understanding would be enhanced if the world's major capital markets all operated under a single set of high-quality accounting standards that elicit comparable, high-quality financial information from public companies.

Most commentators on the roadmap proposal agreed with this notion.

A major potential benefit then is improving comparability of reported corporate financial information across the capital markets of the world. By facilitating cross-border investing, it could also increase liquidity in capital markets and lower the cost of capital for companies. Better international comparability of reported financial information might also improve corporate decision making. For companies operating on a multinational basis, the ability to prepare their financial reports using a single set of accounting standards across the jurisdictions in which they operate would lower costs and could improve quality and consistency in preparing and communicating such information.

Now, I recognize that some people in the United States pose a number of important arguments based on a number of considerations against having a single set of high-quality international accounting standards or even common, but not identical, standards between the United States and other parts of the world. Some maintain that the United States, as the world's largest national economy and capital market, is a world unto its own—that U.S. companies can raise all the capital they need here and that U.S. investors have a cornucopia of U.S. securities they can invest in. Further, as noted in the March 2009 FAF-FASB comment letter on the SEC roadmap proposal, the overall macroeconomic benefit to the United States of moving to IFRS is not clear. Also as noted in the SEC staff's July 2012 final report on its IFRS work plan, in the absence of virtually complete convergence between U.S. GAAP and IFRS, a switch to IFRS would likely entail significant cost and effort by U.S. issuers. U.S. companies are very understandably tired from all the regulatory changes and economic and business challenges they have gone through in recent years: regulatory changes first from Sarbanes-Oxley and, more recently, from the Dodd-Frank Wall Street Reform and Consumer Protection Act, and the effects of the global financial crisis

Chapter 4: International Convergence

and the ensuing economic recession, to name a few. So, the prospect of significant changes in accounting and financial reporting requirements is not one that is welcomed by many in the corporate community.

Some also argue that our more robust financial reporting system gives the United States a competitive advantage and that we could lose this edge if we go to international standards. In their view, the primary goal should be to maintain and improve our system of financial reporting, including our U.S. GAAP accounting standards, seeking convergence only when it would clearly enhance our system and when the benefits of a change clearly exceed the costs. For these and other reasons, I believe that significant political challenges could accompany a decision by the SEC to mandate the use of IFRS by U.S. issuers.

I certainly do not dismiss or underestimate these factors and the continuing challenges in the United States of moving to or toward IFRS. The United States is a very large economy, and our capital markets are large, deep, and liquid. However, I believe the arguments against the United States moving to international standards may not give proper weight to what seem to me to be continuing trends in the global economy and capital flows and to the growing acceptance of IFRS around the world as the recognized set of international accounting standards. The fact is that the U.S. share of global gross domestic product (GDP) and global capital markets has now been steadily declining for many years. One decade ago, we accounted for more than 50 percent of the global equity markets; that has now fallen to approximately 30 percent.[60] Differential growth rates between the slower-growing U.S. economy and those in China, India, Brazil, and other nations in the developing world means that the U.S. share of global GDP has been decreasing and is likely to continue to decrease over the next decade. As a result, U.S. investors seeking the potential for higher returns have been allocating more capital to foreign securities, with overall U.S. portfolio holdings of foreign securities at December 31, 2011, totaling more than $6.8 trillion—more than triple the amount at the end of 2001.[61]

However, my apparent exuberance for IFRS or any set of international accounting standards is tempered by three important considerations:

1. First, the standards must be high quality. It's no good having a single set of standards if those standards don't produce sound financial and transparent information. So, as previously mentioned, the FASB-IASB convergence program is not just

---

[60] Aaron Anderson and Ofori Nkansah, "International Accounting: Should the US Adopt IFRS?" *Financial Executive*, September 2011.

[61] See U.S. Department of the Treasury press release dated 8/31/2012 "Preliminary Annual Report on U.S. Holdings of Foreign Securities" and May 2003 "Report on U.S. Holdings of Foreign Securities as of December 31, 2001" from the Department of the Treasury, the Federal Reserve Bank of New York, and the Board of Governors of the Federal Reserve System.

about convergence; it is also very much about trying to improve standards for the benefit of investors and other users of financial information both in the United States and around the world. In this sense, although there are some continuing gaps in the IFRS literature and particular standards that, in my opinion, are in need of improvement (just as there are in U.S. GAAP), overall I believe IFRS does represent a high-quality set of standards.

2. Second, those standards need to work in the United States with, for good or bad, all the other institutional and cultural forces that affect our financial reporting system. So, even though the U.S. share of global GDP and capital markets is decreasing, we are still a key force and major player in the global economy and financial system, such that a set of accounting standards cannot be truly international if they are not used or do not work in the United States. For them to work in the United States, additional implementation guidance beyond that provided by the IASB and its interpretations committee may be needed in some cases.

3. Third, as previously noted, although having a single set of high-quality accounting standards is a prerequisite for achieving the larger goal of comparable, high-quality financial information across the global capital markets, it is not a sufficient condition for achieving that goal. That goal also depends heavily on sound application of the standards, strong auditing, and proper regulatory review and enforcement across the capital markets of the world. This point is reinforced by the results of the SEC staff's recent review of the consolidated financial statements of more than 180 companies that use IFRS from 22 countries around the world. The November 2011 study[62] found that, although the reviewed financial statements generally appeared to comply with IFRS, there was diversity in practice, in some cases resulting from what appeared to be noncompliance with IFRS requirements. Continuing and cooperative efforts by all parties, including companies, the major global accounting firms, securities regulators, and national accounting standard setters are needed to reduce this diversity in practice over time. But I think that having a single set of international accounting standards or at least common standards provides a better starting point for achieving this goal than having multiple sets of accounting standards around the world.

---

[62] *Work Plan for the Consideration of Incorporating Financial Reporting Standards into the Financial Reporting System for U.S. Issuers: An Analysis of IFRS in Practice.*

Chapter 4: International Convergence

Nobody Said This Would Be Easy

Like most labors of love, this one has had many challenging aspects and will likely continue to face a number of challenges. Although both boards shared a commitment to a common goal, and the members of the boards have generally worked together in a very collegial manner, the fact that we were starting from different places and that we each also had to maintain our existing standards, while also trying to converge, often complicated matters. At times, it was a bit like trying to ride two horses at the same time because as significant reporting issues arose relating to existing standards, both boards had a responsibility to address them, sometimes resulting in short-term fixes that would later need to be revisited in major joint convergence projects. This was particularly the case during the financial crisis of 2008–09.

Each board's existing standards had been developed during the prior 30 years, and although there had been some harmonization efforts, they were largely developed separately. So there were many areas of difference between the two sets of standards. We were clearly starting from different places. That has caused, and continues to cause, differences in the technical agendas and priorities of the two boards. For example, for the IASB, completing a project on accounting for insurance contracts has been viewed as very important because IFRS does not have a standard in this area. In contrast, U.S. GAAP has well-established standards covering insurance companies. Although these may be capable of improvement, it's of less priority for the FASB.

By its very nature, convergence requires change, whether it be through developing common new standards or through one board agreeing to adopt the other's standards in particular areas. Change is not regarded lightly by the boards or their constituents. The benefits of any change must be carefully weighed against the costs of the change. So, for individual board members, balancing the desire for convergence while also trying to ensure that the resulting changes are cost beneficial is a very important, but often a very difficult, exercise. Not surprisingly, because the boards have been starting with different existing standards, the respective constituents of each board often favor continuing with the existing standard (that is, U.S. constituents may prefer sticking with the existing U.S. GAAP approach, and constituents of the IASB may favor continuing with the current IFRS standard). Thus, the cost-benefit evaluations by each board can differ. Understandably, we have seen instances on joint projects (for example, recently with consolidation and offsetting of financial instruments) in which, after significant joint deliberation and input from their respective constituents, each board decided, at least for now, to continue with its existing approach, thereby not achieving convergence in these areas.

For very understandable and valid reasons, people do not always enthusiastically embrace potential change, particularly when they believe a change may disadvantage them relative to the status quo or when a change will require significant cost and effort. So, it is not surprising that both the FASB and IASB have encountered significant opposition to certain of the proposed changes resulting from the convergence effort. Those most opposed to particular changes sometimes attempt to block, delay, or overturn them through political processes. Politicians are not elected by, or accountable to, a global constituency. As the old saying goes, "all politics are local." So, when lobbied by their constituents asking them to intercede against the FASB or the IASB on a particular proposed change, they may not be swayed by the asserted merits of international convergence of accounting standards. As discussed in chapter 3, we experienced that with the accounting for stock options. Similarly, the IASB experienced significant lobbying of the European Commission against IFRS 8 by opponents to that IASB standard that converged the IFRS reporting of segment information to that required by U.S. GAAP. Nevertheless, in both of these instances and notwithstanding the lobbying efforts, converged standards were issued and adopted.

Challenges in the convergence process also arise from the fact that that there are significant differences across the world in the cultural, institutional, economic, business, regulatory, and legal systems that surround the financial reporting system in different countries and jurisdictions. For example, aspects of the U.S. regulatory and legal environment drive some participants in the U.S. reporting system to demand more detailed accounting guidance and clear rules than seems to be the case in other parts of the world. Differences in the cultural, business, regulatory, and legal environments can also result in some proposed changes being more opposed in the United States than in other parts of the world, and vice-versa.

Despite all these challenges, the boards have been making progress in jointly improving and converging their standards. Disagreement within each board and between the boards on particular technical issues are to be expected. In my view, that is a normal, healthy part of the standard-setting process. In a number of cases, with further effort, including joint redeliberation of such issues or by exposing alternative approaches for public comment, these differences have been successfully resolved, but it requires persistence, determination, hard work, and a lot of goodwill. Overall and despite the many challenges, I believe those qualities have been in plentiful supply by board members and the staffs of the two boards and that, although it has not achieved all its goals, the FASB-IASB convergence effort has been something of a shining example of international cooperation.

Now Where?

The effort is a work in process and faces many continuing challenges and opportunities. First, I believe it is critical that the boards successfully complete the major MoU projects. To me, success means standards that are either wholly or substantially converged; that improve upon the existing standards; and that are understandable, operational, and cost beneficial. The major MoU projects were carefully selected as representing those broad areas of accounting standards where both boards, after extensive consultation with stakeholders and regulators, believed improvement was necessary. Successfully completing them would be a major step toward achieving a single set of high-quality international accounting standards. The boards are making progress on these projects, but there will be continuing challenges in getting agreement among the boards and ensuring that the proposed standards truly represent cost-beneficial improvements.

The boards will likely continue to face some opposition from affected stakeholders on some of the more significant changes they propose. For example, opposition to the new proposed leasing standard that would significantly change accounting for leasing transactions has arisen, not surprisingly, from the leasing industry and some companies that are major users of leased equipment. Further, although politicians in particular countries and jurisdictions may try to halt or influence the course of convergence, I believe that powerful geo-economic and global capital market forces will continue to exert pressure on both boards for convergence and on the United States and other countries that have not yet adopted or committed to adopt IFRS. That well over 100 countries, including many major ones, have already adopted, or committed to adopt, IFRS is testament to those forces as have been the declarations coming out of meetings of the G20 leaders from 2009 onward urging international accounting convergence. Regional groups of national standard setters in Europe, Africa, Asia-Oceania, and Latin America have been formed to help provide input to the IASB and foster the implementation of IFRS across their parts of the world. As well, the IFRS Foundation has created a new Accounting Standards Advisory Forum comprising these regional groups plus certain major national standard setters (which presumably would include the FASB).

However, the three largest countries in terms of national GDPs—the United States, China, and Japan—have not yet adopted IFRS or committed to adopt it. The SEC will presumably eventually decide on the course forward in the United States. China developed its own set of standards a few years ago. Although these are largely modeled on IFRS and are asserted to produce financial information that is the same as IFRS, or substantially similar to using IFRS, at this point, China seems committed to maintaining its own set of accounting standards while also continuing to try to maintain substantial convergence with IFRS. Japan now allows certain of its listed companies to use IFRS and had indicated that it intends to make a decision in 2012 on whether to require the use of IFRS by its listed companies starting in 2015 or 2016. However, few Japanese companies have so far elected to use IFRS, and many of the largest Japanese multinationals use U.S. GAAP. Further, following the devastating earthquake and tsunami in 2011 and the resulting challenges Japan is facing, Japanese officials intimated that this timeline might be pushed out further. It also seems that Japan is waiting to see what the United States does about IFRS.

Additionally, as of November 2012, there seems to be some uncertainty about the adoption of IFRS in India. In evaluating IFRS for adoption in India, numerous changes to the standards intended to better suit the Indian environment have been proposed.

So, although the growing use and acceptance of IFRS has been remarkable and has, in my view, greatly enhanced the chances of getting to a common, if not completely identical, set of global accounting standards, the journey is far from over. The FASB-IASB convergence effort has been a very important part of that journey, but that convergence effort should not, in my view, go on for an indefinite period. The movement to IFRS in the United States could be accomplished through the incorporation of IFRS into the legal U.S. GAAP wrapper through completion of the major MoU projects and some sort of endorsement approach thereafter.

Successful completion of the major MoU projects would, in my view, result in IFRS being a high-quality set of standards. It will not, however, result in IFRS and U.S. GAAP being close to being completely converged because numerous differences will remain. Some of these differences are well-known and potentially controversial to U.S. stakeholders, such as the prohibition in IFRS on using last in, first out as a method of inventory accounting. There are also differences in the approaches to the impairment of lived-assets, in the treatment of the costs of developing new products, in accounting by rate-regulated enterprises, in pension accounting, in the extent of "recycling" between other comprehensive income and earnings, in consolidation policy, and in accounting for contingencies. As well, many differences exist in disclosure requirements. These differences and many others, as well as areas in which U.S. GAAP and IFRS are converged or substantially similar, are described in the November 2011 paper[63] issued by the SEC staff, and in their July 2012 final report on the IFRS work plan.[64]

---

[63] *Work Plan for the Consideration of Incorporating Financial Reporting Standards into the Financial Reporting System for U.S. Issuers: A Comparison of U.S. GAAP and IFRS.*
[64] *Work Plan for the Consideration of Incorporating International Financial Reporting Standards into the Financial Reporting System for U.S. Issuers: Final Staff Report.*

Chapter 4: International Convergence

Also, at least for now, it seems the result of certain MoU projects, including accounting for financial instruments, insurance, and consolidation, may not result in substantially converged standards, and ongoing projects by each board may result in creating additional differences between U.S. GAAP and IFRS. Other continuing areas of difference between IFRS and U.S. GAAP may be more obscure but could have significant effects on reported financial information, and there are many differences in disclosure requirements. Ironing all these out through a joint convergence process between the FASB and IASB could take many years, such that achieving complete convergence between U.S. GAAP and IFRS may be not attainable. Even if it were to be attained, could it be maintained?

That suggests if we are indeed serious about the goal of a single set of high-quality international standards, at some point, we will have to move to a single set of standards. Some believe that at least for now a more practical and realistic goal would be to try to achieve common, but not identical, standards that generally produce comparable financial reporting. For example, in the letter dated November 15, 2011, to the SEC, the trustees of the FAF recommended a number of refinements to the condorsement approach that would support "a practical interim goal to achieve highly comparable high-quality accounting standards" that are increasingly based on IFRS while continuing U.S. GAAP as the legally recognized standards in the United States and maintaining U.S. sovereignty over the accounting and reporting standards used in our capital markets. Under this approach, the FASB and IASB would continue to work together to complete projects currently under joint development. The FASB would develop a process to address substantial remaining differences between U.S. GAAP and IFRS and new standards issued by the IASB for potential incorporation of IFRS into U.S. GAAP. Members of the FASB (and perhaps of other major national accounting standard setters) would participate as nonvoting observers in IASB meetings and FASB would not separately undertake new standard-setting projects on topics that are on the IASB's agenda. As envisioned, the FASB and FAF would continue to undertake due process and U.S. stakeholder engagement and postimplementation reviews of IFRS following its long-standing criteria of investor primacy, independent standard setting, robust and participatory due process, benefits exceeding costs, and the need for clarity and adequacy of guidance in the standards.

The approach outlined in the FAF letter seems like a constructive, practical path forward toward continuing convergence between U.S. GAAP and IFRS. However, those favoring global adoption of IFRS as the single set of high-quality international standards may view it as delaying and potentially diluting actual achievement of substantial convergence between U.S. GAAP and IFRS and as potentially jeopardizing ultimate achievement of substantial comparability in financial reporting across the major capital markets of the world. These fears have probably been reinforced by the SEC not having yet made a decision regarding the use of IFRS in financial reporting by U.S. issuers.

When and if it comes, the SEC decision will be very important to the United States and the future of an international reporting system. Whatever the path to incorporating IFRS into U.S. reporting, ensuring that such standards are high quality and work in the United States and that the body or bodies setting those standards are viable, capable, sufficiently insulated from undue political interference, and operate for the benefit of investors and the capital markets is critical. My educated guess at this point is that the SEC will eventually propose an endorsement approach under which the FASB, subject to certain criteria, proper public due process, and reporting protocols, will be charged with reviewing specific IFRS for potential incorporation into U.S. GAAP. I can also foresee the SEC asking for certain changes relating to IFRS and the IASB, including, for example, in the funding arrangements; in the overall governance and accountability of the organization for accomplishing its mission; in the IASB filling in major gaps in its standards; in continuing to enhance the ability of the IASB and its interpretations body, IFRIC, to provide timely guidance on reporting issues; and in continuing active participation by the FASB in the IASB's activities.

I am supportive of an endorsement approach under which the FASB would be charged with evaluating whether the United States should adopt the IFRS approach in these areas, providing it is targeted and not too open-ended in terms of the criteria for evaluating whether a particular IFRS standard is suitable for use by U.S. registrants. In my opinion, those criteria should be focused on assessing whether the application of the IFRS standard provides understandable, decision-useful financial information to investors and other users at a level comparable to, or higher than, existing U.S. GAAP and on whether it is operational and can be implemented in a cost-effective manner in the United States. In many, if not most, cases, I believe those criteria will be met. In that regard, I would note that many other countries have been able to successfully transition to IFRS, including our neighbor to the north, Canada, which adopted IFRS for its listed companies in 2011. Although Canada is certainly not the United States in terms of the size of its economy and depth and breadth of its capital markets or in terms of its regulatory and legal systems, its existing accounting standards were often based on or similar to U.S. GAAP, it has quarterly reporting by its listed companies, and it has capable securities regulators.

As recommended in the FAF letter, continuing proactive involvement by the FASB in the IASB's standard-setting projects could also help minimize the frequency and severity of instances of a new standard

Chapter 4: International Convergence

issued by the IASB getting a thumbs down by the FASB. However, there may be cases, few in number, I hope, when adoption of an IFRS standard may prove problematic in the United States, in which case either the IASB would need to consider changing the standard to address the U.S. concerns, or there will be continuing long-term differences between U.S. GAAP and IFRS. I feel somewhat troubled and torn by the concept of having a permanent standard-by-standard endorsement mechanism by which the FASB, SEC, or some other body in the United States would decide whether the United States should adopt each particular standard issued by the IASB. On the one hand, the longer-term result of such a process could be a U.S. version of IFRS or "GAAPFRS," which, in my view, would encourage other jurisdictions to continue to do likewise, thereby potentially undermining the movement toward a single set of high-quality international standards. On the other hand, I recognize the very thorny issues of national sovereignty and geopolitics under which many other jurisdictions do have IFRS review and endorsement processes and that, therefore, the United States is likely to also retain such a mechanism. Moreover, I believe it is very important for the SEC or the FASB to have the tools necessary to ensure that the standards issued by the IASB are appropriately investor-oriented by counteracting the pressure on the IASB that may come from other parts of the world to gear its standards to other public policy objectives and, when necessary in the interests of the U.S. capital markets, to be able to address reporting issues on a timely basis.

So, just as it did in the formation of the IASB over one decade ago, I believe the United States, in the form of the SEC, FAF, and FASB, needs to continue to take a proactive role in helping shape the global financial reporting system. In doing so, they need to be clear on objectives and desired outcomes and must also be good global citizens by trying to impart the good aspects of our standard-setting regime and financial reporting system into the global system while avoiding trying to impose what may less desirable features of the U.S. system.

Despite protests and threats coming from certain parts of the world over the IASB continuing to work closely with the FASB and delays by the SEC in making a decision regarding the path forward for IFRS in the United States, I believe the United States continues to have a major opportunity to help shape the future of a truly global financial reporting system. I also believe others in the world are looking for us to continue to take an active role in doing so. I think that makes sense both internationally and for the United States. On the one hand, an international reporting system is unlikely to work as effectively as possible without the United States being part of it, and we can help ensure that it works both for us and the global capital markets. On the other hand, in a world where the U.S. share of global GDP and global capital markets continues to trend downward, it may be precarious for us to try to go completely our own way in terms of financial reporting. Thus, I believe the U.S. should not be excluded from or marginalized in actively participating in the ongoing development of the international financial reporting system, nor in my view should the U.S. be indifferent as to the direction and key features of this system.

My hope is that the SEC will continue to support the goal of getting to a single set of high-quality international accounting standards and, with the help of the FAF and FASB, establish a clear process and target timelines for incorporating IFRS into financial reporting by U.S. issuers. To do otherwise could either delay or potentially undermine efforts to develop such a system. It could also result in the United States being on the outside of a system that includes many of the other major capital markets of the world and that may not operate in ways that are satisfactory to U.S. investors who have been increasingly investing in foreign securities. It might also reduce the ability of the United States to influence the future direction of other aspects of the international capital markets and global regulation. None of these outcomes would be desirable. As previously noted, as part of making a decision on the future of IFRS in the financial reporting system for U.S. issuers, the SEC might also stipulate a number of conditions and changes relating to IFRS, the IASB's processes, and the funding and governance of the IASB.

Another important issue confronting the SEC is whether and when to allow all or some subset of U.S. issuers to voluntarily adopt IFRS. I would be supportive of an early adoption option if and when the SEC has established a more concrete plan and timeline for incorporating IFRS into the financial reporting system for U.S. issuers. To allow an option to use IFRS in the absence of a plan to require its use would result in a dual-GAAP system for U.S. issuers, which I do not support. Assuming there is a more concrete timeline for getting to IFRS in this country, an early adoption option would allow U.S. companies wanting to achieve comparability in reporting with international peers and to reduce their cost of producing financial information to do so sooner rather than later. In addition, this could provide valuable information for other U.S. companies considering moving to IFRS and for our overall reporting system. It might also enable U.S. companies to get the change to IFRS behind them rather than going through what could be a set of serial changes resulting from an endorsement process that could take many years to achieve complete or substantially complete convergence between U.S. GAAP and IFRS. As discussed further in chapter 6, the potential movement toward IFRS by U.S. public companies has also raised important questions and issues relating to the accounting standards used by U.S. private companies and not-for-profit entities.

Chapter 4: International Convergence

If we incorporate IFRS into U.S. public company reporting over time, we will also need to consider whether and how those standards are interpreted in the United States and who interprets them. Do we leave it solely up to the IASB and its official interpretations body, IFRIC, or will there be a need for the FASB or the SEC to provide additional interpretative and implementation guidance for U.S. companies? If the FASB or the SEC do provide additional guidance in the United States on IFRS and converged standards, might that effectively create new areas of divergence in how those standards are applied in the United States with how they are applied in other countries? Achieving convergence is one thing, maintaining it is another. In that respect, some of the IASB's constituents have expressed concern that if the United States goes to IFRS, we will inevitably feel the need to provide all sorts of additional complex and detailed implementation guidance for the U.S. reporting system, the use of which might then spread beyond the United States, a potential result that they view as highly undesirable. That led Sir David Tweedie to declare from time to time that if such were to begin to occur, the IASB might need to officially "ring fence" the additional U.S. guidance to prevent it from spreading to the rest of the IFRS world and undermining the IASB's goal of having more principles-based standards. So, it would seem to me that a reasonable and practical approach to dealing with this would be to establish clear protocols that would require the FASB or SEC to refer issues to the IASB for resolution, on the understanding that if the IASB or its interpretations committee chooses not to or is unable to address them in a sufficiently timely manner, the FASB or SEC would need to provide guidance.

There is also a question of whether the FASB or SEC should or would initiate and conduct U.S.-only standard-setting efforts in cases when the IASB is either unable or unwilling to undertake a project that is deemed important by U.S. stakeholders. As the number of countries and jurisdictions served by the IASB increases, it is inevitably facing more numerous requests to undertake various standard-setting projects that may be considered less important in the United States. For example, the subjects of accounting for agriculture, inflation accounting, and accounting for Islamic transactions and instruments are important in parts of the world but probably less so in the United States. On the other hand, there will likely be continuing demands in the United States for standard setting in other major areas. Again, an approach to dealing with this would be for the FASB or SEC to refer such matters to the IASB and embark on major new standard-setting projects only if the IASB is unwilling or unable to do so. Will the IASB be able to balance these competing demands and priorities from various parts of the world in a way that satisfies U.S. stakeholders?

Conclusion

As I have mentioned now a few times, having a single set of high-quality accounting standards, or at least common standards, is just one part of getting to comparable, high-quality financial reporting across the global capital markets. Though not a sufficient condition for achieving the broader objective of high-quality comparable financial reporting around the world, having common standards is a necessary and critical aspect of achieving that goal. So, as described in this chapter, a great deal of time and effort has been devoted by accounting standard setters, regulators, and many other participants in the financial reporting system in the United States and around the world to the convergence of accounting standards and adoption of IFRS. Those activities continue, including major joint projects between the IASB and the FASB, but it seems the once powerful desire to converge U.S. GAAP and IFRS may be waning.

In the meantime, stakeholders in the United States and around the world continue to wait for the SEC to decide on whether, when, and how IFRS will be incorporated into financial reporting by U.S. issuers and how this decision, if and when it comes, will affect the future of financial reporting in the United States and the continued movement to the IFRS across the globe.

Also, very importantly, the SEC and other major securities regulators and capital market authorities need to redouble their efforts on these other fronts to ensure that the potential benefits of having a single set of international accounting standards are not dissipated because of poor and inconsistent implementation of the standards, weak auditing, and lax or nonexistent regulatory review and enforcement. Accordingly, regulatory and other structural changes at both the international and individual country levels may be needed to foster achievement of these goals.

Nobody said this would be easy. But, I continue to believe these are very important goals that are well worth pursuing.

Chapter 5: The Financial Crisis

Accounting Did Not Cause the Financial Crisis, and Accounting Will Not End It

I spoke those or similar words on a number of occasions during the financial crisis. For example, in a speech at the National Press Club in Washington, D.C., on June 16, 2009, I stated,

> There is a general consensus that excess leverage at many levels and lax lending practices fueled the creation of complex and risky structured securities and derivatives that were spread across opaque and unregulated markets around the world. When the risks became evident, the lack of basic supporting infrastructures in terms of timely and accurate information flows, clearing mechanisms, and price discovery compounded the problems, leading to freezing credit markets, plummeting equity markets, and significant downward pressure on economic growth. However, one very welcome development arising from the financial crisis is that a much broader constituency is calling for greater transparency as a necessary ingredient for recovery and the rebuilding of investor and public confidence. Included in this has been the need to improve and strengthen certain accounting and reporting standards. While accounting did not cause the crisis and accounting will not end it, it did reveal a number of areas requiring improvement in standards and overall transparency. And so, over the past 18 months we have responded vigorously with a number of new standards and

enhanced disclosure requirements relating to securitizations and special purpose entities, credit default swaps and derivatives, financial guarantee insurance, and fair value measurements and credit exposures.

That excerpt provides a rather bland summary of what was a hectic, tumultuous, and unforgettable period for me and my colleagues at the Financial Accounting Standards Board (FASB) and many, if not most, people around the world. Although policymakers may not have had an existing playbook to guide their actions, actions were needed in the face of the unfolding, unprecedented events of the time. The SEC, FASB, and IASB needed to take action on financial reporting issues emanating from these events. Recounting all the events in which I was involved in my role at the FASB during the crisis would fill many tomes. Those events and actions included issuing numerous pronouncements, attending many meetings with the IASB, advisory groups, and a broad range of stakeholders in the U.S. and international financial reporting systems, engaging in discussions with senior officials at the SEC and the Department of the Treasury (Treasury) and with bank regulators as specific accounting and reporting issues arose relating to ongoing events and governmental actions, and having various dealings with members of Congress.

In this chapter, I will attempt to recount and provide my perspectives on some of the key events and our actions during the global financial crisis, as well as some important lessons learned and, perhaps, relearned.

Were There Warning Signs?

In the January 27, 2011, press release announcing the official report of the Financial Crisis Inquiry Commission (FCIC), Chairman Phil Angelides stated, "Despite the expressed view of many on Wall Street and Washington that the crisis could not have been foreseen or avoided, there were warning signs." I agree with that statement, but as is often the case, I think the warning signs are now much clearer with the benefit of hindsight than they were at the time.

As an accounting standard setter, the FASB was, in my view, less well-placed than some others, including the companies engaged in particular business and financial activities and the regulators of such entities, to pick up early warning signs of potential issues in the financial system. Nonetheless, a warning sign we were aware of and acted on well before the onset of the crisis related to the rapid growth of nontraditional loans. These seemed to us to pose additional risks to those originating such loans, servicing or guaranteeing them, or investing in such loans or in securities backed by them. So, in December 2005, we issued guidance on disclosure requirements in this area in the form of FASB Staff

Position (FSP) SOP 94-6-1.[1] Paragraph 2 of FSP SOP 94-6-1 states, "The FASB staff is aware of loan products whose contractual features may increase the exposure of the originator, holder, investor, guarantor, or servicer to risk of nonpayment or realization. These features may include repayments that are less than the repayments for fully amortizing loans of an equivalent term and high loan-to-value ratios." The document then goes on to describe the various types of nontraditional loans with increased credit risk, including loans with high loan-to-value ratios, option adjustable rate mortgages with resetting interest rates, negative amortization loans, interest-only, and deferred payment loans. The FSP also lists and discusses the many existing disclosure requirements under U.S. GAAP and SEC rules and regulations in this area. Although that guidance was effective immediately on issuance of the pronouncement, unfortunately, perhaps reflecting the overall exuberance at the time, it did not seem to always elicit the kind of clear disclosures by companies engaging in these activities that might have better informed investors of the risks these companies were undertaking.

That was in late 2005, and although there had been some accounting issues relating to credit issues with commercial mortgage-backed securities, it wasn't until 2007 that accounting issues appeared with increasing frequency with residential mortgage-backed securities with credit problems. Those were a symptom of the emergence of the potential credit issues foreshadowed in our December 2005 document on nontraditional loan products. Of course, what we were not aware of was the alleged widespread lax and fraudulent underwriting practices around these loans. At the time, I also think we were unaware of the extent to which certain major financial institutions had been accounting for these securitizations as sales, thereby removing the underlying loans from their balance sheets and making them part of the "shadow" banking system. In the following sections, I discuss these important issues in greater depth, along with other key reporting issues and debates that arose during the financial crisis.

The Addiction to Off-Balance Sheet Accounting

In the wake of the Enron scandal, the FASB had addressed the accounting for special purpose entities (SPEs) and issued FASB Interpretation No. 46,[2] in 2002 and FASB Interpretation No. 46 (revised

---

[1] *Terms of Loan Products That May Give Rise to a Concentration of Credit Risk*, which is now codified in FASB *Accounting Standards Codification* [ASC] 825, *Financial Instruments*.
[2] *Consolidation of Variable Interest Entities—an interpretation of ARB No. 51*.

147

December 2003).[3] Although these interpretations may have put an end to the types of off-balance sheet structures that Enron engaged in, it became clear from the financial crisis that they did not stop companies, particularly certain major financial institutions, from engaging in such activities. In my opinion, and with the benefit of hindsight, at least some of these off-balance sheet treatments seemed to have resulted from a stretching or even a violation of the accounting rules in FASB Interpretation No. 46(R) and FASB Statement No. 140.[4]

What caused certain major financial institutions to go to such lengths to try to get off-balance sheet treatment for securitizations and other financial structures? From a financial reporting perspective, the treatment of a securitization as a sale of financial assets versus a secured borrowing can result in recording of gains and a smaller balance sheet in terms of reported debt and total assets. Those results boost reported earnings, earnings per share, and returns on assets and lower the reported leverage and debt-to-equity ratios. However, beyond the attractions from a financial reporting perspective, getting off-balance sheet treatment had potentially significant benefits on their regulatory capital requirements (that is, off-balance sheet accounting lowers the amount of capital the bank regulators require a regulated institution to maintain). Having to maintain additional capital is costly and lowers reported earnings. From a systemic point of view, I believe the off-balance sheet treatments became an enabler in the growth of the "shadow" banking system. The July 2010 (revised February 2012) Staff Report No. 458, *Shadow Banking*, of the Federal Reserve Bank of New York defined *shadow banks* as "financial intermediaries that conduct maturity, credit, and liquidity transformation without explicit access to central bank liquidity or public sector credit guarantees." That report discusses the rapid growth of the shadow banking system in the United States in the years leading up to the financial crisis and provides various measures of the size of the shadow banking system, which by 2008 was significantly larger than the official U.S. banking system. Such entities included securitization vehicles of various types, including asset-backed commercial paper (ABCP) conduits, structured investment vehicles (SIVs), and qualifying special purpose entities (QSPEs).

The *Financial Crisis Inquiry Report* of the FCIC describes some of these motivations and the lobbying by banks of bank regulators to obtain off-balance sheet treatments for regulatory capital purposes. For example, in discussing the ABCP conduits sponsored by major financial institutions, the report states the following:

---

[3] *Consolidation of Variable Interest Entities—an interpretation of ARB No. 51*, in 2003 (amended by FASB Statement No. 167, codified in FASB ASC 810, *Consolidation*).

[4] *Accounting for Transfers and Servicing of Financial Assets and Extinguishments of Liabilities—a replacement of FASB Statement No. 125* (amended by FASB Statement No. 166, codified in FASB ASC 860, *Transfers and Servicing*).

> When the Financial Accounting Standards Board, the private group that establishes standards for financial reports, responded to the Enron scandal by making it harder for companies to get off-balance-sheet treatment for these programs, the favorable capital rules were in jeopardy.... In 2003, bank regulators responded by proposing to let banks remove these assets from their balance sheets when calculating regulatory capital. The proposal would have also introduced for the first time a capital charge amounting to at most 1.6% of the of the liquidity support banks provided to ABCP programs. However, after strong pushback ... regulators in 2004 announced a final rule setting the charge at up to 0.8%.... Growth in this market resumed.

Additionally, and as discussed in the FCIC report and in other papers and reports on the financial crisis, in light of some of the accounting issues that surfaced during the crisis relating to securitization transactions and special purpose entities, I am sympathetic with those who assert that securitization and structured finance practices went very awry in the years leading up to financial crisis. Perhaps this view was best summed up on page 10 of the FCIC report by James Rokakis, treasurer of Cuyahoga County, Ohio, who stated "Securitization was one of the most brilliant innovations of the 20th century. It freed up a lot of capital...It worked for years. But then people realized they could scam it."

Off-Balance Accounting 101

So, exactly where and how, rightly or wrongly, did certain major financial institutions get these off-balance sheet treatments for financial reporting purposes? Three areas existed where off-balance sheet accounting was used by major financial institutions: accounting for securitizations involving QSPEs, accounting for certain variable interest entities (VIEs), and accounting by Lehman Brothers for the Repo 105 and Repo 108 transactions. Not surprisingly and quite appropriately, these matters were the subject of Congressional inquiries. Although the following provides an overview of each of these off-balance sheet accounting issues, I would refer those seeking a more in-depth understanding of the first two subjects to my letter dated March 31, 2008, to Senator Jack Reed, then-Chairman of the Subcommittee on Securities, Insurance, and Investment of the Senate Committee on Banking, Housing, & Urban Affairs. Other good resources are FASB Statement Nos. 166[5] and 167,[6] both of which are now codified in FASB ASC 860 and 810, respectively. For additional information on the third issue, see the March 11, 2010, *Report of Anton R. Valukas, Examiner* for the United States Bankruptcy Court Southern District of New York and

---

[5] *Accounting for Transfers of Financial Assets—an amendment of FASB Statement No. 140.*
[6] *Amendments to FASB Interpretation No. 46(R).*

my letter dated April 19, 2010, to Chairman Barney Frank and Ranking Minority Member Spencer Bachus III of the House Committee on Financial Services.

Did They Qualify?

The concept of QSPE was introduced into the accounting literature by FASB Statement No. 125,[7] which was issued in 1996. It was carried forward with certain amendments in FASB Statement No. 140, which was issued in 2000, and replaced FASB Statement No. 125. FASB Statement Nos. 125 and 140 distinguished two types of SPEs: QSPEs and nonqualifying SPEs. The concept of the QSPE was created to consider, in certain transactions, that the assets in a securitization entity are effectively the assets of the investors that hold beneficial interests in the entity. An SPE qualified as a QSPE only if the beneficial interest holders in the entity could sell or pledge their interests, and there were significant restrictions around the powers and activities of the entity. Accordingly, in order to qualify as a QSPE, the entity had to meet a number of specific requirements around the types of assets it could hold and the types of activities it could engage in. These were designed to ensure that the assets held by the entity would not require the servicer to make significant decisions or actively manage the assets, the activities of the entity were very limited and entirely specified in the legal documents establishing the entity, and that the entity could sell or dispose of assets only in automatic response to the occurrence of a narrowly defined set of events. Because they were supposed to comply with these strict requirements, QSPEs were described by some as being on "autopilot" or as "brain dead" entities. In effect, they were lockboxes in which the cash flows from the high-grade and passive financial assets in the entity were collected by the servicer and then remitted to the holders of the beneficial interests in the entity. The bottom line was that if a securitization of financial assets was effected using a QSPE, provided it met certain other criteria, it was treated as a sale, and the assets transferred into the QSPE were removed from the transferor's balance sheet.

Although the FASB received certain implementation and interpretation questions relating to QSPEs and had a project from 2003 onward to address these and other issues relating to FASB Statement No. 140, the requirements relating to QSPEs seemed to generally work as intended for a number of years. That was the case when the FASB addressed issues relating to the use of SPEs in the wake of the Enron scandal. Accordingly, in developing FASB Interpretation No. 46 and FASB Interpretation No. 46(R) in 2002–03, we decided to carry forward the

---

[7] *Accounting for Transfers and Servicing of Financial Assets and Extinguishments of Liabilities.*

special provisions relating to QSPEs, effectively exempting such structures from consolidation.

In the years leading up to the financial crisis, however, trillions of dollars of mortgages and other loans with nontraditional features were originated and securitized. In addition, it has been asserted in numerous reports and official inquiries on the financial crisis that many of these loans had been originated based on lax or even fraudulent underwriting practices.[8] Nevertheless, securitizations of these loans had often been accounted for as sales of the transferred assets to QSPEs and accorded off-balance treatment.

What seems clear to me with the benefit of hindsight is that some, if not many, of these entities were effectively ticking time bombs. As the loans contained in them increasingly experienced credit problems during the course of 2007, all sorts of actions and active management by the servicers became necessary, including attempting to proactively modify the terms of many of the mortgages held in these entities under government-encouraged programs and, in a mounting number of cases, foreclosing on the underlying properties. These actions went beyond those contemplated by the requirements to qualify as a QSPE and beyond the activities that had been specified in the documents establishing the entities. Not surprisingly, we and the SEC staff received increasing requests to clarify and expand the range of permissible activities of a QSPE in order to enable these activities to be conducted without jeopardizing the off-balance sheet treatment of these entities.

To me, it seemed clear by late 2007 that the concept of the QSPE had been stretched to the point where it was no longer workable. So, as stated in paragraph A33 of FASB Statement No. 166, which replaced FASB Statement No. 140,

> The Board believes that because the range of financial assets being securitized and the complexity of securitization structures and arrangements, the application of the conditions of a qualifying special-purpose entity have been extended in some cases beyond the intent of Statement 140, thus effectively rendering the conditions no longer operational in practice.... As a result, the Board decided to remove the concept of a qualifying special purpose entity.

In other words, in light of the evidence of what had been happening, we decided to "kill the Q." The exposure draft *Amendments to FASB Interpretation No. 46(R)* proposing that and other amendments to FASB Statement No. 140 was issued in September 2008. FASB Statement No. 166 was issued in June 2009 and effective in 2010. As an important interim step and in order to quickly increase the transparency around

---

[8] For examples, see chapter 5, "Subprime Lending," and chapter 7, "The Mortgage Machine," in the *Financial Crisis Inquiry Report* of the Financial Crisis Inquiry Commission.

the use of SPEs by companies, we issued new disclosure requirements that took effect starting with 2008 calendar year-end financial reports. These new disclosures significantly expanded the information in the footnotes to a company's financial statements on its involvements with QSPEs and other SPEs.

The removal of the QSPE from U.S. GAAP literature was also a step toward convergence with IFRS in this area because IFRS did not contain a QSPE concept. In developing FASB Statement Nos. 166 and 167 on VIEs, we proactively reached out to, and consulted with, many parties, including the U.S. banking regulators.

SIVs, Conduits, and Other VIEs

So much for QSPEs. Starting in the second half of 2007, significant reporting issues also began to surface with certain other SPEs that had not been treated as QSPEs for accounting purposes. These entities, which included SIVs and ABCP conduits established and run by major banks, involved the active management of financial assets and the related (often, short-term revolving) financing of these assets. So, these entities clearly did not qualify as QSPEs and, accordingly, had been accounted for under FASB Interpretation No. 46(R). As previously noted, that standard was issued in the wake of abuses with off-balance entities by Enron and others under the prior set of rules. The basic concept in FASB Interpretation No. 46(R) was that for thinly capitalized entities that did not meet the QSPE requirements, the party holding the majority of risks or rewards of the entity was deemed to be the primary beneficiary and had to consolidate the entity. The determination of which party, if any, was the primary beneficiary was generally implemented through the use of mathematical modeling techniques to calculate what were called expected losses.

In some cases, the sponsoring banks had entered into support arrangements as a back-stop for investors in the securities issued by these entities. These included liquidity puts and asset buy-back arrangements. Some institutions also sought to structure around FASB Interpretation No. 46(R) by creating and selling so called expected loss notes to hedge funds and other investors in order to transfer a majority of the expected losses of an entity to a third party if and when such losses materialized. By doing so, they asserted they were no longer the primary beneficiary and, as a result, avoided consolidating such entities in their financial statements.

Starting in fall 2007, some of these entities began to experience credit problems with their assets and difficulty in continuing to issue financing for these assets, which triggered or threatened to trigger the support arrangements provided by the sponsoring banks. Perhaps the most noteworthy of these occurred with entities sponsored by Citigroup that eventually had to take tens of billions of dollars of problem financial assets and related financing onto its books.

How had these entities received off-balance sheet treatment under FASB Interpretation No. 46(R)? Again, with the benefit of hindsight, it seems the calculations of the expected losses by the sponsoring institutions either did not always include all the relevant risks or severely underestimated these risks, including the potential credit risks of the assets held by these vehicles and the liquidity risk surrounding the vehicles. A more in-depth discussion of the apparent fallacies in the assumptions used to model such risks can be found in the *Financial Crisis Inquiry Report*.[9] At the FASB, we did not have any regulatory review or enforcement powers, but I also wondered whether the expected loss notes actually transferred a majority of the real risk in these vehicles to third parties. If not, was this just a case of poor estimation or was that by design (for example, through reverse engineering of the terms of these securities to be able to claim they transferred more than 50 percent of the expected losses)?

All of this, plus the effects of eliminating the QSPE, led us to conclude that we also needed to revisit FASB Interpretation No. 46(R). So, during 2008 and into 2009 and in conjunction with our development of FASB Statement No. 166, we also worked on revising and improving the consolidation rules relating to VIEs. The new standard, FASB Statement No. 167, was issued in June 2009 at the same time as FASB Statement No. 166 and also became effective in 2010. FASB Statement No. 167 introduced a more qualitative approach to assess whether an SPE should be consolidated that requires evaluating both the economics of the entity and who directs its activities. FASB Statement No. 167 resulted in the consolidation of trillions of dollars of SPEs, perhaps most notably by the government-sponsored entities (GSEs) Fannie Mae and Freddie Mac, for the trusts that issue mortgage-backed securities guaranteed by the two GSEs.

The Lehman Repo 105 and 108 Transactions

The failure of Lehman Brothers in September 2008 was one of the many noteworthy events that shook the global capital markets during that unforgettable month. In March 2010, the court-appointed examiner Anton Valukas issued his report, *Report of Anton R. Valukas, Examiner*, on the bankruptcy of Lehman Brothers. That report describes in a fair amount of detail the accounting and (lack of) disclosure by Lehman Brothers for Repo 105 and Repo 108 transactions (collectively referred to as Repo 105 transactions in the examiner's report). According to the

---

[9] For example, see chapter 8, "The CDO Machine," of the *Financial Crisis Inquiry Report*.

examiner, Lehman Brothers structured transactions around the ends of reporting quarters to temporarily remove securities inventory from its balance sheet, thereby reducing the leverage it reported in its quarterly financial information. The report states that "Lehman regularly increased its use of Repo 105 transactions in the days prior to reporting periods to reduce its publicly reported net leverage and balance sheet" and that "Lehman never publicly disclosed its use of Repo 105 transactions, its accounting treatment for these transactions, the considerable escalation of its total Repo 105 usage in late 2007 and into 2008, or the material impact these transitions had on the firm's publicly reported net leverage ratio."

When the news broke about this, I was asked by staff of the House Committee on Financial Services to provide my views on the matter, in particular whether the accounting for these transactions by Lehman Brothers prior to its bankruptcy violated U.S. GAAP. My response to that request is contained in my April 19, 2010, letter to Congressmen Frank and Bachus III. As noted in my letter, the FASB does not have regulatory or enforcement powers; so, my views were necessarily based only on publicly available information at the time. Without further information, I was not in a position to conclude whether the treatment by Lehman Brothers had violated U.S. GAAP, which generally requires repurchase transactions to be accounted for as secured borrowings, not as sales, which Lehman Brothers had done in this case:

> The FASB does not have regulatory or enforcement powers. However, whenever there are reports of significant accounting or financial reporting issues, we monitor developments closely to assess whether standard-setting actions by us may be needed. In some cases, a misreporting is due to outright fraud and/or violation of our standards, in which case accounting standard-setting action is not necessarily the remedy. Other cases reveal weaknesses in current standards or inappropriate structuring to circumvent the standards, in which case revision of the standards may be appropriate. In some cases, there are elements of both.
>
> At this point in time, while we have read the report of the Lehman Bankruptcy Examiner, press accounts, and other reports, we do not have sufficient information to assess whether Lehman complied with or violated particular standards relating to accounting for repurchase agreements or consolidation of special-purpose entities. Furthermore, we do not know whether other major financial institutions may have engaged in accounting and reporting practices similar to those apparently employed by Lehman.
>
> In that regard, we work closely with the SEC. We understand that the SEC staff is in the process of obtaining information directly from a number of financial institutions relating to their practices in these areas. As they obtain and evaluate that

information, we will continue to work closely with them to discuss and consider whether any standard-setting actions by us may be warranted.[10]

However, as noted in my letter, from the report of the examiner and press accounts and other public information on the matter, it did seem to me that Lehman Brothers had purposefully attempted to structure in the Repo 105 and 108 transactions so as to try to support the sales treatment. My letter discusses the steps Lehman Brothers seemed to have taken in order to attempt to meet two specific U.S. GAAP requirements for the transactions to be accounted for as sales, not secured borrowings, and raises some questions about whether those steps achieved their intended objective. I also noted in my letter that "[w]hen there are material structured or unusual transactions, disclosure is also very important" and that according to the examiner's report, Lehman Brothers had incorrectly disclosed that it accounted for all repos as secured borrowings.

Unfortunately, history has repeatedly shown that companies do sometimes attempt to structure transactions solely or mainly to achieve desired financial reporting outcomes. I know this all too well from my "Bad Bob" days. This poses a real challenge for just about everyone in the financial reporting supply chain: accounting standard setters, auditors, audit committees and boards of directors, regulators and enforcers, and, most importantly, the investing public. Like outright financial reporting fraud, reports of attempts to loophole accounting requirements, particularly in connection with the failure of major companies, sap public confidence in the integrity of published financial information. I touch upon this very important topic again in chapter 6, "Complexity."

Before I left the FASB, we added a project to address one of the provisions in U.S. GAAP that Lehman Brothers seems to have tried to structure around in the Repo 105 and 108 transactions. That project resulted in a final standard, FASB Accounting Standards Update No. 2011-03,[11] which was issued in April 2011, removing the provision in question from U.S. GAAP. In March 2012, the FASB added a project to undertake a broader review of the accounting and disclosure requirements relating to repurchase agreements, in part because of concerns about the accounting by MF Global that went bankrupt in October 2011 for repo-to-maturity transactions.

---

[10] Letter from Bob Herz to Barney Frank on April 19, 2010.
[11] *Transfers and Servicing (Topic 860): Reconsideration of Effective Control for Repurchase Agreements.*

Fair Value, Mark-to-Market Accounting, and Impairment of Financial Assets

I now move on to discuss the subject of accounting for financial instruments, which is a complex and challenging subject that came to the forefront during the financial crisis. This subject includes the debate between amortized cost and fair value accounting and the controversy about mark-to-market accounting and its role in the crisis. This could well be the subject of another book that might shed more light than heat on a very important subject. During the financial crisis, there was certainly a spotlight on this topic, and it brought a lot of heat on us as accounting standard setters.

I will certainly not be able to do justice to this subject in the discussion that follows because it involves one of the oldest, longest-running, most controversial, and, in my opinion, yet to be properly resolved issues in accounting and financial reporting: how particular assets and liabilities should be measured. For purposes of this discussion, I will confine myself to accounting for financial assets and liabilities, a complex and controversial topic in itself.

Some History

I could go way back in time, but let me start with the savings and loan (S&L) crisis from the 1980s and 1990s. Accounting practices by financial institutions, both under U.S. GAAP and as prescribed by banking regulators, were heavily criticized as having contributed to the crisis. Significant questions were raised about whether the use of amortized cost methods of accounting for financial instruments had enabled S&Ls and other banks to inappropriately defer recognizing losses on underwater loans and investment securities while also generating reported earnings through selective gains trading of appreciated securities.

On September 10, 1990, then-Chairman of the SEC Richard Breeden spoke publicly before the Senate Committee on Banking, Housing, & Urban Affairs about the shortcomings of reporting investments at amortized cost, stating that "serious consideration must be given to reporting all investments securities at market value" for banks and thrift institutions. Similarly, in 1991, the GAO issued to Congress the report *Failed Banks: Accounting and Auditing Reforms Urgently Needed*. That report concluded that "[t]he key to successful bank regulation is knowing what banks are really worth." The report urged the immediate adoption for both U.S. GAAP and regulatory reporting of mark-to-market accounting for all debt securities and rapid study of the potential merits of a comprehensive market value-based accounting and reporting system for banks in order that "banks' true financial condition could be reported promptly."

The FASB was already working on a major project on accounting for financial instruments and accelerated its review of accounting for loan impairments and accounting for investments in debt and equity securities. This resulted in the issuance of FASB Statement Nos. 114[12] and 115[13] in May 1993. FASB Statement No. 114 requires impaired loans that are not held for sale to be measured based on the present value of expected future cash flows discounted at the loan's effective interest rate or, as a practical expedient, at the loan's observable market price or the fair value of the collateral if the loan is collateral dependent. Under this standard, a loan is impaired when, based on current information and events, it is probable that a creditor will be unable to collect all amounts due according to the contractual terms of the loan. Under FASB Statement No. 115, debt securities held as investments can be accounted for in one of three ways: at amortized cost subject to impairment for debt securities that are being held to maturity, at fair value with unrealized changes in the fair value of the debt and marketable equity securities that are available for sale being recorded in other comprehensive income outside of reported earnings, or at fair value with the unrealized gains and losses being recorded in earnings for debt and marketable equity securities classified as being held for trading purposes.

These different treatments were intended to reflect the different purposes and business models used by financial institutions in originating loans and making investments in debt and marketable equity securities.

The FASB passed Statement Nos. 114 and 115 by a 5-2 vote, with the dissenting Board members arguing for more use of fair value in measuring impairments of loans and in accounting for investments in debt and equity securities. For example, the opening sentence of the dissent to FASB Statement No. 115 states

> Messrs. Sampson and Swieringa disagree with the accounting treatment prescribed in paragraphs 6-18 of this Statement because it does not resolve two of the most important problems that caused the Board to address the accounting for certain investments in debt and equity securities—namely, accounting based on intent, and gains trading. They believe that those problems can only be resolved by reporting all securities that are

---

[12] *Accounting by Creditors for Impairment of a Loan—an amendment of FASB Statements No. 5 and 15*, now codified in FASB ASC 310, *Receivables*.

[13] *Accounting for Certain Investments in Debt and Equity Securities*, now codified in FASB ASC 320, *Investments—Debt and Equity Securities*.

within the scope of this Statement at fair value and by including unrealized changes in fair value in earnings.[14]

Commenting on FASB Statement No. 115, noted accounting historian Professor Stephen Zeff stated,

> In the first of three successful lobbying sorties (1990–93), the American Bankers Association (ABA)—abetted by letters sent by the chairman of the Federal Reserve Board, the chairman of the Federal Deposit Insurance Corporation, the Secretary of the Treasury, and two United States Senators—pressured the FASB either directly or indirectly. Even though the FASB had strong SEC support, the ABA pushed the FASB to retreat from a position that it was considering, namely that all marketable securities be shown at fair value and that the year-to-year change in fair value be taken into earnings.[15]

Of course, depending on one's point of view on a particular accounting subject, a specific standard may represent either a retreat or compromise versus a worthwhile improvement.

However, FASB Statement Nos. 114 and 115 would be tested when the accounting for financial instruments again came under stress during the financial crisis of 2008–09. In the intervening years, the FASB (before, during, and after my tenure) issued a number of pronouncements that affected accounting for financial instruments and improved the disclosures on a company's use of, and risks relating to, financial instruments. Perhaps most notable of these were FASB Statement No. 133,[16] issued in 1998 and now codified in FASB ASC 815, *Derivatives and Hedging*, and FASB Statement No. 157, *Fair Value Measurements*, issued in 2006, and as subsequently amended now codified in FASB ASC 820, *Fair Value Measurement*.

In issuing FASB Statement No. 133, which requires derivatives to be measured at fair value, paragraphs 221 and 222 state

> 221. The Board believes fair values for financial assets and liabilities provide more relevant and understandable information than cost or cost-based information. In particular, the Board believes that fair value is more relevant to financial statement users than cost for assessing the liquidity or solvency of an entity because fair value reflects the current cash equivalent of the entity's financial instruments rather than the price of a past transaction. With the passage of time, historical prices become irrelevant in assessing present liquidity or solvency.

---

[14] Dissents of Messrs. Sampson and Swieringa to Financial Accounting Standards Board Statement No. 115, *Accounting for Certain Investments in Debt and Equity Securities*.
[15] Stephen A. Zeff, "'Political' Lobbying on Proposed Standards: A Challenge to the IASB," *Accounting Horizons*. 16, no. 1 (2002): 49–50.
[16] *Accounting for Derivative Instruments and Hedging Activities*.

222. The Board also believes fair value measurement is practical for most financial assets and liabilities. Fair value measurements can be observed in markets or estimated by reference to markets for similar financial instruments. If market information is not available, fair value can be estimated using other measurement techniques, such as discounted cash flow analyses and option or other pricing models, among others.

Contrary to the assertions of some during the financial crisis, FASB Statement No. 157 did not require any new fair value measurements or new uses of fair value in financial reporting and did not change the accounting for loans or for investments in debt and marketable equity securities, including the requirements relating to impairments of these financial assets. Rather, FASB Statement No. 157 was issued to provide a more consistent definition of, and framework for, measuring fair values of both financial instruments and other items and to expand and improve the disclosures about fair value measurements included in the financial statements.

However, at the urging of many parties, including major financial institutions, in early 2007, the FASB also issued Statement No. 159,[17] which is now codified in FASB ASC 825, *Financial Instruments*, that, similar to the existing provisions of IFRS, provided a fair option for financial assets and liabilities. A number of entities, mainly larger financial institutions, voluntarily chose to begin measuring certain financial items at fair value starting in 2008.

Then Came the Crisis

Soon thereafter, with the onset and rapid deepening of the financial crisis during 2008 and into the first quarter of 2009, the fair values of many, if not most, financial assets fell significantly. For financial assets accounted for as trading or under the fair value option, these declines were recorded in earnings. For available-for-sale debt and equity securities, they were recorded in other comprehensive income, subject to an assessment of whether the decline in value was other than temporary. For debt securities that had been classified as held to maturity, no loss was recorded unless and until the loss was judged to be other than temporary. For loans that were not held for sale, additional impairments, either in the form of additional reserves for loan losses or writedowns in loan carrying amounts, followed the provisions of FASB Statement No. 114, which, as previously described, does not generally require a fair value approach to accounting for impairments of loans.

---

[17] *The Fair Value Option for Financial Assets and Financial Liabilities—Including an amendment of FASB Statement No. 115.*

With the falling values and growing concerns over the quality of the collateral backing such securities, liquidity in the markets for many asset-backed securities dried up. Securities that had previously been valued using quoted prices (level 1 valuations under FASB Statement No. 157) became increasingly difficult to value. FASB Statement No. 157 provided guidance on valuing assets in illiquid markets (level 3 valuations under FASB Statement No. 157), involving the use of various techniques, including discounted cash flows. However, prior to the financial crisis, these techniques had generally been used for valuing nonfinancial assets, such as intangibles, and their use in valuing financial assets had generally been confined to valuing private equity investments and illiquid, long-dated derivatives. As market participants became increasingly aware of the problems with the loans backing many mortgage-backed and other asset-backed securities, the markets became less and less active. As a result, there were hundreds of billions, if not trillions, of dollars of these "toxic" securities and credit default swaps and other over-the-counter (OTC) derivatives related to these securities for which current trading prices and quotes became increasingly difficult to obtain. Under these circumstances, it was probably not surprising that a number of parties, including financial institutions holding these financial assets, started to publicly blame mark-to-market and fair value accounting as exacerbating or even causing the financial crisis.

These complaints reached a crescendo in late September 2008 as Congress debated emergency legislation in the wake of the near meltdown of the financial system. Some, primarily financial institutions and their industry associations, lobbied for a repeal or suspension of fair value accounting requirements. Vocal support for this came from a variety of recognized political and economic commentators. For example, commenting in the September 22, 2008, *Washington Times*, Lawrence Kudlow of CNBC stated, "Bad accounting rules like this (mark-to-market) are sinking the financial system." In the September 29, 2008, issue of *Forbes*, former Speaker of the House Newt Gingrich said, "Because existing rules requiring mark-to-market are causing such turmoil on Wall Street, mark-to-market accounting should be suspended immediately so as to relieve the stress on the banks and corporations."[18]

However, many others saw it quite differently. For example, in testimony before the Senate Committee on Banking, Housing, & Urban Development on October 16, 2008, former SEC Chairman Arthur Levitt stated,

> One of the biggest steps we can take to light a fuller picture of companies' financial health would be to expand fair-value accounting to cover all of the financial instruments.... Yet in recent weeks, fair-value accounting has been used a scapegoat by the banking industry—the financial equivalent of shooting the

---

[18] See www.aba.com/Press/Pages/Accounting_FVAQuotes.aspx.

messenger. If financial institutions were accurately marking the books, they would have seen the problems they are experiencing months in advance and could have made the necessary adjustments—and we could have avoided the current crisis.

Many, including investors and investor organizations and the major accounting firms and Financial Accounting Foundation (FAF) Chairman Robert Denham, wrote letters to Congress opposing any legislation that would suspend the fair-value requirements, warning that it could severely undermine investor confidence.

Meanwhile at the SEC and FASB, although not inclined to suspend the requirements, we also recognized the need for additional guidance in what was clearly an emergency situation. Accordingly, we issued a joint SEC-FASB press release on September 30, 2008, that provided additional guidance from our staffs on valuing securities in illiquid and inactive markets.[19] As promised in that release, the Board, following an expedited comment period, issued additional clarifying guidance on these matters on October 10, 2008, in the form of FSP FAS 157-3.[20] I recall that some of the comment letters we received on the proposal that resulted in this document were from individuals making impassioned pleas on both sides of the fair value debate. Exhibit 5-1, "Letters of Comment," shows four of these letters, the first two from people strongly against fair value and the second two urging us to hold the line on fair value. Many more such letters and e-mails were to follow in the months ahead, as well as hundreds of lengthier and more detailed letters addressing the technical accounting aspects of the various proposals we were to issue on financial reporting matters arising from the crisis.

---

[19] Securities and Exchange Commission press release, *SEC Office of the Chief Accountant and FASB Staff Clarifications on Fair Value Accounting.*
[20] *Determining the Fair Value of a Financial Asset When the Market for That Asset Is Not Active.*

Exhibit 5-1: Letters of Comment

Letter of Comment No. 10

From: XXX

May the souls of all of those who developed FASB 157 burn in the 7th circle of Dante's hell. The statement does not reflect economic reality and in fact converts statements to liquidation statements distorts periodic measurement of income, distorts capital and cause bankruptcies where in fact paper entries create a situation the opposite of cash flow. Perhaps this was the intended consequence. I am [sic] old CPA and an investor and I will tell you academic [sic] never done anything but contemplate your navel types that this statement does not help me evaluate investments because in fact [sic] distorts the most important investor issue which is earnings and earnings growth. You have made the income statement a garbage dump of no meaning in favor the balance sheet. Rule bound, every single member of this group and their staff are solely responsible for this non meltdown, meltdown. You are garbage.

XXX

CPA

Letter of Comment No. 12

From: XXX

I've read FAS 157 and your proposed FASB staff position on FAS 157. I've been a CPA for 40 years and I can not [sic] believe what the FASB has done to me personally and to the country as a whole. You've destroyed the retirement of me and my wife and millions of other Americans. Your lame attempt to correct the problem is way too little and way too late. Your arrogance and self righteous approach has cost millions of Americans their financial independence and their futures. I hope you can't sleep at night, because I know I can't. How do I tell my wife that our equity income funds that were to provide our retirement have been decimated because of an accounting rule that makes financial institutions, on paper, insolvent (essentially bankrupt) and makes their stock, even if they have positive cash flow, essentially worthless? You continue to do a great disservice to our country. Shame on you. I hope you can live with yourselves and all of the destruction you've caused.

XXX, CPA (Not very proud of it)

Chapter 5: The Financial Crisis

Letter of Comment No: 8

From: XXX

It is time to draw the line in the sand on the mark-to-market rules. I am deeply ashamed that you would even consider softening these rules when you know that the lack of regulations got us into this financial mess!!!! The lack of enforcement and changes in regulations by the SEC are to blame: changing the leverage rules for investment banks from 12 to 1 and letting them go up to 40 to 1 that is why there are none left, lack of enforcement in short selling rules, reversal of the up-tick rule, reversal of computer program trading restraints on a very bad day, etc. In my opinion I want to know how all these problems happened to the banks with SOX in place and what were the public accounting firms doing????? Why is no one going to jail—no material internal control weaknesses??? DO NOT GET CAUGHT UP IN POILITCS [sic]—WE ARE SUPPOSED TO BE INDEPENDENT!!!!! WHAT DO YOU WANT THE TREASUY [sic] DEPARTMENT TO HAVE AN EXCUSE TO PAY HIGHER PRICES FOR THIS TOXIC DEBT ON THE F/S ON US AND FOREIGH [sic] BANKS!!!! THIS IS A DISGRACE!!!!

XXX

Letter of Comment No. 17

From: XXX

I am concerned that the proposed revisions to the rule could further exacerbate the current financial crisis, rather than help it, by essentially making the financial health of a company that has non-performing assets on its books seem better than it actually is. What the rule is essentially doing is allowing a company to assign a value that is based on "assumptions" to an asset that has no market and is therefore actually, in the real world, worthless.

Furthermore, if a consumer applied for credit and showed a portfolio of securities that had no market as collateral, I don't believe they [sic]would be extended the same leeway in interpretation.

XXX

In response to the controversy, as part of the Emergency Economic Stabilization Act of 2008 (EESA), Congress mandated that the SEC conduct a study on mark-to-market accounting in conjunction with the Treasury and the Board of Governors of the Federal Reserve System. The EESA further authorized the SEC to suspend mark-to-market accounting if it deemed such a move necessary or appropriate in the public interest. As part of its study, the SEC received numerous comment letters; held several public roundtables; and reviewed the effects of the use of fair value accounting on financial institutions. This latter step included reviewing whether and how fair value accounting might have affected the 22 banks that had failed during 2008 (including the 3 largest failures: Washington Mutual, IndyMac, and Downey Savings and Loan) and other major failed or distressed financial institutions (including Bear Stearns, Lehman Brothers, and AIG). During fall 2008, we, together with the IASB, held public roundtables—one in London; one in Tokyo; and one in our offices in Norwalk, CT—to gather input and views from constituents on reporting issues stemming from the financial crisis that needed standard-setting action.

The report by the SEC staff to Congress,[21] was issued on December 30, 2008. Its overall conclusion was

> Rather than a crisis precipitated by fair value accounting, the crisis was a "run on the bank" at certain institutions, manifesting itself in counterparties reducing or eliminating the various credit and other risk exposures they had to each firm.... The Staff observes that fair value accounting did not appear to play a meaningful role in bank failures occurring during 2008. Rather, bank failures in the U.S. appeared to be the result of growing probable credit losses, concerns about asset quality, and, in certain cases, eroding lender and investor confidence. For the failed banks that did recognize sizable fair value losses, it does not appear that the reporting of these losses was the reason the bank failed.

The report noted that investors generally believed that fair value accounting increases financial reporting transparency and that the information it provides helps result in better investment decision making. Accordingly, the SEC staff recommended against suspending FASB Statement No. 157 or existing requirements relating to the use of fair values in financial reporting. However, the report did contain a number of recommendations for potential improvements to the guidance on fair value, as well as some broader recommendations on the need (*a*) to simplify accounting for investments in financial assets and (*b*) for enhancements to the accounting standard-setting process.

I would note that other studies[22] have similarly concluded that the use of fair value accounting was a not a contributing factor to the financial crisis. In that regard, I found a study conducted by an economist at the Federal Reserve Bank of Boston and published on January 31, 2010, to

---

[21] *Report and Recommendations Pursuant to Section 133 of the Emergency Economic Stabilization Act of 2008: Study on Mark-to-Market Accounting.*

[22] Another study with similar conclusions was Christian Laux's and Christian Leuz's *Did Fair-Value Accounting Contribute to the Financial Crisis?*

Chapter 5: The Financial Crisis

be particularly interesting. That study[23] looked at whether, as contended by some, the use of fair value accounting and markdowns of financial assets to fair value during the height of the financial crisis in 2008 was a major contributory force to the financial crisis. Some had argued that fair value accounting caused a procyclical contagion effect that led to a downward spiral in financial asset prices because financial institutions had to sell these assets at ever-falling distressed prices in order to prevent a further destruction of regulatory capital. The study focused on the largest U.S. bank holding companies: those with more than $100 billion in assets because these were the most prone to such write-downs and had the highest amounts of the troubled financial assets. The conclusion of this study states,

> Based on this simple analysis it would appear that fair value accounting had a minimal impact on the capital of most banks in the sample during the crisis period through the end of 2008. Capital destruction was due to a deterioration in loan portfolios depleted by items such as proprietary trading losses and common stock dividends. These are a result of lending practices and the actions of bank managements, not accounting rules. Furthermore, the data suggests that banks were not raising significant capital through asset sales; rather they were relying on government programs as well as debt and equity markets. There was no clear observable evidence to back the assertion that fair value accounting, linked to regulatory capital rules, caused banks to sell investments at distressed prices and thus promote a pro-cyclical effect that accelerated the decline in investment asset prices.

Nevertheless, the assertions that fair value accounting exacerbated or even caused the financial crisis continued, as evidenced by some of the comment letters the FASB received on its May 2010 proposed Accounting Standards Update (ASU)[24] and by the dissenting statement of Commissioner Peter Wallison in the *Financial Crisis Inquiry Report*, who, in discussing his views on factors contributing to the financial crisis, stated,

> The Commission majority did not discuss the significance of mark-to-market accounting in its report. This was a serious lapse, given the views of many that accounting polices played an important role in the financial crisis. Many commentators have argued that the resulting impairment charges to balance sheets reduced the GAAP equity of financial institutions and, therefore, their capital positions, making them appear financially weaker than they actually were if viewed on the basis of the cash flows they were receiving.

---

[23] *Fair Value Accounting: Villain or Innocent Victim, Exploring the Links Between Fair Value, Bank Regulatory Capital, and the Recent Financial Crisis.*
[24] *Accounting for Financial Instruments and Revisions to the Accounting for Derivative Instruments and Hedging Activities—Financial Instruments (Topic 825) and Derivatives and Hedging (Topic 815).*

However, the majority opinion of the FCIC seems to dismiss this view in a comment in the *Financial Crisis Inquiry Report*, "Determining the market value of securities that did not trade was difficult, was subjective, and became a contentious issue during the crisis. Why? Because the write-downs reduced earnings and capital, and triggered collateral calls."

At the time, however, some seemed to have a "shoot the messenger" approach to trying to address what was a very difficult and challenging situation. Being the chairman of the body that was at the center of these assertions and attacks was not always the most comfortable of roles during this period. I recall my then 23-year-old daughter Nicole, who is not an accountant or steeped in finance, observed from reading news accounts and watching cable news shows, "Daddy, there seems to be a lot of people mad at you and the FASB over this mark-to-market thing," and asking, "Why are they so against banks showing what their assets are worth?" I was buoyed by the professionalism and dedication of my fellow Board members and our staff and by the support we received from many quarters, including our trustees, many investors and investor organizations, the accounting profession, the academic community, and others, both for maintaining a line on not suspending the use of fair value and for the importance of independent standard setting. The support of then-Treasury Secretary Paulson, then-SEC Chairman Cox, and then-SEC Chief Accountant Conrad Hewitt who stood firm in favor of these principles was also important in weathering the storm against fair value and independent standard setting in fall 2008. Paulson would later write in his book *On the Brink*

> Some people have also blamed the use of fair-value accounting for causing or accelerating the crisis. To the contrary, I am concerned that had we not had fair value—or as it is sometimes known, mark-to-market—accounting, the excesses in our system would have been greater and the crisis would have been even more severe. Managements, investors, and regulators would have had even less understanding of the risks embedded in an institution's balance sheet.[25]

However, that was certainly not the universal view, and there was more to come in this controversy.

The Year 2008 Draws to a Close

Although the problems in the credit markets seemed to have been at their height during November 2008, neither a rebound in those markets in December 2008 nor the issuance of the SEC report at the end of 2008 dampened the calls from financial institutions and their trade groups for major changes to accounting standards relating to the valuation of

---

[25] Henry M. Paulson, *On the Brink: Inside the Race to Stop the Collapse of the Global Financial System*. Boston: Business Plus, 2010.

investments and, in particular, the standards relating to write-downs of debt securities for what are called other-than-temporary impairments. Under FASB Statement No. 115 and related guidance issued by the SEC staff and the EITF, both held-to-maturity debt securities carried at amortized cost and available-for-sale debt securities carried at fair value through other comprehensive income need to be written down through earnings when an other-than-temporary impairment occurs. Determining what constitutes an other-than-temporary impairment requires judgment based on an assessment of the length and severity of the decline in value of the debt security. Rules of thumb had developed in practice, such as if a security had fallen by more than 20 percent in value below amortized cost for a period of at least one year, it should be written down to its current fair value. Until that point, however, no charge to earnings (and no reduction in regulatory capital) needed to be made for the decline in fair value in the hope there would be a recovery in value.

The declines in the values of many debt securities had begun in the second half of 2007 and continued through much of 2008, with a bit of rebound in some debt securities coming in December 2008. By December 31, 2008, many debt securities had been underwater for more than one year and had significantly declined in value. So, it was not surprising that pressure mounted on us and the SEC to do something to mitigate the resulting write-downs that would need to be taken in the year-end financial statements of financial institutions. The institutions argued that credit markets had become dislocated and dysfunctional, such that the fair values were not representative of the underlying fundamental or true values of the debt securities, and that many of these securities with severely depressed fair values were actually "money good," meaning they were expected to pay off in full. They also argued that auditors were taking an overly conservative approach in forcing their clients to mark these assets down to unrealistic "fire-sale" prices.

I must admit that I had some sympathy for some of these arguments, particularly for the one that auditors may have been requiring overly excessive write-downs based on unrepresentative trades or "non-binding" broker quotes rather than allowing institutions to use other techniques to value what had, in many instances, become illiquid debt securities. In that regard and as we tried to clarify and emphasize in FSP FAS 157-3, the definition of *fair value* in FASB Statement No. 157 is the price that would be received to sell an asset in an orderly transaction and not what would be received in a forced sale or liquidation. The markets for many securitized debt securities had become illiquid. I supported and voted in favor of FSP EITF 99-20-1,[26] that we issued on January 12, 2009.

---

[26] *Amendments to the Impairment Guidance of EITF Issue No. 99-20.*

This FSP modified the rules relating to determining impairments of certain securitized debt interests to make them more consistent with the approach to impairment on other illiquid debt securities by allowing the use of management's cash flow estimates instead of market estimates of cash flows in computing the fair value and resulting impairment of these interests. The FSP was effective for December 31, 2008 financial statements and passed by a 3-2 vote of the Board, with Tom Linsmeier and Marc Siegel dissenting to what they felt was an inappropriate change in the impairment requirements for these assets.

Into 2009—Congress Weighs In

In January and February 2009, we met with many constituents, including our Valuation Resource Group, to discuss further actions we might take in light of the SEC staff's recommendations in their report to Congress and ongoing requests for additional guidance on determining fair values and impairments of financial assets. As a result, on February 18, 2009, I announced in a press release that we added two projects to our agenda: one to provide further application guidance on a number of areas, including when markets had become inactive and on determining when a transaction is distressed, and the other on improving disclosures about fair value measurements used in the financial statements. We had already issued for public comment certain proposed enhanced disclosures in interim reports relating to the fair values of financial instruments. We began work on the two additional projects, with a goal of finalizing the additional guidance on determining fair values in inactive markets and distressed transactions in time to be applied for 2009 second quarter financial reports.

Apparently, that was neither quick enough nor enough of a change for some financial institutions and their trade groups, as well as for certain broader business groups, such as the U.S. Chamber of Commerce (see exhibit 5-2, "Multi-Industry Letter on Mark-to Market Accounting: Practices and Implications"). Now, my experience has been that when companies and business groups oppose particular proposed changes in accounting standards, they often complain the proposal needs more vetting, that the FASB needs to slow down and conduct field tests and additional cost-benefit analyses, and so on. However, in this instance, which was certainly not the ordinary course of business and which, as many have said, was unprecedented, these groups lobbied for the changes they wanted to standards to be done on an emergency basis, with little or no due process by us, the SEC, or Congress.

Exhibit 5-2: Multi-Industry Letter on Mark-to-Market Accounting: Practices and Implications

Release Date: Wednesday, March 11, 2009

March 11, 2009

The Honorable Paul Kanjorski
Chairman
Subcommittee on Capital Markets,
Insurance and Government
Sponsored Enterprises
U.S. House of Representatives
Washington, DC 20515

The Honorable Scott Garrett
Ranking Member
Subcommittee on Capital Markets,
Insurance and Government
Sponsored Enterprises
U.S. House of Representatives
Washington, DC 20515

Dear Chairman Kanjorski and Ranking Member Garrett:

The undersigned business organizations and institutions, which represent entities from across a broad spectrum of the economy and all areas of the financial services industry, thank you for holding this very important hearing tomorrow on mark-to-market accounting practices.

The United States and the global economy have undergone a period of almost unprecedented strain and challenge. The falling prices of real estate related assets have ground the securitization markets to a halt, dried up liquidity, and frozen credit availability. The resulting illiquid and non-functioning markets and related impacts have cascaded throughout the economy, causing severe market dislocations and job losses.

While there are many causes for this crisis, the procyclical impacts of certain mark-to-market accounting principles have exacerbated the situation. Accounting rules did not cause this crisis. However, the inability of businesses, investors, and government to properly value assets in disorderly markets has created uncertainty and a loss of confidence that has led to a self-reinforcing cycle of write-downs and further economic contractions.

We recognize that accounting standards should be developed and governed by the appropriate bodies. Further, we believe the appropriate course is not the wholesale abandonment of appropriate application of fair value accounting principles, but rather immediate correction to better principles-based financial reporting. Each of our organizations has jointly or individually proposed short-term and long-term solutions to the unintended consequences that have arisen from the application of mark-to-market accounting standards. While the Securities and Exchange Commission ("SEC") and the Financial Accounting Standards Board ("FASB") have taken some incremental action to facilitate the use of mark-to-market accounting in disorderly markets, the scope of the changes has not been adequate, nor has the pace been consistent with the crisis conditions that exist.

With the upcoming subcommittee hearing on mark-to-market accounting, we write to you today to express our concerns for the need to correct the unintended consequences of mark-to-market accounting. We do not ask that Congress write accounting rules. Rather, it is incumbent that the appropriate bodies understand that a pace of business-as-usual is unacceptable. Let us be clear, real economic losses should be recognized and are necessary for orderly markets. However, the recognition of losses that do not have a basis in economic reality is unsustainable in any environment. Appropriate changes in mark-to-market accounting should not wait until mid-year or near-end. That will only allow the spiral of accounting driven financial losses to continue.

Our hope is that these hearings ask the tough questions and stimulate immediate action that makes necessary adjustments in both the accounting treatment and guidance so that economic recovery is not impaired by the application of flawed rules. We stand ready to work with all willing participants to bring about this goal in a rational and expeditious manner.

Sincerely,

American Bankers Association

American Council of Life Insurers (ACLI)

American Financial Services Association

Certified Commercial Investment Members Institute

Commercial Mortgage Securities Association

NAIOP, the Commercial Real Estate Development Association

The Council of Federal Home Loan Banks

Financial Services Roundtable

Group of North American Insurance Enterprises

Independent Community Bankers of America
Institute of Real Estate Management
International Council of Shopping Centers
Mortgage Bankers Association
National Association of Home Builders
National Association of Realtors
Pennsylvania Association of Community Bankers
Property Casualty Insurers Association of America
The Real Estate Roundtable
The U.S. Chamber of Commerce
Federal Home Loan Bank of Atlanta
Federal Home Loan Bank of Boston
Federal Home Loan Bank of Chicago
Federal Home Loan Bank of Cincinnati
Federal Home Loan Bank of Dallas
Federal Home Loan Bank of Des Moines
Federal Home Loan Bank of Indianapolis
Federal Home Loan Bank of New York
Federal Home Loan Bank of Pittsburgh
Federal Home Loan Bank of San Francisco
Federal Home Loan Bank of Seattle
Federal Home Loan Bank of Topeka
Cc: The Members of the House Committee on Financial Services

Readers may also recall that during January and February 2009 and into the beginning of March, stock markets precipitously declined. On March 9, 2009, the Dow Jones Industrial Average stood below 6,600, a more than 50 percent drop from its peak in October 2007. The U.S. economy also suffered more than 1.4 million job losses in the first 2 months of 2009. There was panic in the air. And, so, it was at this point that I was asked to testify at a hearing of the Subcommittee on Capital Markets, Insurance, and Government Sponsored Entities of the House

Committee on Financial Services on March 12, 2009, along with others, including James (Jim) Kroeker, the acting chief accountant of the SEC.

From the outset of the hearing, it seemed clear to me this was not going to be a neutral discussion of the issues. In his opening statement, the Chairman of the subcommittee, Congressman Paul Kanjorski, said, "We can, however, no longer deny the reality of the procyclical nature of mark-to-market accounting. It has produced numerous unintended consequences, and it has exacerbated the ongoing economic crisis. If the regulators and standard setters do not act now to improve the standards, then the Congress will have no other option than to act itself." Both my testimony and that of Jim Kroeker tried to explain the existing requirements, including the extent to which mark-to-market accounting and fair value measurements were and were not used by financial institutions, the results and principal conclusions of the SEC's study of the subject, and the actions we had already taken and planned to take to provide additional application guidance for valuing financial assets in inactive markets. I also provided the following observations:

> I would be remiss if I did not briefly comment on the role of financial reporting and economic and regulatory consequences, including assertion by some that the use of mark-to-market accounting and fair value caused banks to fail and has exacerbated the financial crisis. We agree with the SEC's conclusion that fair value did not cause banks to fail. We also agree with the SEC that suspending or eliminating the existing fair value requirements would not be advisable, would diminish the quality and transparency of reporting, and could adversely affect investors' confidence in the markets. The role of accounting and reporting standards is to help provide investors and the capital markets with sound, unbiased financial information on the activities, results, and financial condition of reporting enterprises. So, while financial institution regulators may base computations of regulatory capital on GAAP numbers, [they are able to] and do systematically make adjustments to reported GAAP figures in computing regulatory capital.... Of course, good accounting and reporting can have economic consequences, including potentially leading to what some term as procyclical behavior. Highlighting and exposing the deteriorating financial condition of a financial institution can result in investors deciding to sell their stock in the entity and lenders refusing to lend to it, to the company trying to shed problem assets, and to regulators and the capital markets recognizing that the institution may be in danger of failing and need additional capital. Indeed, individuals and families may take such procyclical actions when they see the falling value of their homes and of their 401ks and decide to spend less and to sell investments in order to raise cash in troubled times. But I think few would suggest that suspending or modifying the reporting to individual investors of the current values of their investment accounts. Thus, to the extent there are

valid concerns relating to procyclicality, I believe these concerns are more effectively and appropriately addressed through regulatory mechanisms and via fiscal and monetary policy, than by trying to suppress or alter the financial information reported to investors and the capital markets.

From what I recall, much of the rest of the hearing that lasted several hours involved certain members of the subcommittee making what I viewed as inaccurate statements about the actual accounting requirements and urging and demanding that either we or the SEC do something. At one point, I recall Jim Kroeker indicating that if the FASB was unable to quickly respond, the SEC might be able to do so. We already had begun our work, and in response to the demands from one member of the subcommittee (I believe it was Congressman Gary Ackerman), I indicated that I thought we could issue additional guidance in three weeks but would have to consult with my fellow Board members on that. My thinking was that it would be better for the FASB to provide such guidance through its open, public due process, albeit on a very fast-track basis, than for the SEC staff to try to do it by quickly issuing guidance with no public due process. I also recall that not all of the discussion was hostile, with some members of the subcommittee asking questions that indicated to me that they were genuinely interested in better understanding the issues. I recall Congressman Alan Grayson defending fair value and comparing the demands to suspend or change it to other ideas, such as changing pi from 3.14 to 4 in order to relieve congestion on the Beltway (the highway around Washington, D.C.); increasing the size of an inch so that Grayson, a tall man, would be shorter and, therefore, more comfortable in an airplane seat; or making the number 98 larger than 109 so that the loss the Washington Wizards basketball team had suffered the prior night would be counted as a win. In summing up, he asked his colleagues, "Does it make sense to kill the messenger?"[27]

I also recall one or more of the members of the subcommittee citing examples of what they asserted to be the ridiculous results of using fair value to measure impairments of debt securities. I do not recall the exact details, but almost one year later, in February 2010, I read a piece by *Bloomberg* columnist Jonathan Weil, "Suing Wall Street Banks Never Looked So Shady," in which he refers back to some of the examples cited by members of the subcommittee and the extent of losses that were subsequently recorded by the specific financial institutions. For example, Weil reported that, in the hearing, Congressman Ed Perlmutter cited what he called an example that was really disturbing: the Federal Home Loan Bank of Seattle that blamed the accounting rules for its needing to take a write-down of more than $304 million on

---

[27] Sarah Johnson and Marie Leone, "Congress Members Fume at Fair Value," *CFO*, 12 March 2009.

its portfolio of mortgage-backed securities, claiming this went well beyond any expected economic losses. According to Weil, in February 2010, the bank said it now expected more than $311 million of actual credit losses on its portfolio and had sued a number of the Wall Street underwriters of these securities. Weil also noted that Chairman Kanjorski pointed to a similar example at the Federal Home Loan Bank of Atlanta that in the third quarter of 2008 had recorded $87 million of write-downs to fair value on its mortgage-backed securities but estimated actual losses would amount to only $44,000. Weil quotes Kanjorski as saying, "I find that accounting result to be absurd. It fails to reflect the economic reality. We must correct the rules to prevent such gross distortions." However, Weil reports that when the bank released its results for the third quarter of 2009, it raised its estimate of credit losses to more than $263 million.

I could say I was shocked by all this, but that would not be true. First and perhaps foremost, the hearing came at a point when, as I previously suggested, there was clearly a sense of deep concern, if not panic, over the state of the financial markets, financial system, and economy. Second, I had previously learned, particularly during the controversy over stock option expensing, that members of Congress and their staffs are bombarded by industry lobbyists who supply them with arguments in support of their desired objectives, including potentially erroneous and misleading data, scripts to use in hearings, and even draft legislation. Don't get me wrong, as I noted in chapter 3, "Stock Option Controversies—Take Two," I also had the honor and pleasure to work with many members of Congress and their staffs, particularly on the Senate side, who cared deeply about the public interest, understanding issues, and doing what they believed to be the right thing. However, I also experienced firsthand some of the less positive aspects of our Congress at work.

Our Response

In any event, later that day and on my return to Norwalk, CT, the next day, I conferred with my fellow Board members and senior staff about whether and how we might respond to the demands from the subcommittee. As I have said before and will reiterate many times in this book, I was very blessed with fellow Board members and staff who, despite differences in views on particular technical matters, were dedicated to our mission and properly fulfilling that mission. So, we decided that with a lot of hard work, we could quickly issue for public comment two documents: one proposing additional guidance on determining fair values in inactive markets and another proposing changes in the accounting for, and presentation of, impairments of debt. We had also already exposed for public comment a proposal to increase the frequency of disclosure of fair values from annually to quarterly.

The next three weeks were to be very challenging, with Board members and staff working very long hours and through weekends to issue the proposals, discuss the proposals with many constituents, carefully review and analyze the more than 700 written comment letters we received during the two-week comment period, and revise the proposals and issue three final documents on April 9, 2009, so they were available for 2009 first quarter reporting. It was a real team effort, and I offer special thanks and my deep appreciation to three members of the FASB staff who worked tirelessly on these documents: Practice Fellows Adrian Mills and Diane Inzano and Valuation Fellow Kristofer Anderson.

FSP FAS 157-4[28] provided guidance on determining fair values when there is no active market or when the price inputs being used represent distressed sales. It reaffirmed what FASB Statement No. 157 states as the objective of fair value measurement: to reflect how much an asset would be sold for in an orderly transaction (as opposed to a distressed or forced sale). It also reaffirmed the need to use judgment to determine if a formerly active market has become inactive and to determine fair value in such circumstances. FSP FAS 115-2 and FAS 124-2[29] provided for a more consistent approach to the timing of impairment recognition and greater clarity on the credit and noncredit components of impaired debt securities that are not expected to be sold. The measure of impairment remained at fair value, but it was required to be split into the estimated credit component, which is charged to earnings, and the remaining noncredit component, which is charged to other comprehensive income. Although not one of our specific goals in establishing this approach, an important practical effect of it for the banks was to take some pressure off their regulatory capital because only the portion of the impairments in debt securities relating to credit would now be charged to regulatory capital. That FSP also expanded the disclosures sought by investors regarding expected cash flows, credit losses, and an aging of securities with unrealized losses. Finally, FSP FAS 107-1 and APB 28-1[30] extended the annual disclosures of fair values of financial instruments to quarterly financial reports. All Board members voted in favor of the first and third documents. Tom Linsmeier and Marc Siegel dissented to the second document that they viewed as an inappropriate change in the impairment requirements.

Reaction to the issuance of these three documents was strong but mixed. Critics of fair value generally said it was a positive step but did

---

[28] *Determining Fair Value When the Volume and Level of Activity for the Asset or Liability Have Significantly Decreased and Identifying Transactions That Are Not Orderly.*
[29] *Recognition and Presentation of Other-Than-Temporary Impairments.*
[30] *Interim Disclosures about Fair Value of Financial Instruments.*

not go far enough. Supporters of fair value saw it as a weakening of the standards and as allowing banks and other financial institutions too much latitude in determining fair values and in deciding what portion of an impairment to charge to report in earnings. We received strongly worded letters and e-mails from both camps: those who saw fair value as the root of all evil and those who, having read some press accounts, believed we had "caved" to the "evil banks" and their water carriers in Congress.

To me, the documents represented a genuine attempt by us to provide helpful guidance at a very challenging juncture for the capital markets and economy while preserving the underlying principles of fair value and greatly expanding the disclosure of information that professional investors had been seeking. Most of all, I will remember the sheer hard work and dedication we put into the efforts, making sure we also preserved our public due process. I take pride in the effort, but I certainly do not recommend it as a permanent mode for setting accounting standards.

The World Goes On, but It's Not the Same

Starting from the lows in early March 2009, stock markets began to rebound. The credit markets also continued to slowly strengthen, with bond spreads significantly tightening. Some of the most vocal critics of fair value have attributed all this to what we did in April 2009. As tempting as it would be to take some credit for the recovery, I do not believe that would be honest. Other developments, including the perceived stimulative effects of government fiscal and monetary policies and supply of cheap funds to the banking sector, along with the stress tests conducted by the banking regulators on the largest U.S. bank holding companies, were probably important factors. In any event, it began to seem that we had collectively averted going over the cliff.

The financial crisis has left an indelible mark on many people and many aspects of the financial system. I believe this also was true for the accounting standard setters and our joint efforts. Throughout the financial crisis, we and the IASB had endeavored both to address specific reporting issues from the crisis while also moving forward together on our major joint projects. Achieving the latter become very challenging, particularly for the areas of accounting and reporting that were the most relevant in the financial crisis, namely accounting for financial instruments and accounting for securitizations and involvements with SPEs. As previously discussed, these are key areas in accounting and reporting by financial institutions and were the areas requiring the most attention by us during the financial crisis. In looking back, I believe the principal challenges arose from the fact that we were starting from different places in terms of our existing standards; therefore, necessarily, there were some different fixes we each needed to put into place. Unfortunately but quite understandably, neither our regulators nor politicians on either side of the Atlantic were willing to accept a response in the heat of the crisis that, "We will deal with these issues over the next few years in our major joint projects on accounting for financial instruments, derecognition, and consolidation." Nevertheless, we met frequently, considered each other's actions, and, whenever possible, tried to achieve common, if not converged, responses (for example, in the guidance on determining fair values in inactive markets and in improving disclosures around fair value measurements). We also held joint public roundtables and jointly formed a Financial Crisis Advisory Group (FCAG) that I discuss later in this chapter.

The crisis had an effect on our convergence efforts. Certainly, it delayed progress on some major joint projects because we each had to devote significant time and resources to addressing the reporting issues arising from the crisis.

Also, having each put some fixes to these issues in place, it becomes more difficult to make another round of changes within a few years. Thus, for example, having issued FASB Statement Nos. 166 and 167 that took effect in 2010, it would not be fair to require U.S. companies to then make another round of major changes in their reporting in these areas within a few years. The IASB had already issued proposals in these areas that contained a number of significant differences from FASB Statement Nos. 166 and 167. Similarly, the exigencies of the financial crisis caused the two boards to take differing approaches to addressing accounting for financial instruments. In such circumstances, bringing things back together requires time and a rational and systematic approach. The June 2010 revised Memorandum of Understanding (MoU) attempted to do that. Time will tell whether it and subsequent efforts by the boards prove successful in achieving converged high-quality standards in these areas.

Some Lessons Learned

For me, many lessons were learned, and some were relearned. I say relearned because as the title of my June 2009 speech at the National Press Club states, "History doesn't repeat itself, people repeat history." Clearly, some of the key lessons from this financial crisis are not new, including the perils of excess leverage and inadequate capital, the importance of liquidity, particularly in a crisis, and the importance of incentives in driving the behavior of corporate managers and market participants. I also think some other important lessons were learned from this crisis.

First, as I have already said but cannot say too often, I was often amazed and constantly uplifted by the sheer dedication, professionalism, and willingness of my fellow Board members and staff to put in long hours in what sometimes seemed like an endless barrage of difficult issues we needed to deal with during the crisis. Having had the opportunity to work with people at the SEC and the Treasury, particularly during the height of the crisis, I can also attest to their dedication and tireless work on behalf of our country. People band together in a crisis in order to try to respond to the challenges and to try to get through it.

I was also very much impressed by, and learned a great deal from, the deliberations of the FCAG that we and the IASB formed to consider and advise us on financial reporting issues stemming from the crisis. The FCAG was co-chaired by former SEC Commissioner Harvey Goldschmid and Hans Hoogervorst, the head of the Netherlands Authority for the Financial Markets. (Hans later became the Chair of the Monitoring Group over the IFRS Foundation and succeeded Sir David Tweedie as the Chairman of the IASB starting on July 1, 2011.) The FCAG consisted of 18 recognized leaders from around the world from financial institutions and other major corporations. It also included leaders from the investment, accounting, and regulatory communities, with various official observers from major regulatory bodies and the FASB's and IASB's main advisory councils. It met 6 times between January and July 2009, addressing a broad array of issues relating to effective financial reporting, the limitations of financial reporting, convergence of accounting standards, and standard setters' independence and accountability. The FCAG provided important recommendations to us and policymakers.[31]

Reflecting the global scale of the financial crisis, the FCAG was, by design, a group comprising senior people from around the world. I believe the financial crisis clearly demonstrated the many connections between financial markets and economies around the world and the increasing need for international cooperation and coordination in addressing issues that arise in financial markets.

I am very grateful to the members of the FCAG for their willingness to serve on such a body at a time of crisis and for their candid views and constructive recommendations. Certainly, I learned a great deal from listening to and participating in the deliberations of this group. For example, I think the problems with QSPEs provide a clear example to standard setters of the perils of creating exceptions, however narrowly

---

[31] See July 2009 *Report of the Financial Crisis Advisory Group.*

constructed, that confer highly desirable reporting outcomes. I believe history has shown that in an effort to avail themselves of the exception, over time, it gets stretched and abused to the point where standard setters or regulators have to shut it down. It happened with fixed-price employee stock options, pooling of interests accounting for business combinations, and the QSPEs.

I also believe that the crisis reinforced the importance of understanding the potential behavioral effects of standards. The rather simple definition of *fair value* as the price a holder would receive in a sale of an asset in an orderly transaction may work just fine in normal times. It came under real stress during the crisis as markets broke down, and important questions arose over what constituted an orderly transaction versus a distressed one. Although FASB Statement No. 157 provided guidance for valuing illiquid assets, it did not contemplate what happened in the financial crisis, so we had to provide several rounds of additional guidance to help preparers, auditors, and regulators deal with the situation in order to obtain reasonable valuations that were consistent with the principles of fair value.

That brings up what I believe to be one of the major lessons learned from the crisis. We (politicians, regulators, and the private sector) cannot again allow trillion dollar markets that lack proper infrastructures in terms of price discovery, clearing mechanisms, transparency of financial information, and appropriate regulation. Balanced and effective regulation, oversight, and enforcement are also key ingredients of sound markets as is the appropriate exercise of due diligence and proper risk management by financial institutions. Although regulation should not stifle innovation and risk taking, it should help create needed infrastructures, standards of conduct, and transparency in markets. Unfortunately, in the years leading up to the crisis, the exploding markets for asset-backed securities and OTC derivatives lacked the most basic of infrastructure elements and "rules of the road" that, as a country, we worked hard to put into place throughout many decades in our public equity and debt markets. In modern times, the effective operation of capitalism depends on the existence of infrastructures that support transparency and the orderly functioning of markets. Far from constraining markets and capitalism, these are essential elements in its effective operation and in public trust in the system. So, it is not surprising and, in my view, is appropriate that the Dodd-Frank Wall Street Reform and Consumer Protection Act contained a number of provisions aimed at addressing these issues.

In terms of financial reporting, some of the most difficult accounting and reporting issues from the financial crisis stemmed, at least in part, from the lack of proper information infrastructures around the "dark markets" for structured credit products and derivatives. Under such conditions, accounting and valuation are significantly challenged. Proper accounting and valuation require that companies and market participants are able to identify, understand, and reasonably calibrate risk and returns originating from financial assets and obligations and to ascertain transaction prices in exchange markets. It is not surprising that in the financial crisis there were significant issues surrounding the determination of fair values in inactive and dislocated markets, the recognition of impairments of financial assets in such markets, and the quality and timeliness of disclosures of risk.

To me, all this reinforces the fundamental importance of transparency and accountability. A lack of transparency makes it more difficult to spot growing problems. Even when the problems become evident, the lack of transparency and proper information makes it harder to understand, pinpoint, and address the problem. It also makes it harder to identify who to hold accountable. In short, transparency is not just a buzz word or cliché. It is a fundamental and an absolutely essential attribute of sound financial markets. Relevant, trustworthy, and timely information is the oxygen of financial markets. It creates trust and confidence in markets, promotes market liquidity, and reduces costs to market participants. Depriving markets of relevant, trustworthy, and timely information, or polluting that information, can have adverse consequences on individual companies and their stakeholders and on overall confidence in the financial system.

Now, in regard to the merits of providing greater transparency in a crisis, what I am about to say may be a big oversimplification of a complex subject. At times, during the crisis, it seemed to me that the mindset of some bank regulators was that greater disclosure by banks could be harmful, whereas the approach of accounting standard setters and securities regulators was that more public disclosure is important and helpful. As former SEC Chairman Arthur Levitt stated in testimony on March 26, 2009, before the Senate Committee on Banking, Housing, & Urban Development, "What serves the health of banks may run exactly counter to the interests of investors—and we have seen situations where bank regulators have kept information about poorly performing assets from the public in order to give a bank time enough to dispose of them." This difference in perspectives would seem to stem from, and reflect some fundamental differences in, the role of bank regulators on the one hand and the role of securities regulators and accounting standard setters on the other hand. Bank regulators are charged with overseeing the safety and soundness of the institutions they regulate and with the stability of the financial system. The role of accounting standard setters and securities regulators is to provide investors and the capital markets with the information they need to make informed investment decisions to promote efficient allocation of capital across the economy. Both missions are critical to the operation of a sound financial system and healthy economy. The work of bank regulators, securities regulators, and accounting standard setters can be challenging, all the more so during a major financial crisis.

During the crisis (and perhaps even now) there seemed to be some confusion in the media and elsewhere between the accounting standards used for financial reporting to investors and the capital markets and the regulation of financial institutions. For example, accounting standards do not prescribe or directly determine the levels of capital that banks are required to maintain; the bank regulators do. However, under the laws enacted by Congress in the wake of the S&L crisis, the determination of regulatory capital by the bank regulators starts with the U.S. GAAP numbers. The bank regulators have some discretion to make adjustments in computing regulatory capital, and they have other tools to address the capital adequacy, safety, and solvency issues of financial institutions. For example, it has been the long-standing policy of bank regulators to exclude unrealized gains and losses included in other comprehensive income from the computation of regulatory capital.

So, regulators have a natural interest in accounting standards; likewise, investors have an interest in both accounting standards and the impact of regulatory requirements and actions on the institutions in which they invest. In that regard, I publicly commended the U.S. bank regulators on the transparency they provided on the results of the "stress tests" of major U.S. bank holding companies in spring 2009. I believe it was well received by the markets and contributed to help stabilize the financial system at a critical juncture. I would encourage this type of transparency by prudential regulators on an ongoing basis and applaud the efforts of the Federal Reserve to provide this under the annual Comprehensive Capital Analysis and Review program for the largest U.S. bank holding companies.

It is important for accounting standard setters and prudential regulators to work together to share information and to try, whenever possible, to develop common solutions to reporting issues arising in the financial system, particularly in times of financial and economic stress. These common solutions help minimize unnecessary differences between financial reporting and regulatory reporting and the additional costs to regulated institutions resulting from such differences. However, because of the differences in the roles and missions of accounting standard setters and prudential regulators, it is also important that both be able to conduct their work in an independent manner, without one being subordinated to the other. In my opinion, the regulators should not be handcuffed by accounting standards developed with a different purpose in mind nor should the needs and perspectives of the regulators drive accounting standards because to do so could degrade the financial information available to investors and reduce public confidence in the capital markets.

The importance of maintaining independently established accounting standards was tested in fall 2009 as the House of Representatives debated the financial services reform bill. Congressmen Perlmutter of Colorado and Lucas of Oklahoma planned to introduce an amendment that would have allowed the new Financial Stability Oversight Council (FSOC) to effectively override and modify accounting standards and reporting to investors and the capital markets to achieve bank regulatory and financial stability objectives. That possibility generated a quick, strong, and broad-based response against such a measure from the FAF trustees and others in the business, investor, and accounting communities such that it was modified to allow the FSOC to comment on financial accounting and reporting matters but not override or modify the standards. In the end, I believe that episode served to reinforce the importance of independent accounting standard setting. Certainly, when push came to shove, I felt very good about the level of support for that principle and for the need for sound financial reporting and transparency as important public policy goals.

Measuring Financial Instruments— Amortized Cost Versus Fair Value

I think that the fact that it got to this point also evidenced the continuing controversy and debates over how to measure and report financial instruments. So, what are my thoughts on that important subject? First, let me make it clear that I am neither a fair value zealot nor an ardent defender of amortized cost accounting for most financial instruments. At times, depending how I voted on a particular document, I was characterized in some of the business press as caving to the banks and their arguments against fair value; at other times, I was painted as a champion or strong advocate of mark-to-market accounting for everything. Neither characterization accurately captures my perspectives on what I view as a complex subject. So, I will expound a bit further both on the arguments for and against the use of amortized cost and fair value for financial instruments and on my views.

As previously noted, the subject of measurement in accounting is a complex one and one on which informed and reasonable people can and do disagree. My own view is that there are pros and cons to both amortized cost and fair value, depending on the facts and circumstances, and that other measurement attributes may be appropriate in certain circumstances. I think most people agree that fair value is the most appropriate measure of financial assets that are being traded or held for sale in the relatively near term, for financial liabilities that are part of a trading activity, and for derivatives. Where most of the disagreement seems to focus is on financial assets and financial liabilities with fixed principal amounts (that is, debt securities and loans) that are being held for collection or payment of contractual cash flows. For example, banks and other financial institutions originate loans and, in some cases, debt instruments as part of their customer lending and financing activities and will often hold these for collection of cash flows rather than selling or securitizing them. Companies may invest part of their treasury activities in fixed income instruments and hold them for collection of cash flows. Similarly, most companies obtain loans and debt financing for their operations, making interest and principal payments over the life of the instruments and either cannot or do not intend to sell or otherwise transfer such obligations to third parties.

Some Arguments for Using Amortized Cost

In such circumstances, supporters of amortized cost believe it produces the most relevant and reliable reporting. They argue that showing a financial asset at what it could be sold for today is not relevant when the company does not intend to sell it and can result in unnecessary and misleading volatility and "noise" in reported results and financial position. For example, if a bank makes a 10-year $300,000 loan at, say, a 5 percent annual interest rate and expects to collect all the contractual cash flows on the loan for its life, it should carry the loan on its balance sheet at $300,000 despite any interim changes in the value of the loan due to changes in market interest rates and other market factors. It will report $15,000 of interest income each year and the loan at the $300,000 due at maturity. Only credit risk matters such that the carrying value of the loan should be reduced only to the extent it becomes impaired and is not expected to pay off in full.

Some also argue that, counter to the efficient market theory, markets are far from always being rational such that basing values on current market prices can lead to significant overstatement of underlying economic values of assets in times of irrational exuberance and significant understatement of the economic values of assets in times of financial crisis. Therefore, they assert and are concerned that reporting based on fair values can have significant procyclical effects that accentuate market bubbles and market downturns. They view the recognition of unrealized "paper" gains and losses as distorting reported income, stockholders' equity, and other key metrics, such as leverage. They are also concerned that it can cause undesirable behavior by financial institutions, including in times of market run-ups to the payment of excess compensation to management and excess dividends and stock buybacks. Ultimately, they fear it could potentially cause banks to curtail making long-term fixed-rate loans and mortgages in an effort to avoid having to report volatile financial results arising from having to fair value their financial assets. When active markets do not exist for particular financial instruments, as was the case in the financial crisis for certain debt securities and is the case for many loans, coming up with fair values is highly subjective, difficult to audit, and costly, often requiring the involvement of valuation specialists. They also note the counterintuitive result of reporting gains on financial liabilities measured at fair value of financially distressed companies, as was the case with Lehman Brothers in the months leading up its demise.

Some Arguments for Using Fair Value

On the other hand, supporters of using fair value to measure and report all financial instruments believe it produces the most relevant and useful reporting because it provides for a more consistent and comparable approach based on current market and economic conditions, not on past costs and prices. They point to a number of academic studies that support this view. They also believe that the measurement of financial instruments should not depend on a company's intent or business model. Rather, they view fair value as the measure most consistent with the objective of financial reporting to provide information that is useful to predicting the amounts, timing, and uncertainty of future cash flows. Also, some believe that by showing the opportunity cost of not selling financial assets, fair value measures are better at holding managements accountable and, as a result, better accomplish the stewardship role of financial reporting. Amortized cost measurements, they believe, do not accomplish this because they are based on past transactions and do not reflect changing circumstances and opportunities.

They also believe fair value measurements incorporate and, so, better reflect the various risks that financial institutions face—credit risk, interest rate risk, and liquidity risk—than do amortized cost measurements. Amortized cost measurements reflect only credit risk and then only management's view of credit risk, which history has proven often lag and underestimate actual credit risks. In that regard, it is interesting to note that in the recent financial crisis, as was the case two decades earlier in the S&L crisis, many, if not most, of the hundreds of banks that failed reported positive net worth and regulatory capital just prior to their failure. That seemed due, in considerable measure, to the apparent overstatement of their capital resulting from the use of historical cost accounting methods and highly subjective, potentially biased and inadequate loan loss reserves as determined by banks' managements. The 1991 GAO report on the S&L crisis *Failed Banks: Accounting and Auditing Reforms Urgently Needed* stated

Accounting rules are flawed in that they allow bank management considerable latitude in determining carrying amounts for problem loans and repossessed collateral. Recognizing decreases from historical cost to market value has an adverse effect on a bank's reported financial condition. This gives bank management an incentive to use the latitude in accounting rules to delay loss recognition as long as possible.

Also, because fair value reflects the effect of all risks inherent in financial instruments, some proponents of fair value believe that broadening its use would promote better risk management practices by financial institutions.

So, Who Is Right?

I could further elaborate on the arguments asserted on either side of this debate, but who's right? To some degree, I think they are both right. There are pros and cons to both amortized cost accounting and fair value measurements and reporting, many of which I believe were in evidence during the financial crisis. I have been involved in the accounting and auditing of financial instruments and financial reporting by financial institutions most of my career and have seen a variety of issues and problems depending on particular instruments and economic and market conditions. During the financial crisis of 2007–09, it seemed to me that amortized cost measures of financial assets with impairments based on management estimates generally lagged market prices in reflecting the growing breadth and severity of the crisis. The other-than-temporary threshold also resulted in delays in recognizing impairments of investments in debt and equity securities. However, once the credit markets started to freeze, it also seemed to me that the fair values based on exit prices of certain financial assets may have overstated the extent of impairment. In any event, starting in 2008 and continuing into 2009, a few things combined to make challenging the valuation of many financial assets in terms of determining fair values and the extent of impairments under amortized cost accounting: the lack of ready price discovery for many asset-backed securities, the sheer complexity of instruments such as investments in collateralized debt obligations (CDOs) and CDOs squared and derivatives tied to these assets, and uncertainty about the magnitude of the contagion effects and about the potential effects of government actions and policies during the crisis.

The real questions for standard setters are, "What set(s) of information will be most useful to investors in understanding the performance, financial condition, and risks and opportunities of reporting enterprises and can be provided by companies at a reasonable cost and effort? In a crisis, should the required or allowable measurement approaches change, or are additional or special disclosures needed?" It is also important to understand the inherent limitations of the information that can be captured by any accounting model that deals with single-point, point-in-time measurements and the limitations of the information that can be reasonably provided in financial reports regarding the often complex and dynamic nature of the risks faced by major financial institutions, particularly during a financial crisis.[32]

During the crisis, both the FASB and the IASB made certain targeted changes in the accounting standards relating to specific types of financial instruments and added a variety of new disclosures requirements. In our November 2009 MoU update with the IASB,[33] we agreed on a number of principles to guide our broader work on accounting for financial instruments. The fourth of those principles stated, "For financial instruments with principal amounts that are held for collection or payment of contractual cash flows rather than for sale of settlement with a third party information about amortized cost and fair value is relevant to investors." That statement was agnostic and left open how to present the information on amortized cost and fair value. It could be done, consistent with current requirements, by using amortized cost in the financial statements and disclosing fair values either parenthetically on the face of the balance sheet or in the footnotes, or vice versa. It could also be done by incorporating both amortized cost and fair value measurements in the financial statements, which was the approach in our May 2010 proposed ASU.[34] It might be done by providing two sets of financial statements: one on an amortized cost basis and another using fair values, which is what some parties have recommended from time to time. Each of these alternatives has pros and cons and potentially different costs and benefits.

Another Alternative

Those who closely follow the deliberations of the FASB will know that I actually favored using a present value of cash flows approach (that is, projected cash flows discounted at current interest rates) to measure the value of assets and liabilities with contractual principal amounts that are being held for cash collection or payment, with the interest income or expense on such instruments being reported in net income, but with other changes in the present values of these instruments being reported in other comprehensive income, not in net income or earnings. Under

---

[32] For a more in-depth discussion of these limitations and some suggestions for potential enhancements in the accounting information relating to financial institutions, see paper by Trevor S. Harris, Robert H. Herz, and Doron Nissim, "Accounting's Role in the Reporting, Creation, and Avoidance of Systemic Risk in Financial Institutions," January 2012, available on SSRN.

[33] *FASB and IASB Reaffirm Commitment to Memorandum of Understanding.*

[34] *Accounting for Financial Instruments and Revisions to the Accounting for Derivative Instruments and Hedging Activities—Financial Instruments (Topic 825) and Derivatives and Hedging (Topic 815).*

this approach, floating rate loans and debt securities and floating rate liabilities would generally continue to be reported at their principal amounts, but the carrying value of fixed rate loans and debt securities being held for collection of cash flows and fixed rate borrowings would change as market interest rates change. Those changes, however, would not be included in reported earnings or earnings per share.

To me, at a conceptual level, both amortized cost and fair value, although providing important information, miss the mark in terms of measuring the value of financial assets and financial liabilities that are being held for collection or payment of contractual cash flows.

In reporting the financial condition of an entity or as between entities, amortized cost fails to properly distinguish between different instruments with different cash flows. For example, consider the following 4 high credit-quality loans that are being held for collection of contractual cash flows: loan A with $100 principal due in 15 years and annual interest of $4; loan B, a 30-year loan that was originated 21 years ago at the then prevailing interest rate, with $100 principal due in 9 years and 8 percent annual interest; loan C with $100 principal due in 6 years and 5 percent annual interest; and loan D, a variable rate loan with $100 due in 3 years.

The total cash to be collected on each of these loans is quite different: $160 for loan A, $172 for loan B, $130 for loan C, and say $112 for loan D based on the current 3-year yield curve. The discounted present values of each of these loans based on current rates is also quite different: approximately $90 for loan A, $125 for loan B, $103 for loan C, and $100 for loan D. In amortized cost accounting, all 4 loans are measured and reported at $100, the amount of the principal, even though the 4 loans are very different in terms of interest rates, total cash flows, present values, term, and duration because under amortized cost accounting for these loans, contractual cash flows are discounted at the contractual interest rates of each loan (that is, for loan A, the cash flows are discounted at 4 percent; for loan B, they are discounted at 8 percent; and so on). Now, it is also important to note that whether one uses amortized cost or fair value or discounted cash flows to measure the loans, the 2 financial statements that are intended to present period flows, namely the income statement and statement of cash flows, will properly reflect the actual interest income and cash income received on each loan (that is, $4 for loan A, $8 for loan B, and so on). That's good and properly reflects the differences in interest income and cash flows for each of the loans, but the balance sheet, which is supposed to be a statement of financial condition, does not reflect the fact that each of these loans is very different. It shows them all at $100. To critics of amortized cost, this seems to violate basic principles of finance and economics.

To the supporters of fair value, the preceding suggests that fair value is the remedy for this problem. In my view, fair value, which represents the amounts each of the loans could be sold for today, can sometimes overcorrect for the problems inherent in amortized cost measurements. To illustrate this, consider the following example that contrasts a 15-year high credit-quality marketable debt security with principal of $100 and annual interest of $4 with the preceding loan A. The timing and amounts of contractual cash flows on both instruments are the same and both are high credit quality, but the fair value of the debt security is likely to be a bit higher than the fair value of the loan, reflecting the fact that the debt security is marketable and can be easily sold in the market, whereas the loan is illiquid and cannot be easily sold. The fair value of the debt security may also be affected by other factors and forces in the market. The key question is whether those differences should matter in valuing the 2 instruments if both are being held for collection of contractual cash flows. At a conceptual level, I think not because the amounts and timing of cash flows that will be derived from holding both instruments is expected to be the same.

When we also consider the liabilities that fund interest rate-bearing assets held for collection of contractual cash flows, further useful information can be derived from using discounted cash flows versus amortized costs. For example, consider the following 2 hypothetical cases involving the funding of the preceding loan A. First, assume loan A is funded with a fixed-rate borrowing with principal of $100 due in 15 years and requiring annual interest payments of 3 percent. In other words, the bank has "matched funded" loan A with a borrowing of the same amount and with the same maturity, effectively locking in a spread of 1 percent per annum for the next 15 years. Each year for the next 15 years, the bank will report $4 of interest income, $3 of interest expense, and net interest income (NII) of $1 under both the discounted cash flow approach and amortized cost. However, the discounted cash flow approach to valuing both loan A and the borrowing will also reveal the value (that is, the present value) of the locked-in spread, whereas using amortized cost does not capture this. Now, let's assume that loan A is funded with a 3-year certificate of deposit bearing 2 percent annual interest. The bank's current NII is now 2 percent, but that NII is only locked in for the next 3 years. After that, the bank will need to find new funding for the remaining 12 years it will be holding loan A (that is, the bank has a duration mismatch between its asset and the liability funding that asset). It is therefore exposed to interest rate risk, and if interest rates have risen 3 years from now, it will report a lower and potentially negative NII going forward. With amortized cost accounting, the balance sheet of the bank looks the same in both cases, with loan A and the funding relating to loan A both shown at $100. However, using discounted cash flows to measure loan A and the funding reflects the differences in the present values of the future cash flows between the 2 situations and can help reveal the difference in the sustainability of the current NII and the differences in the exposures to interest rate risk between the 2 situations.

The preceding examples are very simple ones, and in the real world, financial institutions may have a myriad of loans and debt securities they are holding for cash collection and that are funded in various ways. I think that real-world complication makes the arguments even more compelling for measuring the value of such financial assets and liabilities using a common yardstick of discounted cash flows. In my opinion, discounted cash flows provide a common yardstick without introducing some of the conceptual issues and practical challenges associated with developing fair value exit prices for illiquid instruments that are not being traded or held for sale.

Supporters of fair value note that its use would also help reveal duration mismatches and exposures to interest rate risk. Moreover, they believe that fair value provides a better a common yardstick for measuring financial instruments because it captures all the attributes of a financial instrument, including its liquidity and the impact of other current market factors on its value. They also believe that in valuing a financial instrument, it should not matter what a company plans to do with it or what its business model is, noting these can and sometimes do change (for example, in response to liquidity needs or changes in market conditions). They are concerned that allowing the use of anything short of fair value or mark-to-market for financial assets can result in "mark-to-make-believe accounting." (Although it seems that even a requirement to carry particular financial assets at fair value does not always result in such accounting, as suggested in the August 4, 2011, letter from Chairman of the IASB Hans Hoogervorst to the European Securities and Markets Authority about the apparent accounting, counter to the requirements of the IFRS, by certain major European financial institutions for holdings of distressed sovereign debt, including Greek government bonds, classified as available for sale at values in excess of prevailing market prices.)

In any event, the potential use of discounted cash flows to measure the current value of financial assets and liabilities an entity intends to hold for collection of cash flows is discussed in paragraphs BC61–BC68 of the 2010 proposed ASU on accounting for financial instruments.[35] For the reasons stated in paragraphs BC66–BC67 and based on feedback from a majority of constituents that current value was not sufficiently defined, the Board decided not to pursue trying to further develop that approach:

---

[35] *Accounting for Financial Instruments and Revisions to the Accounting for Derivative Instruments and Hedging Activities—Financial Instruments (Topic 825) and Derivatives and Hedging (Topic 815).*

BC66. The Board obtained feedback from users, preparers, auditors, and others about the potential operationality and usefulness of a current value measurement method. Although there was some support for current value, a majority of the input received was that current value was not sufficiently defined, resulting in wide-spread confusion about what it was meant to represent. Overall, there was little support for its use as an alternative to either fair value or amortized cost.

BC67. The Board believes that to implement current value measurement, it would need to develop a robust definition for consistent application, similar to the exercise undertaken in defining fair value in Topic 820. The Board decided not to undertake a project to further define *current value* because of the perceived limited usefulness of current value as an alternate to fair value or amortized cost. Therefore, the Board decided that it would consider only amortized cost as a potential alternative to fair value measurement for financial instruments.

In other words, I was unable to persuade my fellow Board members of the merits of doing so, although, as previously noted, there was some support among constituents for that kind of approach. As I quipped in public Board meetings when this subject was discussed, "I don't seem to be selling many tickets for this approach." So, reflecting on that input and the very extensive feedback received on the proposed ASU,[36] the FASB has continued to focus on fair value and amortized cost as the principal measurement approaches in accounting for financial instruments, trying to delineate the circumstances under which different accounting methods should apply.

And, as discussed in chapter 4 on international convergence, the FASB and the IASB have been working together to develop a common approach for classifying and measuring financial instruments that incorporates both amortized cost and fair value measurements depending on the type of financial instrument and company business models. They have also been working together and separately, with the help of experts, to develop better approaches to accounting for credit impairments of loans and debt securities than the incurred loss model under which such impairments are not recorded until they become probable. Pointing to the financial crisis, critics of the incurred loss approach maintain it had procyclical effects by inappropriately forcing banks and other financial institutions to delay recognizing expected credit losses and to not being able to build a proper level of reserves in the "good years" as a buffer against the losses they suffered when the crisis occurred. Thus, the boards have been exploring various potential approaches to accounting for impairments of loans and debt securities that would result in earlier recognition of expected credit losses. The

---

[36] *Accounting for Financial Instruments and Revisions to the Accounting for Derivative Instruments and Hedging Activities—Financial Instruments (Topic 825) and Derivatives and Hedging (Topic 815).*

FASB is also working on improved disclosures about interest rate risks and liquidity risks.

Continuing Conceptual Challenges

Although all this work is very important and will, I hope, ultimately result in improved and converged standards on accounting for financial instruments, I believe continuing fundamental conceptual issues need to be addressed, particularly in regard to measurement. As noted, the subject of measurement in accounting is a challenging and complex one, so it is not surprising that informed and reasonable people can and do differ. That is another important lesson learned or perhaps relearned. Accounting and financial reporting are not exact sciences. They are human constructs that attempt to capture and report the financial effects of transactions and events on reporting entities, as best we can based on concepts and cost-benefit considerations and with available tools and technology. Because informed and reasonable people can differ in their views on particular accounting and reporting matters, having a conceptual framework to guide the decisions of the accounting standard setter is important. Otherwise, accounting standards may be prone to become a collection of ad hoc and inconsistent results based on the personal conceptual frameworks of the various members of the standard-setting body. That may confuse constituents and can undermine the credibility of the standard-setting process and resulting standards. As stated in the preamble to FASB Statement of Financial Accounting Concepts No. 1,[37] issued in 1978,

> This is the first in a series of Statements of Financial Accounting Concepts. The purpose of the series is to set forth fundamentals on which financial accounting and reporting standards will be based. More specifically, Statements of Financial Accounting Concepts are intended to establish the objectives and concepts that the Financial Accounting Standards Board will use in developing standards of financial accounting and reporting.... However, knowledge of the objectives and concepts the Board uses should enable all who are affected by or interested in financial accounting standards to better understand the content and limitations of information provided by financial accounting and reporting.... That knowledge, if used with care, may also provide guidance in resolving new or emerging problems of financial accounting and reporting in the absence of applicable authoritative pronouncements.

The bulk of the existing FASB Conceptual Framework was developed in the 1970s and 1980s. Although the guidance contained in those concepts statements has been helpful, experience has also shown that many

---

[37] *Objectives of Financial Reporting by Business Enterprises.*

cross-cutting issues continue to arise in developing standards for which the existing Conceptual Framework does not provide clear guidance. These cross-cutting and recurring issues often involve the subject of measurement (that is, what measurement attribute to use in a particular circumstance) because this was an area that was not fully developed in the existing Conceptual Framework. Certainly, measurement has been a central, challenging, and controversial aspect in the many years (indeed decades) of deliberation by the FASB, IASB, and other standard setters on accounting for financial instruments.

As noted in chapter 4, in 2004, the FASB and IASB agreed to jointly undertake a project to improve and converge their respective conceptual frameworks. Measurement constitutes one of the phases of the joint conceptual framework project. Unfortunately, as discussed in chapter 4, it is still very much a work in progress; thus, the boards have been addressing the complex subject of accounting for financial instruments and the measurement issues that are central to that subject without the benefit of a developed conceptual framework on measurement to guide their decisions.

If I had only one do-over as FASB Chairman, it would be to try to get the improved conceptual framework completed or at least to have made more progress on the project. As I will again touch on in chapter 7, "Looking Back and Moving Forward," wrestling these conceptual issues to the ground represents a real opportunity to further improve what I believe is already, overall, a very good process for establishing accounting standards and, over time, to enhance the conceptual consistency and logical coherence across the body of accounting standards. That is one of the more important insights I believe I gained, not only in terms of the financial crisis and accounting standards but from my years as a standard setter.

Chapter 6: Complexity

Does It Need to Be So Complex?

> Our reporting system, while probably the best in the world, is too complex and is capable of providing more transparent, more understandable, and more useful information to investors and the capital markets.[1]

I think few people involved in financial reporting would disagree that U.S. GAAP and SEC reporting and disclosure requirements are complex and that, overall, we have a relatively complex financial reporting system with lots of detailed standards, rules, and regulations. Although opinions differ about the reasons, sources, and causes of this complexity and what can and should be done about it, there seems to be general agreement that the system is complex. That said, many in this country also believe we have the best financial reporting system in the world, a system that provides for more reliable, consistent, and comparable financial reporting than any other in the world. Some in the United States seem to have a view of financial reporting in other countries as lacking sufficient rigor, comparability, and transparency.

This is in contrast with what I have sensed in my international travels. Many overseas see the U.S. reporting system as overly and unnecessarily complex and as reflecting the forces of greed and litigiousness they believe pervade American society, business, and regulation. For example, I have found that to be a quite common view among many accountants, accounting standard setters, financial executives, regulators, and others in the United Kingdom, where I started my career and have spent a fair amount of time over the years. Indeed, many times, I

---

[1] Robert H. Herz in a speech on December 6, 2005, at the 2005 AICPA National Conference on Current SEC and PCAOB Developments.

have been with fellow Chartered Accountants in England, listening to them espouse the virtues of principles over rules and decry what they view as the mad world of quarterly reporting that creates a culture of short-termism. They also perceive that the U.S. has an overly lawyer-driven approach to regulation and enforcement that, in their view, inevitably results in a rules-based system of accounting and auditing and "box ticking" that they lament has also begun to overtake their beloved system of professional judgment, substance-over-form financial reporting, and true and fair views. They believe the U.S. approach has undermined professionalism in financial reporting, has produced accountants who are "rule seekers and template hunters," and inevitably fosters the use of structuring to achieve form-over-substance accounting outcomes.

As stated by Jeremy Hand, Chairman of the British Private Equity & Venture Capital Association, "It is hard to get useful business information from a set of U.S. GAAP financial statements. In the U.K., the situation is better, but is deteriorating. We support principles based standards, involving the application of judgments and common sense."[2]

From time to time, a similar chorus of laments is heard on our own shores by those longing for a return to a time when accounting was simpler, financial statements and SEC filings were shorter and seemed less complicated, and professional judgment in financial reporting prevailed. I have some sympathy and empathy with these views because, perhaps as a result of my training and experience in the United Kingdom in what now seems like a simpler time, I too sometimes yearn for a return to those days of accounting and reporting (and when I had more hair on the top of my head).

For better or worse, the world of business and finance has clearly moved on and very significantly changed over the past four decades. It is more dynamic and complex than it was in those days, so it is understandable that accounting and reporting, in an attempt to properly reflect and keep pace with these changes, would also become more complex. But in the process, have the accounting standards and reporting requirements become unnecessarily complex and led to a system that has become overly rules based?

The Reporting Scandals and the Sarbanes-Oxley Act of 2002

Enron, WorldCom, and other financial reporting scandals that came to light in 2001 and 2002 shook our collective confidence in the U.S.

---

[2] Quoted in *Getting to the Heart of the Issue: Can Financial Reporting Be Made Simpler and More Useful?*

financial reporting system. In addition to concerns about the integrity of corporate managements and the effectiveness of audits of public companies, some people raised questions about whether U.S. accounting standards had become too rules based, full of very detailed implementation guidance on every conceivable situation and arbitrary criteria and bright lines, which enabled some companies to circumvent the intent of a standard through structured transactions that achieved form-over-substance accounting results. In my opinion, these were very legitimate questions because I had participated in this sort of activity in my "Bad Bob" days working in Corporate Finance Advisory Services. I had also continued to address such situations in my role as a "gamekeeper" in the national office of Coopers & Lybrand (C&L) and PricewaterhouseCoopers (PwC). All of this had given me an appreciation of the double-edged sword that results from lengthy and detailed standards. On the one hand, these detailed standards often provide a ready answer to accounting issues faced by companies looking to ensure that they are complying with the requirements. This can enhance reliability, consistency, and comparability of financial statements. On the other hand, they provide an opportunity, some would say an invitation, for those desiring a particular reporting outcome to structure accounting treatments around specific rules and bright lines, which undermines the relevance, reliability, consistency, and comparability of reported financial information. Further, as discussed in chapter 2, "Charting Course," I had formed strong views about the overall unwieldiness of the U.S. accounting literature.

So, it was not surprising to me that, among its many other provisions, Sarbanes-Oxley required the SEC to conduct a study and report back to Congress on the potential merits and feasibility of adopting a principles-based accounting system in the United States. For our part, soon after I joined the FASB, we got to work on responding to the concerns about the quality and transparency of financial reporting resulting from the increasing level of detail and perceived complexity of accounting standards. In October 2002, we issued a proposal[3] for public input. That proposal discussed potential elements of more principles-based accounting standards, including having few, if any, exceptions and less interpretive and implementation guidance. It also discussed some of the possible costs, benefits, and challenges of moving to more principles-based standards. We held a public roundtable on the proposal in December 2002, and based on the input received in the roundtable and through comment letters, we decided to pursue a number of initiatives aimed at improving the quality of FASB standards, as well as elements of the standard-setting process. Although there was general support for our proposal, many commentators also pointed to the need for additional actions, including moving toward

---

[3] *Principles-based Approach to U.S. Standard Setting.*

greater centralization of U.S. accounting standard setting through FASB, and providing a sounder foundation for a principles-based approach in the United States by improving the Conceptual Framework and coordinating the work of the FASB, SEC, and PCAOB.

In July 2003, the SEC staff submitted to Congress its study[4] on the adoption of a principles-based accounting system in the United States. The core recommendation of the study was that accounting standards should be neither principles-only nor entirely rules-based. Rather, they should be objectives oriented by more clearly articulating the accounting objectives of the standard and avoiding exceptions and bright lines while also providing sufficient detail and structure, so the standard can be operationalized and applied on a consistent basis:

> In our minds, an optimal standard involves a concise statement of substantive accounting principle where the accounting objective has been included at an appropriate level of specificity as an integral part of the standard and where few, if any, exceptions or conceptual inconsistencies are included in the standard. Further, such a standard should provide an appropriate amount of implementation guidance given the nature of the class of transactions or events and should be devoid of bright-line tests. Finally, such a standard should be consistent with, and derive from, a coherent conceptual framework of financial reporting.

The recommendations in the SEC study were generally consistent with the Board's proposal on principles-based standards and the initiatives we had decided to undertake. They were "mid-Atlantic" to my way of thinking, somewhere between the U.K. approach of high-level principles and relatively little official detailed guidance and the U.S. approach of supplementing the principles in a standard with reams of interpretive and implementation guidance.

Conceptual Controversy and Complexity

I think it is interesting and noteworthy that the SEC report to Congress on a principles-based accounting system addressed head-on one of the most fundamental and controversial issues about accounting and financial reporting: the debate about whether accounting should be based on an asset and liability view or a revenue and expense view. This is an age-old debate that I believe is at the center of many of the controversies and misunderstandings that divide constituents in the financial reporting system. This debate continues to challenge the development of a coherent and internally consistent set of accounting

---

[4] *Study Pursuant to Section 108(d) of the Sarbanes-Oxley Act of 2002 on the Adoption by the United States Financial Reporting System of a Principles-Based Accounting System.*

and reporting standards. So, I think it is worth taking a bit of a detour here to explain further for those who may not be steeped in accounting theory. The following explanation will not do full justice to what is a deep-seated controversy and somewhat complex subject.

Asset and Liability View

Under the asset and liability view, income is a measure of the increase in net resources of an enterprise during a period, defined primarily in terms of increases in assets and decreases in liabilities. This view is grounded in the economic theory of wealth and income under which income is a measure of the change in wealth during a period. Therefore, the accounting implementation of this approach starts with determining and measuring the assets and liabilities of an enterprise and the changes in the assets and liabilities during a period in order to determine the income for that period.

Critics of the asset and liability view argue that it places undue weight on determining current measurements of assets and liabilities, which can often be difficult and subjective; that it results in reported income that can be highly volatile due to changes in macroeconomic and market conditions; and that it makes the income statement less useful in understanding an enterprise's actual earnings during a reporting period and over time.

Revenue and Expense View

In contrast, under the revenue and expense view, income is the difference between outputs from and inputs to an enterprise's earning activities during a period. Therefore, the accounting implementation of this approach starts with determining the amounts of outputs (revenues) and inputs (expenses) during a period in order to determine the income for that period. That often requires allocations of inflows and expenditures over a number of accounting periods in order to produce a "matching" of reported revenues and expenses over time (for example, the cost of a machine that is used in manufacturing a company's product is allocated over the useful life of the machine, resulting in a series of annual deprecation charges over those years).

Critics of such "matching" and of the revenue and expense view argue that these allocations are often, by necessity, arbitrary and not grounded in the underlying economics; that it results in inappropriate measures of certain assets and liabilities that are the result of these interperiod allocations and that render the balance sheet less useful in portraying the current financial position of the reporting enterprise; and that it adds to the overall complexity of accounting procedures and impedes an understanding of financial reports.

Although much of accounting practice until the 1970s was based on the revenue and expense view, since then, the FASB, IASB, and other national accounting standard setters have generally adopted the asset and liability view in their conceptual frameworks, viewing it as the conceptually correct and best way to develop standards that are coherent and internally consistent. Reed K. Storey, a senior staff member of the FASB who worked heavily on the development of the FASB's Conceptual Framework, and Sylvia Storey summarized how to apply the asset and liability view (see figure 6-1, "Framework of Financial Accounting Concepts and Standards"). However, many stakeholders in the reporting system, particularly preparers of financial statements do not agree, arguing that the revenue and expense view is the more conceptually appropriate and practically viable approach. Some are also concerned that the asset and liability view portends the expansion of fair value measurements in financial statements, which, for a variety of reasons, they oppose.

Figure 6-1: Framework of Financial Accounting Concepts and Standards[*]

The result of applying the asset and liability view is an internally consistent, well-defined system of elements in Concepts Statement 6 that make it clear that in accounting for a transaction or other event, these are the right questions to ask, and this is the right order in which to ask them:

> What is the asset?
>
> What is the liability?
>
> Did an asset or liability change, or did its value change?
>> Increase or decrease?
>>
>> By how much?
>>
>> Did the change result from:
>>> An investment by owners?
>>>
>>> A distribution to owners?
>>>
>>> If not, the change must be comprehensive income
>>>
>>> Was the source of comprehensive income what we call:
>>>> Revenue?
>>>>
>>>> Expense?
>>>>
>>>> Gain?
>>>>
>>>> Loss?

To start at the bottom and work up the list will not work.

[*] Reed K. Storey and Sylvia Storey, The framework of financial accounting concepts and standards. Norwalk, Conn.: Financial Accounting Standards Board, 1998. p. 87.

For good or bad, although accounting standard setters have attempted over time to bring standards more in line with the asset and liability view, that has by no means been a consistent effort. As a result, I believe the current set of accounting standards, whether they be U.S. GAAP or IFRS, reflect a hodgepodge of the two conceptual approaches and views of the balance sheet and income determination, which, in my opinion, makes financial statements less understandable and complicates financial analysis. This mix of the two approaches can be found, for example, in the U.S. GAAP standards relating to accounting for pensions and other postretirement costs and obligations and in the various FASB and IASB standards on accounting for financial instruments.

In any event, the SEC study[5] came down squarely in favor of the asset and liability view, stating,

> the revenue/expense view is inappropriate for use in standard setting—particularly in an objectives-oriented regime. [H]istorical experience suggests the asset/liability approach most appropriately anchors the standard setting process by providing the strongest conceptual mapping to underlying reality.... FASB should maintain the asset/liability view in continuing its move to an objectives-oriented standard setting regime.

That study has not, in my opinion, ended the controversy.

My Opinion

What do I think? Well, at university in England, I was instructed in economic concepts and theory before I started learning accounting. So, I was very familiar with the economic theories of wealth and income before I was taught debits and credits, management accounting, budgeting, and so on. No doubt, that has influenced my thinking on this matter, so I am more in the asset and liability camp, believing it is important to start first with the determination and measurement of assets and liabilities.

However, I do not think the two views are irreconcilable, just that the translation of economic theory into accounting concepts and practice may have become a bit confused and muddled. Observers of FASB Board meetings will have heard me, on many occasions, talk about the need in accounting to more clearly define and separate the two components of economic income: namely, the "flows" for a period and the changes in the "stocks" during that period. Under the economic concepts of wealth and income, income (being the change in wealth for a period, excluding contributions of additional capital and withdrawals of capital by owners during the period) consists of two components: the flows to the enterprise (both positive and negative) during the period and the changes in the stocks (that is, assets less liabilities) for the period. Although I believe the distinction between these two components of economic income is somewhat akin to the distinction between earnings and other elements of comprehensive income (other comprehensive income), as described in the FASB Conceptual Framework, I do not find the existing, rather lengthy, explanation in the Conceptual Framework particularly crisp or conceptually robust. Existing accounting standards, both U.S. GAAP and IFRS, have not implemented the distinction in a consistent fashion, and there does not seem to be a clear concept on what is included in earnings or net income versus what is included in other comprehensive income.

---

[5] *Study Pursuant to Section 108(d) of the Sarbanes-Oxley Act of 2002 on the Adoption by the United States Financial Reporting System of a Principles-Based Accounting System.*

An Example

So, let me use an example (albeit a simple one relating to personal finances, not a large, complex business enterprise) to illustrate the concepts of wealth, income, stocks, and flows. Let's suppose, as people are sometimes asked to do by a prospective lender, to prepare a set of personal financial statements. You would prepare a balance sheet showing your net worth. It would show your assets (for example, your home, your investments, and cash in banks) and your liabilities (for example, the mortgage on your home and some outstanding credit card balances). The assets would presumably be shown at their current fair market value and the liabilities at the balances outstanding. The total of your assets less your liabilities is your net worth. Your balance sheet, in an economist's terms, shows your "stocks" of assets and liabilities, and your net worth is your "wealth."

You may also be asked to report your annual sources and amounts of income and expenditures (to an economist, your annual "flows"). Those would include what you earn from your job in terms of compensation, the dividends and interest you receive on your investments and any interest on your cash in banks, less taxes, interest payments on your mortgage, and living expenses. Say the value of your investments increased since last year, and your equity in your home (that is, the value of the house less the amount owed on the mortgage) also increased. Those changes in the value of your "stocks" increase your wealth, or net worth, and to an economist, they are another element of your income for the period.

I think we would all agree that the two types of income—your "flows" and the changes in your "stocks"—are quite different in character, somewhat akin to the tax concepts of ordinary income and capital gains (though, for tax purposes, capital gains are generally recognized only when realized). Yet the combination of your "flows" for the year and the change in the value of your "stocks," including unrealized appreciation or depreciation in the value of the equity in your home and in the value of your investments, add up to the change in your net worth from one year to the next and are needed to reconcile that change.

Back to Concepts

One more important conceptual point: valuation theory says that the value of an asset at any point in time is based on the discounted present value of the estimated future cash flows from that asset. Those cash flows might be realized over time from holding the asset or selling or otherwise monetizing it. The main point is that the value encompasses the estimated future "flows," but the "flows" for a period are the ones that actually occurred during that period. Determining and measuring the "flows" that occur during a period can be done in a number ways, including on a cash basis or an accrual basis that adjusts cash flows for amounts payable and receivable at the end of a period. Thus, for example, if your salary is $10,000 per month, and during the year ended December 31, you have received payments from your employer totaling $110,000 (11 months x $10,000) but had not received your $10,000 for the month of December, your salary "flows" for the year would be $110,000 on a cash basis but $120,000 on an accrual basis. That's easy to understand.

However, accounting for many business transactions involves various allocation approaches that have been developed to determine what part of a receipt or expenditure relates to the current period from what part relates to future periods. Proponents of the asset and liability view argue that these approaches inevitably involve arbitrary rules that result in a distortion of both the reported earnings for a period and the amounts reported as assets and liabilities on a balance sheet. For example, they would argue that in changing economic, business, and market conditions, depreciation of a fixed asset based on its historical cost inevitably results in misstating both the economic expense of using an asset for a year and the amount shown on the balance sheet for that asset because it is based on the cost of the asset, not the value of the future flows to be derived from the asset. Proponents of the revenue and expense view would counter that the depreciation represents an appropriate allocation of the cost of the asset that is needed to achieve proper matching with the revenues generated from using the asset each year and that the balance sheet at any date correctly shows the remaining amount of unallocated (that is, undepreciated) cost relating to future periods.

Theory and Practice

Perhaps because of my training in economics, to me, the key conceptual questions in developing accounting standards revolve around the determination and measurement of assets and liabilities (the "stocks") and resulting net worth (wealth) and defining, determining, and more clearly separating the changes in net worth, or wealth, that relate to the "flows" for the period from those that relate to changes in "stocks" for the period. Conceptually, these questions and the order in which you ask them are simple, and if it were possible to accurately and easily answer each of them, accounting and financial reporting could be much simpler.

Alas, in practice, especially when applied to complex business enterprises and complicated transactions and arrangements, reality is often not that simple. I believe that standard setters (including yours truly) have, for reasons that always seem important and valid at the

Chapter 6: Complexity

time, developed standards that reflect a myriad of approaches to recognizing and measuring assets and liabilities. Those reasons have involved considerations around operationally, auditability, and overall cost-benefit of alternatives, resulting in what some may regard as departures from the conceptually correct approach and in the inclusion in standards of exceptions, options, and bright lines. Over time, accounting standard setters have also developed various approaches to defining, measuring, and presenting "flows" and changes in "stocks." To me, these approaches sometimes seem to mix or conflate flows for the current period with changes in the values of stocks that relate to estimated flows in future periods. For example, loan loss allowances and certain impairment charges are based on estimations of cash flows in future periods but are reflected in the earnings for the current reporting period. Therefore, the resulting financial statements represent an "intertemporal hodgepodge of approaches" to defining, measuring, and reporting assets and liabilities on balance sheets and on what goes into reported net income, or "earnings."

By more clearly defining "flows" and separately displaying them from the changes in "stocks," I think it may be possible to better capture and report both current performance and estimates of future "flows" in the financial statements. I believe the FASB-IASB project to improve the Conceptual Framework and the project on financial statement presentation provide opportunities, but by no means a panacea, to address these fundamental issues and to begin to try to reconcile the asset and liability view and the revenue and expense view. As suggested in the SEC study,[6] more consistently applying the asset and liability approach as a starting point would seem to be an important element in moving to a more principles-based or objectives-oriented accounting system and to more understandable financial statements. However, as previously mentioned, other priorities have delayed progress on these important projects.

I offer all this knowing full well that, for many decades, there have been and continue to be different views and no shortage of suggestions on what should be the conceptual underpinnings of accounting and financial reporting.

Suggestions on an Overhaul of the Accounting Framework

Indeed, some contend that an overhaul of the whole accounting model and approach to accounting standard setting are needed, both to reduce

---

[6] *Study Pursuant to Section 108(d) of the Sarbanes-Oxley Act of 2002 on the Adoption by the United States Financial Reporting System of a Principles-Based Accounting System.*

complexity and to improve the relevance, reliability, and overall usefulness of reported financial information, but there are differences in opinions on what would be needed to accomplish that.

On one hand and as touched on in chapter 5, "The Financial Crisis," some believe that the increasing use of fair value measurements is eroding the reliability and usefulness of financial statements. Those who believe this advocate historical cost accounting, the revenue and expense view and the "matching" principle, and conservatism as the proper foundations of accounting theory and practice, particularly for nonfinancial assets and liabilities and enterprises that produce and sell goods and services. For example, in the article "Accounting at a Crossroad" in the December 2005 issue of *The CPA Journal*, Eugene H. Flegm, former general auditor for General Motors Corp., discusses what he views as the perils to the reliability and credibility of financial reporting and the accounting profession resulting from the increasing use of fair value measurements. Flegm advocates that the SEC should "reaffirm the use of historic cost as the measurement base" and concludes that if "we continue the march to fair value, the result will be major frauds and probably the end of an independent public accounting profession." As discussed later in this chapter, the AICPA is developing a new financial reporting framework for use by small and medium-sized private companies that emphasizes the use of historical cost accounting and the matching principle.

On the other hand, others strongly favor a much broader, across-the-board move to fair value accounting. For example, the July 2007 publication *A Comprehensive Business Reporting Model: Financial Reporting for Investors* from the CFA Institute advocates a movement to comprehensive fair value accounting, stating,

> If asset exchanges and financial decisions are based on fair values, then market efficiency would be enhanced if the information upon which such decisions are made is reported at fair value. The implication is that items in the balance sheet should be reported at *current* fair value. Furthermore, changes in these values should be reported in the income statement as they occur.... Currently, financial statements include some items reported at historical cost while others are measured at fair value, the so-called mixed-attribute system. Consequently, investors who rely on fair values for decision making must expend considerable effort trying to restate to fair value those decision-relevant financial statement items that are measured at historical cost.... Most, if not all, of this effort would be eliminated if the financial reporting standards were to require that companies record assets and liabilities at fair value at inception with periodic revaluation.

Similarly, David Mosso, who has had a long and distinguished career as an accounting standard setter as a member and Vice Chairman of the FASB and Chairman of the Federal Accounting Standards Advisory Board, has strongly argued that there is an urgent need for a paradigm shift in accounting and financial reporting to what he terms a wealth measurement model. In his 2009 book *Early Warning and Quick Response: Accounting in the Twenty-first Century*, Mosso strongly criticizes the current accounting model as broken and beyond repair and incapable of properly presenting an entity's true financial condition and health. He proposes that the objective of accounting should be to measure and present an entity's wealth and changes in that wealth (income) by measuring all recognized assets and liabilities at fair value. In this way, he believes balance sheets would show the real economic worth and financial health of entities, and income statements would portray the true change in their financial condition from period to period. Mosso contends that such a change would set the stage for a new accounting standard-setting model and process, one based on a set of core principles that would pave the way for much more coherent, less complex, and more relevant accounting standards and financial reporting and that would provide an early warning signal of looming financial crises. In Mosso's view, this would better enable regulators, standard setters, and policy makers to spot developing threats to the health of the financial system on a timely basis and to respond to them more quickly.

In my opinion, addressing and trying to better resolve these and other fundamental conceptual issues surrounding accounting theory and practice is a necessary and an important first step in getting to a less complex, more useful, coherent, understandable, and more principles-based accounting and reporting system. Additional key conceptual issues include whether and how to distinguish between instruments that should be accounted for as liabilities from those that should be treated as equity, when to recognize and derecognize assets and liabilities, whether and how to incorporate the effects of uncertainty into accounting and financial reporting, and various other matters related to recognition and measurement of items in financial statements. That is why I believed it very important for the FASB and IASB to revisit and try to improve, complete, and converge our conceptual frameworks and why, as I note a number of times in this book, I was disappointed that we did not make further progress toward that goal during my years in accounting standard setting.

Can We Handle a More Principles-Based System?

Even if standard setters were inclined and able to resolve these issues and agree on a clear and complete conceptual model for accounting and financial reporting and to consistently apply it in developing accounting standards, other thorny issues would need to be addressed and resolved in adopting a principles-based accounting system in the United States because accounting standards are part of the financial reporting supply chain. The ultimate product of that supply chain, reported financial information, is the result not only of the accounting standards but also of how they are implemented and how the resulting information is audited, regulated, and enforced, as well as the corporate governance and legal frameworks around the system. Writing standards that are more "principles-based" or "objectives-oriented" does not ensure that the result will be improved, conceptually consistent, and principles-based financial reporting. That may not be the result if, for example, the principles are not implemented faithfully by companies, or if auditors, in fear of being second guessed, do not accept reasonable judgments made by companies on reporting matters and create and impose their own set of accounting rules on the companies, or if regulators create and impose additional rules to facilitate their enforcement of standards. It would take all key parties in the financial reporting system, working together, to truly achieve the potential benefits of a more conceptually coherent, principles-based accounting system.

That necessary harmony was a key theme I emphasized in many of my speeches and presentations as FASB Chairman. For example, in December 2003, at the annual AICPA Conference on Current SEC and PCAOB Reporting Developments, I stated,

> The changes under Sarbanes-Oxley and the related reforms have, in my view, put in place the right kinds of structural and procedural mechanisms, incentives and penalties that are necessary for us to be able to begin moving forward toward the promised land of a better reporting system.... But as necessary as these reforms have been, they will not in and of and by themselves, be sufficient, in my view, to ensure that as we embark on this journey we are truly moving in the right direction. Because there are many players in the system—standard setters, preparers, auditors, Boards and audit committees, regulators and enforcers, legislators, investors, analysts and other stakeholders and consumers of corporate information—it is not only necessary that we each attend to our particular role in the system, but equally important that we have a common understanding of the role of others and of our collective responsibilities so that we can move the system forward in an

Chapter 6: Complexity

orderly and constructive way.... In short, it will take a sense of partnership and a shared commitment to the importance of quality financial reporting to the system.

However, it also seemed clear to me that other aspects of the system were not changing. Indeed, I sensed that the development of a more principled-based approach was being hindered by the behavior of some participants in the reporting supply chain in reaction to the legal, regulatory, and environmental factors that came in the wake of the reporting scandals. For example, the swift and cataclysmic demise of Arthur Andersen and the creation of a new organization, the PCAOB, to regulate and oversee the auditors of public companies surely had an effect on the operating, risk management, and quality control processes of the major accounting firms and on the psyches and behaviors of individual audit partners and partners in the national offices of the accounting firms. Don't get me wrong. I am not criticizing those changes. They were clearly needed, but they also have, in my view, very understandably, engendered some behaviors that may not be consistent with moving to a more principles-based system.

So, in my speech at the December 2004 AICPA SEC Conference, I set forth what I viewed as some key challenges and cross-currents facing the financial reporting system. In one of these, under the heading "Give me principles, but make sure there's no doubt how to apply them (and make sure they don't change what I'm currently doing)," I explained,

> This is the issue of whether we should be moving to more of a so-called "principles-based" system or what the SEC staff has called "objectives-oriented" standards. On the one hand, there has been lots of talk and calls for the standards to be more clearly cast in terms of overarching principles, and to get away from detailed rules, bright-lines and exceptions. On the other hand, given the very important and in my view necessary reforms under Sarbanes-Oxley, there is clearly a heightened sense of attention to getting the financial statements right by companies, auditors, and audit committees and Boards. That's terrific! But there also seems to be a real fear of being second-guessed by regulators, enforcers, the trial bar, and the business press and that has, at least for now very understandably seemed to reinforce the demand for detailed rules, bright-lines and safe-harbors.... So implementing a more principles-based or objectives-oriented approach is very challenging and will require steadfast determination not only by standard setters, but also some important behavioral changes by others.

In another passage in that speech, under the heading "The heck with relevance, give me accounting numbers I can nail to the wall!" I said,

> We hear this in many guises, mainly from preparers, but also from some auditors and other parties. Again, part of this no doubt relates to the fear of second-guessing and the attendant

207

desire to be able to point to something exact, something directly vouchable or verifiable, if called upon to defend one's accounting or auditing. And again, that's very understandable.

So, although I personally favored the adoption of a more principles-based accounting system in the United States, I was also well aware of, and did not discount, the hurdles in properly implementing such an approach in this country. As I would say in a number of speeches, the situation reminded me of Jack Nicholson's line in the movie *A Few Good Men*. Tom Cruise, who was interrogating Nicholson in the court martial scene, states, "I want the truth!" to which Nicholson retorts, "You can't handle the truth!" The question was (and I believe still is) whether in the United States we can handle a more principles-based accounting system.

In fall 2003, my friend and former partner at PwC, Don Nicolaisen, became the chief accountant of the SEC. In addition to our many discussions about international convergence and our experiences during the stock option expensing episode, we chatted regularly about many other matters involving accounting and financial reporting, including about what would become known as the issue of complexity in the U.S. financial reporting system. As we discussed this subject with others in our organizations and among stakeholders in the reporting system, I think it became clear that something more formal and concerted should be done to address the issue.

A Call to Action

Although Don left the SEC in fall 2005, then-SEC Chairman Christopher Cox had also become convinced of the need for action on this front. So, at the December 2005 AICPA SEC Conference, in his keynote address, then-Chairman Cox announced a war on complexity in accounting standards and disclosure requirements, SEC rules, regulations, filing requirements, and forms, a theme he reiterated a few days later in a major speech to the Economic Club of New York.

For my part, I devoted my speech at the December 2005 AICPA SEC Conference to this subject by focusing my comments on a number of fundamental structural, institutional, cultural, and behavioral forces that I and others at the FASB believed were continuing to generate complexity in the U.S. financial reporting system and impeding more transparent reporting. I pointed to various factors, including

1. the detail and volume of accounting, auditing and SEC reporting requirements that had engendered a "check the box" mindset.

2. a form-over-substance approach to financial reporting.

3. the unacceptably high number of restatements of financial statements that were resulting in a lack of transparency and analytical complexity for users of financial information.
4. the conflicting perspectives and agendas of different participants in the reporting system.
5. complex accounting methods that departed from economics.
6. gaps in the education and training of accountants.
7. a palpable fear of the potential consequences of being second-guessed by regulators, enforcers, and the trial bar.

In my view, these factors created a constant demand for detailed rules, bright lines, and safe harbors that deterred preparers, auditors, audit committees, and boards from exercising professional judgment on reporting issues, that resulted in boilerplate and overly legalistic disclosures, and that failed to effectively communicate important information.

I ended the speech with a call to action by stating,

> I believe it is time to stop observing the problem and start thinking about how to solve these issues. For I am concerned that failure to take action will inevitably lead to more complexity, less transparency, and potentially less relevance of reported financial information. Accordingly, we have been discussing with the SEC and the PCAOB the idea that as a first step the SEC, the FASB, and the PCAOB create a senior level advisory panel comprising leading representatives of the various constituencies in the reporting system. I believe such a group is needed to examine the issues and challenges facing the system and to make specific recommendations on appropriate actions to reduce complexity and improve the transparency and overall quality of the reporting system.... I issue this call to action in full knowledge that it could result in significant changes in our reporting system, including institutional and structural changes some of which could impact the FASB. But from where I sit, I believe the status quo is neither acceptable nor sustainable. Our reporting system, while probably the best in the world, is too complex and is capable of providing more transparent, more understandable, and more useful information to investors and the capital markets.

Eighteen months later, in June 2007, the SEC announced the formation of the Advisory Committee on Improvements to Financial Reporting (CIFiR), which also became known as the Pozen Committee after Robert Pozen who chaired the effort. Why did it take 18 months to get it up and running? It was certainly not for lack of broad support for such an effort among key constituencies in the financial reporting system. I believe the delay was mainly due to turnover of key people at both the

SEC and the PCAOB and other priorities that needed to be addressed. As I noted, Don Nicolaisen left the SEC in fall 2005. Alan Beller, the director of the SEC Division of Corporation Finance, had also been involved in the conception of this initiative, but he left the SEC in February 2006. Bill McDonough, Chairman of the PCAOB, had also been involved in these discussions, but he retired from the PCAOB in fall 2005. It took a while for new people to fill all these roles: John White succeeded Alan Beller in February 2006, Mark Olson became the new Chairman of the PCAOB in June 2006, and Conrad Hewitt became the chief accountant of the SEC in July 2006. However, for the PCAOB and the SEC, there were other high-priority matters, including revising the SEC regulations and the PCAOB standard around Section 404 reporting on internal controls by companies and auditors. So, it was not until spring 2007 that the effort to establish and organize CIFiR began in earnest.

I also believe that some impetus for the effort and for establishing a related Department of the Treasury Advisory Committee on the Auditing Profession (ACAP) came out of the March 2007 Summit on Capital Markets Competiveness hosted by then-Treasury Secretary Paulson at Georgetown University. That gathering, attended by such luminaries of the business and financial world as Warren Buffett, Alan Greenspan, Michael Bloomberg, Charles Schwab, Paul Volcker, Jeff Immelt of General Electric, and Jamie Dimon of J.P. Morgan Chase, as well as leaders of various governmental departments and agencies, Mark Olson from the PCAOB, and me, included a session to discuss the issues relating to the financial reporting system.

CIFiR

CIFiR comprised 17 members representing key constituencies in the U.S. capital markets: investors, public accountants, issuers, members of audit committees, academia, and securities attorneys. The FASB, IASC Foundation (now known as the IFRS Foundation), PCAOB, Department of the Treasury, and Board of Governors of the Federal Reserve System representing U.S. banking regulators had observer seats on CIFiR. CIFiR's charge was to examine the U.S. financial reporting system and provide recommendations to the SEC about how to improve its usefulness for investors and reduce unnecessary complexity. The SEC, the PCAOB, and the FASB provided staffing for the CIFiR. I served as our observer, and I and fellow FASB Board members and staff participated in meetings of the subcommittees of CIFiR.

CIFiR had 8 public meetings between August 2007 and July 2008. It solicited and received public input and took testimony from more than

Chapter 6: Complexity

30 witnesses. A good deal of the work was done through 4 subcommittees on substantive complexity, the standard-setting process, the audit process, and compliance and delivering financial information. That enabled CIFiR to examine and develop recommendations on a broad range of areas relevant to its charge.

The final report of CIFiR[7] was issued in early August 2008. It contains 25 wide-ranging recommendations, as well as many important and insightful observations on the U.S. financial reporting system. Although the report was addressed to the SEC, the recommendations covered matters relating to accounting standards and accounting standard setting, auditing matters, recommendations relating to SEC rules and regulations and staff processes and procedures, and delivery of financial information via eXtensible Business Reporting Language (XBRL), corporate websites, and earning releases.

The report also contains a number of important observations about the sources and causes of complexity in our reporting system. Some of those sources and causes include those relating to increasingly sophisticated and complex business and financial transactions and activities, the design and content of accounting standards, audit and regulatory systems that complicate the use of professional judgment, shortcomings in the education and training of accountants, and issues and challenges in the delivery of information to investors and the capital markets.

In regard to accounting standards, the report makes what I believe is an important and useful distinction between the unavoidable complexity in standards that is necessary to properly reflect complex transactions and activities of reporting entities and the unnecessary, or avoidable, complexity in standards that creates complexity in accounting and reporting that goes beyond the underlying business, financial, and economic complexities. The report contains a number of what I believe are good recommendations to help reduce avoidable complexity in accounting standards. In my view, some of the best recommendations include setting standards on the basis of business activities rather than for specific industries, trying to use a consistent approach for measuring all the assets and liabilities of a business activity, avoiding alternative and optional accounting treatments, and improving the display of reported financial information in the way the FASB and IASB were exploring in the joint project on financial statement presentation.

Although I will not go over each of the specific recommendations in the CIFiR report, I believe they represent the result of a very thorough, well-organized, and objective look at the U.S. financial reporting system by a cross-section of knowledgeable and experienced people in financial

---

[7] *Final Report of the Advisory Committee on Improvements to Financial Reporting to the United States Securities and Exchange Commission.*

reporting. As such and as someone who had advocated undertaking such an effort, I believed it was important that the FASB seriously consider and, wherever possible, work to implement the CiFiR recommendations addressed to us. In that spirit, around the one-year anniversary of the issuance of the report, we issued a public status report on how we were addressing, or planned to address, these matters. In the status report,[8] we described

1. our progress in implementing CIFiR recommendations on enhancing investor input into accounting standard setting.
2. greater field testing of proposals.
3. implementing postadoption reviews of standards.
4. undertaking a project to develop a disclosure framework.
5. linking the XBRL U.S. GAAP taxonomy to FASB *Accounting Standards Codification*™.
6. enhancing the Financial Accounting Foundation's (FAF's) oversight over the standard-setting process.

However, we also noted that we had not experienced any significant change in the demand for detailed implementation guidance, bright lines, and exceptions to standards, suggesting a possible need for further changes to the institutional, legal, and cultural factors driving these demands. Accordingly, we expressed our support for the CIFiR recommendations for the establishment of a Financial Reporting Forum (FRF) and for the SEC and the PCAOB to develop and issue policy statements on how they evaluate the reasonableness of accounting and auditing judgments (what some have referred to as a professional judgment framework). I (and I believe others who participated in the CIFiR process) viewed implementation of these two recommendations as potentially central to the effort to reduce the overall complexity of our reporting system.

As envisioned by CIFiR's report,[9] the FRF would bring together key stakeholders from the user, preparer, and auditor communities with senior representatives of the SEC, FASB, and the PCAOB "to discuss pressures in the financial reporting system overall, both immediate and long-term, and how individual constituents are meeting those challenges." Establishing an FRF would, I believe, help surface issues in the reporting system more promptly, addressing them in a logical,

---

[8] *Recommendations of the Advisory Committee on Improvements to Financial Reporting to the United States Securities and Exchange Commission: A Response by the Financial Accounting Foundation and the Financial Accounting Standards Board.*

[9] *Final Report of the Advisory Committee on Improvements to Financial Reporting to the United States Securities and Exchange Commission.*

Chapter 6: Complexity

coordinated, and effective way, and help provide overall strategic direction to the U.S. financial reporting system. It might also help the SEC, FASB, and the PCAOB decide whether and how best to address other key recommendations in the CIFiR report. Such recommendations included those relating to the professional judgment framework, to continuing to harness the power of technology in making financial reports more understandable and useful, and to expanding and enhancing the reporting of information on key performance indicators, business opportunities, risks, strategies, and plans.

With regard to the recommendation that the SEC and the PCAOB develop and issue policy statements on the professional judgment framework, the CIFiR report contains an extensive discussion of the potential benefits of establishing and clearly articulating such a framework and the kinds of factors that might be encompassed by it. In discussing why and how such a framework might contribute to reducing complexity and improving the quality of U.S. financial reporting, the CiFiR report states,

> While preparers appear supportive of a move to less prescriptive guidance, they have expressed concern regarding the perception that current practice by regulators in evaluating judgments does not provide an environment in which such judgments may be generally respected. This, in turn, can lead to repeated calls for more rules, so that the standards can be comfortably implemented.... Regulators assert that they do respect judgments, but also express concerns that some companies may attempt to inappropriately defend certain errors as "reasonable judgments." Identifying how regulators evaluate judgments may provide an environment that promotes the use of judgment and encourages consistent evaluation practices among regulators.

Some may be concerned that implementation of this recommendation could open the door for greater leeway on the part of companies and auditors on accounting and reporting matters and ultimately lead to a deterioration in the quality of financial reporting. I do not see it that way because I believe that the steps and considerations in such a framework, if followed and properly documented, could help improve the discipline and quality of decision making on accounting and reporting issues. Perhaps this recommendation should be rebranded as establishing a framework for robust decision making on accounting and reporting matters.

Over the past few years, a number of the recommendations of CIFiR have begun to be implemented. For example, the FAF has established a formal program for postimplementation review of both FASB and Governmental Accounting Standards Board standards. Also, in 2011 the SEC staff announced they would be holding periodic roundtables (the Financial Reporting Series) that, akin to the FRF envisioned by CIFiR, will bring together a cross-section of representatives from the various stakeholder groups and senior representatives of the SEC staff, FASB, and the PCAOB to discuss emerging issues and risks arising in the U.S. financial reporting system. However, as of late 2012, so far only one roundtable has been held. The SEC has proceeded with the mandatory phase-in of XBRL-tagged financial information in filings. However, some other important recommendations of CIFiR, including the promulgation of professional judgment frameworks by the SEC and the PCAOB, have not yet been implemented.

To "celebrate" the third anniversary of the CiFiR report, Edith Orenstein of Financial Executives International (FEI) posted a very good piece to the FEI Financial Reporting Blog on July 29, 2011, titled "Hey There Bob Pozen!" with an accompanying music video.[10]

> "Hey There Bob Pozen!" sung to the tune of "Hey There Delilah"
> VERSE ONE
> Hey there Bob Pozen
> Chairing the SEC Committee
> To improve financial reporting
> And reduce complexity
> That's you
> Union Station has seen a lot of you
> I swear it's true.
> VERSE TWO
> Hey there Bob Pozen
> I am worried about convergence
> Should we move from GAAP to IFRS
> And a principles-based system
> My oh my
> Investors don't like surprise
> Neither do I
> CHORUS THAT COMES AFTER VERSE TWO:
> Oh too much complexity
> Oh too much complexity
> Oh too much complexity
> Oh too much complexity
> Too much complexity

The article summarizes the work of the Pozen Committee and the positive influence its recommendations have had on recent developments in U.S. financial reporting. The article concludes by thanking the members, observers, and staff of the Pozen Committee for their dedication to the goal of improving financial reporting and reducing complexity and by observing that the report of the committee can continue to serve as a useful reference in this endeavor.

---

[10] See http://financialexecutives.blogspot.com/2011/07/hey-there-bob-pozen.html.

As noted, at approximately the same time CiFiR was formed and began meeting, the Treasury formed ACAP.[11] Co-chaired by Don Nicolaisen and former SEC Chairman Arthur Levitt, ACAP focused on examining and making recommendations on improving accounting education and strengthening human capital in the auditing profession, enhancing the governance, transparency, responsibility, communications, and audit quality of audit firms, and increasing competition and auditor choice in the market for audit services. I served as an official observer to ACAP, and although its charge did not directly involve complexity in the U.S. reporting system, some of those issues inevitably also came up in its deliberations.

Disclosure Overload

For many years, some participants in the financial reporting system have expressed concerns over the growing volume of detailed disclosure requirements and the increasing length of company financial reports and SEC filings that, in their view, have negatively affected the overall understandability and usefulness of these documents. For example, in 1994, Ray Groves, the CEO of Ernst & Young, commented, "The sheer quantity of financial disclosures has become so excessive that we've diminished the overall value of these disclosures."[12]

A number of groups and special committees have studied this issue and included various recommendations for addressing it. For example, the AICPA Special Committee on Financial Reporting (or Jenkins Committee) issued a 1994 report[13] that suggested more flexible disclosure standards that would be responsive to the particular circumstances of different companies. During the early 1990s, the FASB had a disclosure effectiveness project. And, as mentioned in chapter 1, in 2000–01, I headed a working group as part of the FASB's business reporting research project that specifically identified various redundancies between the disclosures contained in the financial statement notes and the information contained in other parts of SEC filings. Our working group also suggested ways to better organize and streamline annual reports on Form 10-K.

During my years at the FASB, we issued a number of standards that, in response to the requests of professional investors and financial analysts, contained additional disclosure requirements relating to matters such as an entity's use of, and involvement with, special purpose entities

---

[11] See October 2008 *Final Report of the Advisory Committee on the Auditing Profession to the U.S. Department of the Treasury.*
[12] Ray J. Groves, "Financial Disclosure: When More Is Not Better" *Financial Executive*, May 1994.
[13] *Improving Business Reporting—A Customer Focus.*

(SPEs), securitizations and other off-balance sheet arrangements, fair value measurements, derivatives, and credit exposures. Some of these new requirements resulted from users' complaints and concerns about what they viewed as inadequate disclosures of these matters, particularly during the financial crisis. For public companies, some of these new disclosure requirements extended to both the annual financial statements and quarterly financial statements. Although, in theory, companies are allowed to make materiality judgments in deciding which of these disclosures to provide in light of their particular circumstances, in practice, most companies and auditors, perhaps fearful of being questioned by the SEC, seem to have adopted a checklist approach to meeting disclosure requirements, regardless of materiality. The inevitable result has been continued growth in the length of financial statements and SEC filings, perhaps most notably for financial institutions.

In partial response to this issue and in order to improve the overall relevance, coherence, and quality of disclosures, more-recent FASB standards, including those jointly issued with the IASB, have contained higher-level disclosure objectives and principles and a list of minimum disclosures needed to meet these objectives and principles. Additionally, the boards have required more of the information to be provided in tables in order to improve the accessibility and usability of the footnote information to users and to facilitate XBRL tagging of footnote information required by the SEC.

CIFiR's report[14] also addressed the issue of disclosure overload and recommended that the SEC and the FASB work together to develop a disclosure framework to "[i]ntegrate existing SEC and FASB disclosure requirements into a cohesive whole to ensure meaningful communication and logical presentation of disclosures, based on consistent objectives and principles. This would eliminate redundancies and provide a single source of disclosure guidance across all financial reporting standards."

The FASB had also received requests to develop a disclosure framework from others, including its Investors Technical Advisory Committee, who suggested the outline of a potential framework for enhancing the comprehensiveness, consistency, and usability of information in the financial statement notes desired by professional users. So, in July 2009, after consultation with my fellow Board members, I added a project to the FASB's technical agenda to develop a disclosure framework. In announcing the new project, I stated,

> Many constituents have expressed concerns about so-called "disclosure overload." While clear and robust disclosures are essential to informative and transparent financial reporting—a

---

[14] *Final Report of the Advisory Committee on Improvements to Financial Reporting to the United States Securities and Exchange Commission.*

critical component in maintaining investor confidence in the markets—improving the way such disclosures are integrated can help decrease complexity. The Board will embark on this project to create a principles-based disclosure framework that will enable companies to communicate more effectively with investors and also help eliminate redundancy or otherwise outdated GAAP disclosure requirements.[15]

I added this project to our agenda believing such a framework could provide the FASB with a more consistent approach to developing disclosure requirements and might also help entities make more coherent and better organized disclosures in their financial reports. I also hoped it would move financial reporting toward more effective communication between reporting entities and the users of their financial information, that it might facilitate the XBRL tagging of footnote data that the SEC had begun to mandate, and that it might more generally explore ways to exploit technology to improve the organization, delivery, and usability of reported financial information. In short, I believed this project had potential to both improve financial reporting and reduce complexity.

So it was with great interest that I read the July 2012 FASB discussion paper *Disclosure Framework*. This preliminary stage document is a thoughtful exploration of the issues that raises a number of interesting and thought-provoking ideas on the approach the FASB might take in the future to develop disclosure requirements for annual and quarterly financial statements. It also explores how companies might go about deciding, based on their particular circumstances, which disclosures to provide in the notes to their financial statements. In effect, it introduces the possibility of a more flexible, situationally based, and dynamic approach to disclosure. As with the concept of principles-based accounting standards, a key issue will be whether an approach requiring the exercise of more judgment by preparers, auditors, and regulators can work in our reporting system. Also, because the scope of the discussion paper is limited to the disclosures in the notes to financial statements and does not extend to other financial information contained in SEC filings, it is not fully responsive to the CIFiR recommendation. Although the discussion paper explores and suggests some ways to improve the organization and formatting of information in the financial statement footnotes, I believe these largely reflect a paper-based way of thinking and do not, as I had hoped, contemplate the potential for technology to make a difference in this area. Nevertheless, I believe the discussion paper represents a good start on this important project, and I am hopeful it will lead to the kinds of improvements envisioned when I added the project to the FASB's agenda.

---

[15] July 8, 2009, Financial Accounting Standards Board (FASB) press release, *FASB Initiates "Disclosure Framework" Project Aimed at More Useful, Organized, and Consistent Disclosures.*

Can Technology Help?

My answer is, "Yes." As I more fully discuss in my February 2012 column "Embracing Technology in Financial Reporting" in *Compliance Week*, I believe the power of technology can be put to use to improve the delivery, accessibility, and overall usability of reported financial information and, in the process, can help solve some of the issues associated with complexity and perceived disclosure overload. As I note in my column, financial reporting has been affected by some important technological advances, including accounting software packages, enterprise resource planning systems, electronic audit working papers, and various software tools used in financial analysis. However, I question whether technology has yet had the kind of transformative effects on accounting and financial reporting that it has had on many other aspects of life and business.

Certainly, the Internet, social media, smartphones, tablets, and the proliferation of apps have revolutionized the accessibility and usability of all sorts of information. In contrast, our official system of financial reporting continues to reflect a paper-based approach and mindset. For some time, certain accounting futurists have predicted that our financial reporting system would evolve from the periodic filing of highly structured financial and regulatory reports to a system of continuous reporting and auditing, with corporate financial data stored in electronic data warehouses into which investors and financial analysts could plug in their own models. Although that has yet to occur, I believe that the advent of XBRL-tagged financial information and interactive data, coupled with the use of other technologies, such as drop-down menus, click-throughs, and search capabilities, might help address some of the challenges on the limitations of our current reporting system, including some of the issues relating to complexity and disclosure overload.

I can envision how, using XBRL, drop-down menus, click-through technology, and search capabilities in electronically delivered financial reports, information could be tiered, structured, and organized to better cater to the needs of different types of users. For example, the top page of an electronically delivered financial report might consist of condensed financial statements and key performance metrics, which might satisfy the needs of an average investor. For professional users, more detailed information could be available through drop-down menus and click-throughs that allow them to drill down several levels. So, for example, clicking on the "revenues" line in the condensed income statement might reveal a drop-down menu of more detailed information about the revenues, such as the accounting policies, revenues by segment, and management's commentary on the changes and trends in sales. In turn, clicking on revenues by segment might reveal a secondary drop-down menu with more granular information, such as revenues by major product line within the segment. Such technologies could also be used to provide alternative presentations of reported data to suit the particular needs of different categories of users (for example, credit analysts versus equity analysts).

So, although a number of critical and potentially very challenging issues would certainly need to be addressed to transform financial reporting along these lines, including issues relating to data capture, legal liability and safeguards, or the possibility of providing potentially proprietary and sensitive information, I believe we should continue to actively explore ways to better harness the power of technology to enhance the quality and usability of reported financial information.

Private Company Reporting

Although CIFiR specifically looked at the issues of improving relevance and transparency of reporting and reducing complexity in the context of reporting by U.S. public companies, some of the same concerns and themes have also been present in discussions over private company reporting in the United States.

This is a very important topic that could well have been the focus of an entirely separate chapter. I chose to address it in this chapter because some of the central issues relate to the subject of complexity in financial reporting. To put the importance of this subject in context, there are some 28 million businesses in the United States, but approximately only 14,000 of these are public companies.[16] Clearly, private companies are a very important segment of the U.S. economy and the source of a majority of job growth in this country. The vast majority of U.S. private companies are not required to provide financial statements prepared in accordance with U.S. GAAP. Some prepare financial statements based on another comprehensive basis of accounting (OCBOA), such as the income tax basis or cash basis, and many others provide financial information requested by lenders, suppliers, and other parties through copies of tax returns and Dun & Bradstreet and other credit reports. However, many, possibly millions, are still required to provide full U.S. GAAP financial statements annually by their lenders or other providers of capital, or for other reasons. Therefore, in establishing accounting standards that cover private companies, it is important to try to ensure that they result in financial information that is relevant and useful to the users of that information and that can be provided in a cost-effective manner.

---

[16] January 2011 Blue-Ribbon Panel on Standard Setting for Private Companies, *Report to the Board of Trustees of the Financial Accounting Foundation.*

In that regard, some, including many involved in accounting and reporting by private companies, argue that the needs of users of private company financial statements sometimes differ from those of public company financial statements. The users of private company financial statements, which include lenders, trade creditors, sureties, individual investors, venture capitalists, and private equity investors, often have the ability to obtain the information they want directly from management of the company. The capital structure of private companies is often quite different than that of public companies, with the capital generally being illiquid and viewed as a long-term investment. Also, very importantly, private companies often have fewer resources dedicated to preparing financial information and implementing new accounting standards than public companies and often have to rely on their outside accountants for help in this process. So, for many years, there has been a debate concerning whether there should be a different or simplified set of accounting and reporting standards, sometimes termed the Big GAAP/Little GAAP issue. The issue has been studied many times for the past 35 years by various groups and has been a challenging one for the FASB and the trustees of the FAF. I think the following passage from the "Standard-Setting Organizations" section of chapter 1, "Financial Accounting Regulations and Organization" of the seventh edition of the *Accountants' Handbook* captures the issue well:

> One pervasive political problem that just will not go away is standards overload. Originally, this phrase described the issuance of numerous detailed standards, but more recently it has come to encompass the issuance of complex standards that are difficult to implement, especially by smaller nonpublic companies.... The FASB's dilemma is that too much emphasis on SEC registrants seems to ignore the constraints affecting private companies, yet too much emphasis on private companies ignores the needs of the SEC and the public for effective capital markets. Because the SEC exerts the greatest influence, it seems likely that that the FASB will continue to focus on the needs of more sophisticated users and will issue standards that that may be difficult for private companies to implement. This choice leaves the state Boards [of accountancy] and the AICPA in a difficult relationship with some of their constituents and members, but there does not appear to be any way out of this dilemma.

This passage was from 1990 and, with the benefit of hindsight, seems rather prophetic. In recent years, this issue has taken on renewed importance and a sense of urgency due to perceptions of the increasing complexity of U.S. GAAP and questions about the relevance and cost effectiveness for private companies of certain accounting standards and also due to the possibility of the United States moving to IFRS for public company reporting.

The Private Company Financial Reporting Committee, IFRS for Small and Medium Enterprises, and Other Initiatives

During my years at the FASB, we took a number of steps to try to obtain greater input from stakeholders representing the small and private business communities and the not-for-profit community into our standard-setting activities. In 2004, we increased private company representation on the EITF by appointing Lawrence Weinstock, the CFO of a private company, to the group. In 2005, we established the FASB Small Business Advisory Committee comprised of a cross section of financial statement users, preparers, and practitioners that focused on private and small public companies. We met with that group twice a year and we also met periodically with the Technical Issues Committee of the AICPA's Private Company Practice Section to discuss private company reporting issues. As we issued standard-setting proposals, we began soliciting specific input on private company considerations.

In 2007, together with the AICPA, we formed the Private Company Financial Reporting Committee (PCFRC). That committee provided the FASB with specific recommendations on potential differences in particular accounting standards that should be made to better meet the needs of users of private company financial statements or in light of cost-benefit considerations. The PCFRC was formed in response to the 2006 report of the AICPA Private Company Financial Reporting Task Force (the Castellano Report) that found that although users of private company financial statements generally placed value on U.S. GAAP financial statements, they believed existing U.S. GAAP did not deliver relevant information for their purposes in a number of areas.

The PCFRC comprised 12 part-time members representing the key stakeholder groups in U.S. private company financial reporting (4 users, 4 preparers, and 4 CPA practitioners). It was chaired by Judith O'Dell, a CPA practitioner and owner of a private consulting business, who was formerly both a member of the AICPA board of directors and a trustee of the FAF. The PCFRC was staffed by professionals from the FASB and AICPA.

To provide additional focus by the FASB on the work of the PCFRC, as well as on private company and not-for-profit reporting issues in general, we hired staff members with extensive experience in these areas, including Paul Glotzer, who had been a partner in a small accounting firm serving private companies. In 2009, I appointed one of our experienced assistant directors, Jeff Mechanick, to oversee our efforts in these important areas. Also in 2009 we established a Not-for-Profit Advisory Committee.

The PCFRC met four to five times per year and provided various recommendations to the FASB on specific modifications it felt should be made to particular standards to either better meet the needs of users of private company financial reports or based on cost-benefit considerations. Based on these recommendations, the Board provided for a number of differences for private companies, generally involving different effective dates and, in some cases, fewer disclosures by private companies. However, in other cases, the Board, based at least in part on gathering further information and additional outreach, including outreach to users of private company financial reports, decided against modifications to standards recommended by the PCFRC. These generally related to proposed modifications that would have created differences in recognition or measurement between U.S. public companies and U.S. private companies, which I believe some FASB Board members viewed as conceptually indefensible.

Regardless of whether one agrees with particular recommendations the PCFRC made to the FASB, I believe the Board deciding not to act on more of them, particularly those relating to differential recognition and measurement for private companies, was disappointing to PCFRC members and many stakeholders in the private company reporting community. At the FASB, I sensed from comments at Board meetings an apparent frustration on the part of certain Board members and staff with PCFRC recommendations that they believed were not sufficiently supported by evidence of differential user needs or by adequate evaluation of cost-benefit considerations by the PCFRC.

There has also been an increasing use of exceptions to U.S. GAAP in private company financial statements in which the users of the reports agreed to accept financial statements with specific departures from U.S. GAAP (for example, for the nonconsolidation of subsidiaries holding the real estate used in a family-owned private company). To some, this demonstrates that the market for private company financial statements is functioning effectively (that is, that preparers and users are able to negotiate and agree upon customizations to the financial statements). To others, however, this greater use of allowed exceptions threatens to undermine the general acceptance of U.S. GAAP for private company reporting.

Some in the private company reporting community have also voiced significant concerns that some of the major proposed standards relating to the FASB-IASB Memorandum of Understanding (MoU) may add unnecessary cost, effort, and complexity to accounting and reporting by U.S. private companies. These included concerns over the perceived expansion of fair value accounting requirements and the additional costs and effort associated with developing such measurements. In addition to these factors, the many issues that could arise for U.S. private company reporting if and when we were to move to IFRS for U.S. public companies also added impetus to calls for a focused look at the subject of private company financial reporting in the United States. Interestingly, experience in countries that have moved to IFRS for public company reporting is mixed. Some of these countries have adopted the IFRS for Small and Medium Enterprises (SMEs) standards for their private companies, but others have chosen to retain a version of their existing national standards for private company financial statements:

> It has been over a year now since the new IFRS standard for non-publicly accountable entities ("IFRS for SMEs") was issued. In that time, many governments around the world have been considering whether to allow or even prescribe the SME standard for non-listed entities, or whether they would prefer to continue with local accounting standards....
>
> Like all ready-made solutions, the SME standards may not be usable straight out of the box in some circumstances. The UK, for example, is considering adopting the SME standard but has run into issues regarding compliance with EU Directives.
>
> To get around this, they are proposing to adopt a "tweaked" version (and, like Hong Kong, have replaced the tax section with IAS 12). France, and to some extent Germany, have rejected the SME because it does not fit with their integrated tax and accounting frameworks, which have only recently been overhauled. South Africa on the other hand has embraced the SME with open arms, adopting the standard while it was still in draft.
>
> The Caribbean and some countries in South and Central America are very supportive and are considering quick adoption of the SME standard as their local GAAP. Some of these countries currently apply IFRS as the only standard. Some countries in South East Asia have already made the step towards the SME standard.
>
> This highlights one of the difficulties that the SME faces—fitting into local legislation and requirements. You could argue that the impact is much reduced if we end up with many flavours or variants of the SME, although the prospect of international harmony probably falls way down the priority list of those that are not multinational already.
>
> In any case, there is quite an appetite for the standard, although not everyone is convinced yet. According to the IASB, some 60 jurisdictions have adopted the SME standard or have made a public statement that they plan to adopt it. That's not bad for a standard that has been in place now for around 15 months only.[17]

---

[17] "IFRS for SMEs—Gathers Momentum." PwC IFRS blog. 11 November 2010. http://pwc.blogs.com/ifrs/2010/11/ifrs-for-smes-gathers-momentum.html.

Blue-Ribbon Panel

During 2009, the FAF board of trustees and senior leadership of the FAF conducted a "listening tour" meeting with a diverse range of constituents to obtain views on U.S. accounting standard setting and financial reporting. Many stakeholders in the private company community expressed continuing concerns relating to accounting standard setting for private companies and disappointment with the results of the efforts between the FASB and the PCFRC. Accordingly, toward the end of 2009, the FAF, together with the AICPA and the National Association of State Boards of Accountancy (NASBA), formed a Blue-Ribbon Panel (BRP) to examine these issues and make recommendations to the FAF. The BRP was chaired by Rick Anderson, Chairman of the accounting firm Moss Adams LLP and an FAF trustee, and it comprised a cross-section of constituents involved in private company financial reporting. It met a number of times during 2010, reviewing prior studies on the subject, learning about how other countries have addressed these matters, and gathering input and discussing the issues. The BRP issued its *Report to the Board of Trustees of the Financial Accounting Foundation* in January 2011.

The report of the BRP called for significant changes to the U.S. system of establishing standards for private companies in order to improve the relevance and overall cost effectiveness of accounting standards relating to U.S. private companies. These changes included the creation of a new board to be overseen by the FAF to specifically focus on making exceptions and modifications to U.S. GAAP for private companies. In making this recommendation, the BRP report stated,

> Based on both the FASB's history and the competing standard-setting pressures on the FASB that are emanating from the public sector, including those related to the FASB's joint projects with the International Accounting Standards Board (IASB), a supermajority of BRP members believe that the FASB will not be able to fully assess and respond sufficiently and appropriately to the needs of the private company sector.

The panel also recommended the development of a differential framework that would provide a set of decision criteria to guide the new board in making exceptions to U.S. GAAP for private companies.

It is important to note that the panel did not recommend, as certain parties have advocated, that there be a separate self-contained U.S. GAAP for private companies. Also, a minority of the BRP opposed the establishment of a separate accounting standards board for private companies, believing it to be premature. They were also concerned that it could lead to too many differences between private company and public company accounting standards and other unintended consequences, including increasing complexity in the U.S. reporting system. Instead, they proposed structural changes in the FASB and its processes to better focus on the private company sector, including having at least one Board member with primarily private company experience. Additionally, one member of the BRP dissented to the report on the basis that the panel was not provided with compelling evidence of a need for differences in standards for private companies or the need for a separate accounting standards board to establish such differences. In the words of this member of the BRP, "the Panel has not been presented with arguments or evidence that private company financial statements do not meet the needs of users. In fact, the push for differential reporting has not been driven by users of private company financial statements, suggesting that the financial statements are providing decision-useful information."

Others voiced concerns over the recommendations of the BRP. For example, PwC issued a public Point of View,[18] stating that it believes the creation of a separate private company accounting standards board would reduce the quality of information provided to users and create undue cost and complexity in the U.S. financial reporting system. Instead, it advocated an approach that would continue the current single U.S. standard-setting board and complement recent changes in the FASB's composition and processes to support greater private company input into the development of standards.

FAF Working Group and Increased FASB Focus on Private Companies

In March 2011, the FAF formed a working group of several trustees and senior FAF members to further consider accounting standard setting for U.S. nonpublic entities (private companies and not-for-profit entities). The working group received input from many constituents through various meetings with stakeholders and unsolicited letters, considered the recommendations of the BRP and relevant academic research on these matters, and reviewed the FASB's processes for gathering input from the needs and concerns of private companies and not-for-profit entities.

In the meantime, the FAF trustees also expanded the FASB Board back to seven members, and one of the new members, Daryl Buck, was the CFO of a private company and a member of the PCFRC and the BRP. Another new FASB Board member, Hal Schroeder, had experience investing in and auditing private companies. Although that's not new because other FASB Board members have had such experience (for example, throughout my career, I had significant involvement in investing in and auditing private companies), I think it shows a sensitivity by the FAF trustees to this issue in appointments to the

---

[18] *Setting private company accounting standards: Recent recommendations miss the mark.*

FASB. The FASB also took various steps to improve its focus on private companies, including holding public roundtables to obtain views from stakeholders in private company financial reports on specific issues; stepping up educational efforts with private company stakeholders and creating methods of obtaining their input on issues; undertaking a project to reexamine the definition of *nonpublic entity* in order to more clearly define what constitutes a private company for standard-setting purposes; and, consistent with a recommendation by the BRP, developing a white paper aimed at setting forth criteria in a differential Private Company Framework that might be used in evaluating potential differences in accounting standards between public and private companies

In July 2012, the FASB issued the invitation to comment, *Private Company Decision-Making Framework: A Framework for Evaluating Financial Accounting and Reporting Guidance for Private Companies*, that contains a set of initial recommendations from the FASB staff on criteria for determining whether and under what circumstances it would be appropriate to adjust U.S. GAAP requirements for private companies.

FAF Proposes Establishing a Private Company Standards Improvement Council

In October 2011, the FAF board of trustees issued a request for comment[19] that was intended to improve the U.S. accounting standard process for private companies. It proposed the creation of a new Private Company Standards Improvement Council (PCSIC) that would replace the PCFRC and would be chaired by a FASB member and comprise 11–15 other people with significant experience in private company financial reporting. The FASB would provide full staff support for the PCSIC.

Working jointly with the FASB, the PCSIC would develop criteria for identifying and evaluating potential exceptions and modifications to U.S. GAAP for private companies, obtain input from constituents on these matters, and deliberate and formally vote on them in public meetings attended by FASB Board members. Changes to U.S. GAAP for private companies proposed by the PCSIC would then be forwarded to the FASB for its consideration and ratification, exposed for public comment, and redeliberated by the PCSIC at public meetings attended by FASB members. If approved by at least a two-thirds vote of the PCSIC, the final changes would be sent to the FASB for ratification and codification as part of U.S. GAAP. The operations of the PCSIC would be overseen by the FAF board of trustees through periodic in-person reports to a newly

---

[19] *Plan to Establish the Private Company Standards Improvement Council.*

Chapter 6: Complexity

created Private Company Review Committee of certain trustees and quarterly written reports to the full board of trustees.

Following three years of operation of the PCSIC, the FAF trustees would assess the overall effectiveness of the new process and whether further changes were warranted in accounting standard setting for private companies.

For accounting standards for not-for-profit entities, the FAF working group concluded that the FASB should continue to fulfill this important role and continue to seek advice from the Not-For-Profit Advisory Committee (NAC) it established in 2009. Indeed, in November 2011, based on input from the NAC, the FASB added two projects to its agenda. One project is exploring ways to enhance certain presentations and disclosures in the financial statements of not-for-profits, and the second, a research project, looks at best practices used by not-for-profits to communicate their financial story to donors and other users of their financial information.

In making the October 2011 proposal on private company accounting standard setting, the FAF trustees seemed to believe it represented a balanced approach that would put in place important structural and process changes that would increase and elevate the FASB's focus on private companies and strengthen and improve its procedures for establishing accounting standards that are responsive to the needs and concerns of stakeholders in private company reporting and to many of the BRP's recommendations while avoiding the potential for creating a Big GAAP/Little GAAP system in the United States. The proposal was welcomed and supported by the leadership of NASBA, but it was quickly and strongly criticized by AICPA leaders in a press release issued on October 4, 2011, the same day the FAF proposal was published. In that press release, AICPA President Barry Melancon stated

> Three thousand private company constituents and a majority of the state CPA societies, representing more than a quarter million CPAs, have spoken. They want a separate independent standard setting board and they have sent letters to FAF asking for change. Over the years, FASB's main focus has understandably been on the needs of publicly traded companies. The pent up frustration we are witnessing by the private company constituency is a direct result of that public company focus and not seeing that differences can be and are appropriate for private companies and their financial statement users.

The FAF Establishes the Private Company Council and a New Process for Setting Private Company Accounting Standards

The FAF's PCSIC proposal was exposed for public comment. The FAF received thousands of comment letters on the proposal, the vast majority of which were form letters following a template developed by the AICPA. After considering the many letters received and other input on the proposal, the FAF trustees voted unanimously in May 2012 to establish a new group called the Private Company Council (PCC) to improve the process of setting U.S. GAAP accounting standards for U.S. private companies. The new structure incorporates a number of significant changes from the proposed PCSIC based on suggestions made by constituents. These include that the PCC chair will not be a FASB member and that FASB will follow a formal and transparent endorsement process for deciding on whether to approve, reject, or suggest changes to the exceptions and modifications to U.S. GAAP for private companies recommended by the PCC.

The PCC will have 9–12 part-time, noncompensated members selected and appointed by the FAF, including users, preparers, and practitioners with significant experience in private company reporting. Members will be appointed for a 3-year term and may be reappointed for an additional 2-year term. Working together, the PCC and FASB will agree on criteria for determining whether and when exceptions or modifications to U.S. GAAP are appropriate for private companies. Using these criteria and in consultation with the FASB and with input from constituents, the PCC will, by a two-thirds vote, determine which areas to consider for possible exceptions and modifications to U.S. GAAP for private companies. The PCC will also serve as the FASB's primary advisory group on the treatment for private companies of technical agenda items being actively deliberated by the FASB and on the new Private Company Decision-Making Framework that the FASB has been developing. During its first 3 years of operation, the PCC will hold at least 5 meetings annually. The deliberative portions of these meetings will be open to the public, and all FASB members will be expected to attend. The PCC will discuss proposed exceptions and modifications to U.S. GAAP for private companies, vote on them, and, if approved and endorsed by a majority of the FASB, expose them for public comment. After the conclusion of the public comment period, the PCC will redeliberate the proposal and forward its final decisions to the FASB for endorsement. If the FASB endorses the PCC's decisions, they will be incorporated into U.S. GAAP. If it does not endorse the PCC decisions, the FASB Chairman will provide the PCC with a written explanation, including potential changes for the PCC to consider in order to obtain FASB endorsement.

Chapter 6: Complexity

The FAF trustees will create a special Private Company Review Committee to oversee the new structure and process to help ensure that there is adequate consideration of private company issues in the U.S. accounting standard-setting process. Following its first three years in operation, the FAF trustees will conduct an assessment of the new structure and process and determine whether further changes are warranted.

In the May 23, 2012, press release announcing the FAF trustees' decisions, FAF President Teresa Polley said

> The plan approved by the Trustees strikes an important balance. One the one hand, the plan recognizes that the needs of public and private company financial statement users, preparers, and auditors are not always aligned. But at the same time, the plan ensures comparability of financial reporting among disparate companies by putting in place a system for recognizing differences that will avoid creation of a "two-GAAP" system.

The AICPA expressed support for the FAF's decisions, noting the important changes the trustees had made in response to input received on the PCSIC proposal. However, the AICPA also announced that it will develop a separate, stand-alone *Financial Reporting Framework for Small- and Medium-Sized Entities* (FRF for SMEs) that do not have to prepare U.S. GAAP financial statements. In effect, the FRF for SMEs will be a new OCBOA that is intended to be less complex and less costly for small and medium-sized private companies to implement and that will meet the needs of the users of such information. In November 2012, the AICPA issued the proposed FRF for SMEs for public comment. The proposed FRF for SMEs emphasizes the use of historical cost accounting and matching of revenues and costs and proposes a number of differences from GAAP that are intended to increase the relevance of the information reported by private company SMEs to bank lenders and other users. The proposed FRF for SMEs is also intended to reduce the cost and complexity of the accounting by, for example, allowing the use of certain accounting methods for tax purposes in preparing the financial statements, not requiring certain derivatives to carried at fair value, and not requiring consolidation of variable interest entities.

In September 2012, the FAF announced the names of the 10-member PCC, comprised of experienced private company users, preparers, and practitioners, and chaired by Billy M. Atkinson. Billy was a long-time partner and colleague at C&L and PwC with a great deal of experience in serving private company clients and was a recent Chairman of NASBA. The first meeting of the PCC occurred in December 2012.

I commend the FAF and FASB, the AICPA, and NASBA, as well as other stakeholders, for systematically working through what has been a very important, long-standing, controversial, and challenging issue in

U.S. accounting standard setting and financial reporting. Although I believe the new structure and process approved by the FAF trustees provides a balanced, well-developed approach, time will tell whether it achieves the stated goals of addressing and satisfying the concerns of private company stakeholders while also avoiding the creation of a two-tier Big GAAP/Little GAAP system in the United States. Time will also tell if the new FRF for SMEs that the AICPA develops gains a widespread acceptance such that there could effectively be multiple tiers of financial reporting in the United States comprising public company U.S. GAAP, private company U.S. GAAP for some private companies, and FRF for SMEs for other private companies. Certainly, it will be interesting to see how this all develops, including which kinds of private companies choose to report under GAAP as modified by the PCC and FASB and which adopt the AICPA's FRF for SMEs. The extent of differences in the financial statements prepared under these two sets of standards, the level of acceptance of each of these approaches by lenders and other users of private company financial information, and their overall branding in the marketplace will also be interesting.

So Where Are We on Complexity?

My short answer to that question is that although I believe we have made some progress on this front, it continues to be a work in process. In my opinion, the U.S. financial reporting system has been going through and continues to go through some very major challenges, crosscurrents, uncertainties, and changes that have affected and will likely continue to impact the complexity issue.

The reporting scandals a decade ago shook confidence in U.S. public company financial reports, revealing a number of systemic issues, including deficiencies in certain accounting standards, reporting practices at certain major U.S. companies that, either through fraud or abusive accounting practices, resulted in reporting misleading financial information to the public, and weaknesses in internal control processes and corporate governance practices. The reporting scandals also raised concerns about the quality of independent audits of financial statements.

Congress, through Sarbanes-Oxley, enacted significant reforms in the U.S. financial reporting system. In terms of accounting standards, improvement in standards to more faithfully reflect the economics of transactions and events, trying to make the standards more principles-based and, when appropriate, seeking convergence with international accounting standards, was a theme in SOX and follow-up studies by the SEC mandated by SOX. Two SEC studies—one on the feasibility of a principles-based accounting system of accounting and the other on off-balance sheet arrangements—pointed to the need to improve accounting standards in a number of major areas. The results of these studies were an important source of input to FASB and the IASB in developing the list of projects included in the MoU.

At the same time, the creation and activities of the PCAOB in overseeing and regulating auditors of SEC registrants, coupled with expectations of stronger review and enforcement of reporting practices by the SEC, greater diligence by auditors and audit committees, and the ever-present threat of litigation relating to reported financial information, have, in my view, had both very positive and some unintended negative effects on the U.S. financial reporting system. On the positive side, the overall quality of U.S. public company financial reports has improved during the last decade. That is a welcome and very important outcome.

On the negative side, the increased fear by companies, audit committees, and auditors of being second-guessed on accounting and reporting matters has, at times, very understandably, been a force creating resistance to change and inhibiting our country moving toward less complex and more transparent financial reporting. Similarly, although the enhanced focus on internal controls has helped raise the overall quality of accounting and financial reporting, it has also upped the cost of implementing changes in accounting and reporting requirements, which affects both the overall receptivity to change and the cost-benefit analysis on proposed changes in accounting and disclosure standards.

I believe these realities of the U.S. public company financial reporting system were expressed well in the following excerpts from a letter dated November 5, 2010, from Marie Hollein, president and CEO of FEI, a U.S.-based, leading organization of senior financial executives, to Sir David Tweedie, Chairman of the IASB. The letter expressed the FEI's concerns on the perceived rapid pace of development of standards under the MoU and otherwise by the IASB:

> [I]t is important to understand that the U.S. regulatory environment is very demanding in terms of its expectations about application of accounting standards. This includes, but is not limited to, evaluations of the process followed in interpreting and implementing new standards, the development of high quality repeatable and sustainable processes and controls, and thoroughness and transparency of related disclosures that enable investors to fully understand the nature and effect of the required changes. It is also noteworthy that these reporting processes occur every quarter in the U.S. rather than the semi-annual or annual reporting cycles typical in other reporting regimes. Meeting these expectations and timetables causes companies to incur significant compliance costs, both in terms of internal and external technical accounting resources as well as systems and audit-related costs.... It is important to remember

that, due to the long lead times necessary to meet U.S. compliance requirements, companies and audit firms will commit enormous resources to implementing these standards as soon as they are issued final.

These and other issues relating to complexity and improving financial reporting were the focus of CIFiR. However, as previously discussed, although some of CIFiR's recommendations have been or are in the process of being implemented, other ones that could be important to help address the complexity issue have not yet been implemented.

Convergence and the possible move to IFRS have further added to the crosscurrents and uncertainties in the U.S. financial reporting system. As I said in speeches and public meetings and discussed in chapter 4, "International Convergence," we have been "riding two horses" in terms of accounting standard setting, working on convergence in major areas while also responding to U.S. reporting issues relating to existing standards and to the concerns of private company stakeholders. As noted in chapter 4, that has been challenging, not only for the FASB but, more importantly, for many stakeholders in the U.S. reporting system.

The potential move to or towards IFRS for U.S. public company reporting coupled with concerns over the suitability for private companies of some existing and proposed standards have added impetus to renewed calls for differential accounting standards in this country. In response, the FAF trustees have instituted changes in the process for developing U.S. GAAP for private companies, and the AICPA is developing a new reporting framework for small and medium-sized private businesses that are not required to prepare U.S. GAAP financial statements.

Some say the solution is to have less complex accounting standards for both public and private companies. That may well be part of the answer because I certainly believe, as CIFiR recommended, that accounting standard setters should strive to avoid creating avoidable complexity in developing standards. But what constitutes avoidable versus unavoidable complexity is subjective and may involve some different considerations for public versus private company reporting. For example, the recent standards on consolidation of SPEs and uncertain tax positions were developed in response to specific problems in public company financial reporting and at the urging of the SEC staff. So, going back to the prior accounting in those areas would not seem advisable for public company reporting. Yet, those are two of the areas where many private company constituents have voiced significant concerns over the relevance and cost-benefit of recent standards, so reevaluating differences in those standards for private companies would seem to be in order. Perhaps they can be simplified for both private and public companies in a way that does not weaken reporting

Chapter 6: Complexity

by public companies. In that regard, the FASB, in responding to concerns expressed by private company stakeholders, has recently issued standards that provide a simplified approach to the testing of impairments of goodwill and other indefinite-lived intangibles for impairments that apply to both private and public companies.[20] However, as is the case in some other countries, such as Canada and the United Kingdom, and with *International Financial Reporting Standards for Small and Medium-sized Entities* (IFRS for SMEs), it may be time in the United States to develop a stand-alone set of accounting standards specifically for use by private companies. This is the approach of the AICPA for private companies that do not have to prepare U.S. GAAP financial statements, but is not the approach adopted by the FAF trustees for U.S. GAAP for private companies.

Additionally, although the FASB-IASB program to develop common standards focuses on areas that the boards, users of public company financial reports, and regulators have cited as requiring improved standards, the prospect of significant changes in these areas have added to the concerns voiced in the private company sector. For example, the FASB and IASB have been working to address perceived deficiencies in current lease accounting standards that enable lessees to exclude leased assets and obligations from their balance sheets. That was a significant issue raised in a 2005 SEC report to Congress on off-balance sheet arrangements and an area that most users of public company financial reports seem to believe needs fixing. Doing so will likely add additional cost and complexity to the accounting by lessees, and that additional cost and effort could fall disproportionately on small and private companies. When and if it comes back onto the active standard-setting agenda, the FASB-IASB project on financial statement presentation could result in significant changes in the format of the basic financial statements and in the level of disaggregation in the statements, two areas of change that seem to be favored by many users of public company financial reports. However, many stakeholders in the private company reporting community, including some users of private company financial reports, generally seem to believe that such changes to private company financial statements would not be cost beneficial.

In short, there are some important crosscurrents, competing objectives, and trade-offs in trying to make accounting standards and financial reporting both more relevant and less complex. As previously noted, I believe those considerations and trade-offs can and do sometimes differ between public and private company reporting. This difference creates potential opportunities to simplify U.S. GAAP for both public and private companies, as the FASB demonstrated through recent revisions

---

[20] FASB Accounting Standards Update (ASU) No. 2011-08, *Intangibles—Goodwill and Other (Topic 350): Testing Goodwill for Impairment*, and FASB ASU No. 2012-02, *Intangibles—Goodwill and Other (Topic 350): Testing Indefinite-Lived Intangible Assets for Impairment*.

to the accounting for impairment of goodwill and other indefinite-lived intangibles. Add to the mix the issues concerning whether, how, and when to move to, or incorporate, IFRS for U.S. public companies, we clearly have a rather interesting and challenging situation facing the U.S. financial reporting system.

So, in the face of these crosscurrents, competing objectives, uncertainties, and overall complexity, is there a path forward to the improved and less complex accounting and reporting that many, including me, have called for? Although I have my own thoughts and preferred solutions on paths forward, first and foremost, I think it will require addressing and resolving all the major crosscurrents and uncertainties previously discussed. Is this likely to happen? I hope so but probably not completely in the short term. Understandably, in the wake of the recent financial crisis and economic recession, many parties have more pressing issues to deal with. U.S. companies have been working hard to cope with basic business and financial challenges, and public companies, particularly those in the financial services sector, face a plethora of regulatory changes from the Dodd-Frank Wall Street Reform and Consumer Protection Act (Dodd-Frank Act). They are understandably not looking forward to the prospect of significant changes in accounting and reporting requirements, whether as a result of the completion of major convergence projects or by the SEC deciding to either adopt or incorporate IFRS into our system.

The SEC has had scores of regulations to promulgate and studies to conduct under the Dodd-Frank Act and the Jumpstart our Business Startups (JOBS) Act of 2012. So addressing major challenges facing the U.S. financial reporting system, including recommendations of CIFiR and providing greater clarity about the path to the potential use of IFRS in the United States, may not be a priority for the SEC right now. Also, as I have previously discussed, there is a real need to continue the Conceptual Framework project to provide a better foundation for accounting standard setting, including dealing with the fundamental controversies surrounding the asset and liability view versus the revenue and expense view and with the controversial subject of measurement. There is also a need to get on with the FASB's disclosure framework project as part of the effort to make the information communicated in financial statements more relevant and understandable. However, the FASB and IASB clearly have very full plates right now, working hard to try to complete major convergence projects, so significant near-term progress on these fronts is very challenging.

For the future of private company financial reporting in the United States, I view this as a very significant and interesting public policy issue of national importance. My own experience and leanings suggest to me that we are better off continuing with a vertically integrated system of accounting standards and financial reporting between U.S. public and private companies. I believe our country has benefitted from having common accounting standards that, with a few differences for private companies and not-for-profit entities, apply across the system. As an economist might say, this approach would seem to result in significant network externalities (for example, in the education and training of accountants and in the use of accounting information by capital providers and financial analysts). Also, there could be important implications on capital formation in the United States if we were to have very different accounting and financial reporting for public companies and private companies.

However, consistent with the recommendations of the BRP and the October 2011 FAF proposal, the new PCC structure and process adopted by the FAF trustees in May 2012, and the FRF for SMEs that the AICPA is developing, I also believe there are more opportunities for justified differences in accounting standards and disclosure requirements for private companies to better address differences in user needs and cost-benefit considerations. During my years at the FASB, we attempted to build mechanisms and processes to better gather input from constituents in private company financial reporting and to evaluate potential differences in standards, but those clearly fell short of the expectations of many private company stakeholders. So, as previously noted, the new PCC structure and process offers the prospect of a better solution to this long-standing and important issue. We will see whether that new PCC structure plus the new FRF for SMEs that the AICPA is developing will provide a comprehensive, satisfactory, and durable resolution of this issue.

Conclusion

These are all complex and interrelated issues whose resolution will determine the future of accounting standards and standard setting in the United States, with potentially significant ramifications for our financial reporting system, capital markets, and economy. The work of the SEC staff in considering whether, how, and when to incorporate IFRS into the U.S. public company reporting system and the new PCC/FASB/FAF and AICPA FRF for SMEs standards and processes for private company accounting standard setting and reporting are critical components of this journey.

Because the issues are interrelated, I believe there needs to be close coordination by all the relevant parties to ensure that the end result is accounting standard setting and financial reporting that work effectively for our country. I can see some danger that we could be heading toward a rather complex and fragmented system of financial reporting in this country, with foreign companies listed on our stock exchanges and, perhaps, some U.S. companies reporting under full IFRS; all or most U.S. public companies reporting under U.S. GAAP that, over time, may incorporate more and more IFRS; some private companies reporting under U.S. GAAP for private companies that, over time, contains a growing number of differences with the standards used by public companies; and other private companies reporting using the AICPA-developed FRF-SME that could also be quite different than the U.S. GAAP standards used by other private companies.

So, although there might be a certain richness to such a system that allows for differential financial reporting that may better fit different segments of the market, it also carries with it the potential for increased complexity and confusion and higher overall system-wide costs. I believe we need to proceed carefully with eyes wide open about the potential benefits, risks, and costs of having a multitiered financial reporting system.

I also believe we must continue to seek ways to reduce the overall complexity and enhance the effectiveness of communication in public company financial reports and that, although we have made progress toward these goals, there is still much to do. In that regard, I believe that resolving some of the long-standing, crosscutting conceptual issues in accounting standard setting, continuing to move toward more principles-based or objectives-oriented accounting standards, developing a disclosure framework, formalizing and promulgating the professional judgment framework advocated by CIFiR, and continuing to harness the power of technology in financial reporting all provide significant opportunities to make meaningful progress toward reducing complexity and improving the overall relevance and usability of reported financial information. From my own experience as an accounting standard setter and my decades of working in financial reporting, I can certainly attest to the challenges in making progress along these fronts. It takes vision, leadership, a sense of direction, and willingness by stakeholders in the system to change. Without change, there can be no progress and we will continue to confront these issues over and over again.

However, we must also be careful in making such changes to ensure that our reporting system continues to meet the needs of participants in our capital markets and business community for relevant, timely, understandable, and trustworthy financial information.

Chapter 7: Looking Back and Moving Forward

> Robert Herz has had a more interesting career than any accountant deserves.[1]

As I write this, it is now over two years since I retired from the FASB on September 30, 2010. In some ways, that marked the end of a major chapter in my career and life. For many years, much of my work (and life) revolved around accounting, auditing, and financial reporting issues and related policy matters: as the senior technical partner of Coopers & Lybrand (C&L) and PricewaterhouseCoopers (PwC), leading and serving on various professional committees and groups, as an accounting standard setter on the Emerging Issues Task Force (EITF) and the International Accounting Standards Board (IASB), and as Chairman of the FASB.

Looking back, overall, it was wonderful—demanding but interesting and engaging, full of opportunities and challenges, working with terrific colleagues, and personally very satisfying. An article in *The Economist* on September 30, 2010, on my years at the FASB quipped, "Robert Herz has had a more interesting career than any accountant deserves." Perhaps so, but the time had come to move on, and I was looking forward to a change and, most of all, being able to spend more time with my family. I explained my thinking in the following question and answer session with Mary-Jo Kranacher of *The CPA Journal*:[2]

---

[1] "Beancounter there, done that," *The Economist*, 30 September 2010.
[2] Mary-Jo Kranacher, "Recollections on Standard Setting, Convergence, and Crisis: An Interview with Former FASB Chair Robert H. Hertz," *The CPA Journal*, February 2011.

Accounting Changes: Chronicles of Convergence, Crisis, and Complexity

The CPA Journal: First, let's get the 800-pound gorilla out of the room: Some people were surprised by your sudden departure from FASB, especially given FASB's full agenda and the sensitive timing for IFRS convergence efforts. Why did you choose this time to leave?

Robert H. Herz: Well, the FASB agenda has been very full since the first day I started there—or even before, with the Enron and WorldCom scandals, and of course with the big spotlight on financial reporting my first month at the FASB, during which the Sarbanes-Oxley Act took shape and was quickly passed. The agenda has been very full throughout my eight-plus years as chairman of the FASB. Certainly, it was really full during the financial crisis, and we had to vigorously respond to a number of reporting issues that emanated from that. And the successful completion of the Codification marked an important milestone. It was time to move on. To put it in perspective, I was at the FASB as chairman for more than eight years and before that I was a member of the International Accounting Standards Board. Together, that was just about a decade of accounting standards setting. That's not counting the years I was on the Emerging Issues Task Force, chairman of the AICPA SEC Regulations Committee, chairman of the IFAC Transnational Auditors Committee, or a member of the FASB Financial Instruments Task Force from the late 1980s on. So, it's been 20-plus years that I have been involved in standards setting. It's been a wonderful experience, particularly the years at FASB and the IASB—two very good organizations with terrific people working on a very important mission. But I'm looking forward to different challenges and new experiences in life.

As I have discussed in this book, over my career and, in particular, during the last decade, there have been significant developments and changes in the financial reporting landscape, both in the United States and globally. In terms of accounting standards, the objectives of improvement and international convergence have been the driving forces behind many of the changes. Responses to reporting issues emanating from, and revealed by, crises and breakdowns in the financial system have also been an important source of change in accounting standards and in broader aspects of the environment in which financial reporting occurs.

I feel privileged to have been an active participant in these developments. They gave me a deep appreciation for the dynamics of our capital markets and the broader financial system and for the many, often complex, challenges that policymakers face. It also reinforced for me the fundamental importance of sound accounting and reporting and transparency across the financial system to help foster the health and vibrancy of our capital markets and economy.

Chapter 7: Looking Back and Moving Forward

I also count myself very fortunate to have been able to work with many talented and dedicated professionals and to have met many interesting people, not only during my years as an accounting standard setter but throughout my career. That starts with the people I have worked with the closest, who, over much of the last decade, were my fellow FASB and IASB Board members and the terrific members of our staffs, but also extends to many others who served as trustees of the Financial Accounting Foundation (FAF) and International Financial Reporting Standards (IFRS) Foundation, members of our various standard-setting advisory groups, and countless others who contribute to the accounting standard-setting process. I had the privilege to work with many at the SEC, including several SEC chairmen and chief accountants, members and staff of the PCAOB, several U.S. Treasury secretaries and their staff, senior officials at the banking regulatory agencies and the IRS, many members of Congress and their staffs, and many investors and other users of financial information, financial executives, and public accountants. The increasingly international aspect of our work also enabled me to work with and meet many very interesting people from around the world, including those at other major national accounting standard setters, foreign governments, and international organizations.

Ultimately, it is the people I have met and worked with that I think I will remember most about my years in the accounting profession and as a standard setter. As has been my good fortune throughout my career, I count many of these people as friends.

I suspect those who know me well would be very surprised if I did not end this book with some overall thoughts about my years in accounting standard setting and recommendations on the future of accounting standards and financial and corporate reporting. Indeed, in the time since I have left the FASB, I have been interviewed several times and have, through public speaking engagements and other venues, met with many people who seem genuinely interested in my thoughts on these matters. One such interview from October 2010 can be found in exhibit 7-1. The questions I seem to be asked most frequently include the following:

- What do you think were the most important accomplishments during your tenure as Chairman of the FASB?
- What were your biggest disappointments, regrets, and mistakes?
- What advice would you give to your successors and other key players in accounting standard setting and financial reporting?
- What are you doing now, and does that include staying involved in accounting standard setting and financial reporting?"

Let me try to answer these questions. In doing so, I will try to be brief, so my answers will reflect those matters that seem the most significant to me as I look back and as I contemplate the future.

Exhibit 7-1: Alix Stuart. "After Eight Years at FASB, Herz Looks Back," *CFO.com*, 4 October, 2010. www.cfo.com/article.cfm/14528858/c_14529070.

On September 30, Robert Herz stepped down as Chairman of the Financial Accounting Standards Board, leaving board member Leslie Seidman as acting Chairman. Neither FASB nor Herz would comment on why he retired after more than eight years in the job, but it probably wasn't due to any lack of popularity. Nearly all of those who worked with the 57-year-old Herz commend his blend of intellect and calm. Herz has done a "terrific job," says Dennis Beresford, accounting professor at the University of Georgia's J.M. Tull School of Business and a former FASB Chairman himself. "He's dealt with tough issues and tough board members—not all of them are easy to work with—and he's been able to get the board to resolve some very difficult issues."

"I don't think there was ever a raised voice when Bob spoke," says Mark Ellis, CFO of luxury goods retailer Michael C. Fina and a six-year veteran of the FASB small business advisory committee. "He truly had the intellect to understand both sides of an argument and explain the reasoning behind decisions made that both sides would understand and appreciate."

In an exclusive interview with *CFO*, conducted via e-mail, Herz reflected back on his tenure at FASB and speculated about his future. The following is an edited version of the interview.

As you look back over your years at FASB, what do you think is your legacy?

I can point to the scores of pronouncements we issued, but I'm also very proud of many other things we did over the last eight years to improve accounting standard-setting. Those included rationalizing the standard-setting structure in our country so that most pronouncements now come out from the FASB versus the four-legged stool of the FASB, AICPA, EITF, and SEC before. I'm also very proud of the codification effort, which has [created] a much better organized and more accessible set of U.S. GAAP literature.

We also significantly broadened our outreach to various constituencies through new advisory groups with investors and with small business and private companies. We strengthened our staff ... and we stepped up our involvement with the accounting academic community by reinstituting an accounting academic fellowship program and through our Financial Accounting Standards Research Initiative.

We also did things to make the process more transparent and open, including making our standards available on the Web free of charge and audiocasting our meetings for free on the Web. Finally, and very importantly, there has been the whole international convergence effort.

Which accounting pronouncement made the greatest single improvement to the accounting literature during your tenure?

It's hard to single out any particular one. [One] example of what I think was [a] good and interesting pronouncement [is] Statement 157. Before that standard there were many different definitions and approaches to fair value measurements. What that standard did was to provide a common definition of fair value, how to approach it in different circumstances, and standardized disclosures around fair value measurements included in the financial statements.

The second standard I'd mention is Statement 167, which is the recent changes to the guidance on consolidation of variable interest entities. What I like about that particular pronouncement is that it sets out clear principles and then provides a good set of implementation guidance, particularly in the form of examples.

When comparing U.S. generally accepted accounting principles and international financial reporting standards, it seems as though some rules will be impossible to converge, such as those that pertain to LIFO inventory accounting and revaluation of property, plant, and equipment [PP&E], among others.

There are a number of specific continuing differences between U.S. GAAP and IFRS that do pose challenges ... but I believe that with continued [cooperation], solutions can be found. Sometimes the solutions may not just involve accounting answers. For example, in the case of LIFO inventory, the IRS is aware of this issue, and one solution might involve changes to the tax code. Regarding the revaluation of PP&E, FASB is now looking at the use of fair value for investment properties.

In 2003, you stated that FASB's implementation of fair-value standards wouldn't outstrip the ability of people to properly implement the concept. In hindsight, considering the liquidity crisis of 2008, do you think FASB met this challenge?

Just as many other parties did during the financial crisis, I'd [note] that we didn't have an existing playbook for what many termed an "unprecedented" crisis. Nevertheless, I believe we dealt pretty vigorously with issuing guidance on how to deal with the challenges of fair-value measurements and impairments of financial assets.

You spent quite a lot of time on the hot seat before Congress, especially during the crisis. Would you say that during your tenure things got better, worse, or remained unchanged with respect to political influence over accounting standards and the independence of FASB?

While I was certainly on the proverbial hot seat during the financial crisis...I actually appeared many more times in front of Congress during the debate on accounting for stock options a number of years ago. I feel that things have gotten a little bit better over the last eight years. I believe that, overall, there's been respect for our due process and the importance of it remaining thorough, objective, and as unbiased as possible.

What was the toughest battle you had to face?

I don't like using the word "battle," but the most challenging situation in terms of trying to improve the accounting in an important area related to accounting for employee stock options, in 2003-2005. Members of the high technology and venture capital communities strongly opposed our proposal to require the recording of compensation expense related to the granting of executive and employee stock options. They had many lobbyists and PR firms. It got so far as the House passing a bill that would have effectively blocked the expensing of stock options.

Fortunately, we also had very strong support from a number of quarters for making the accounting change. In the end, we were able to make that needed change, which was an important outcome for financial reporting.

Under current GAAP, there are individual revenue-recognition accounting rules for about 25 different industries. The joint FASB-IASB revenue-recognition exposure draft [ED] standardizes many of those rules. Still, with 25 industries arguing that they need specialized rules, how likely is the ED to remain in its current form?

I think the ED provides a good basis for a broad standard on revenue recognition. During the development of the ED, we and the IASB held a number of workshops with companies from around the world to beta-test a variety of different transactions and arrangements across different industries. [We wanted] to understand whether the model could be applied, and I think we generally found that it could.

That's not to say that the exposure draft is perfect. Some challenging issues revolve around the definition of transfer of control, because that's key to revenue recognition under the proposed model. [Another challenge is] around the cost side of the accounting, because we decided it

Chapter 7: Looking Back and Moving Forward

was important to address the related costs in order to properly portray profit margins.

There are a few industries we've heard from for which the proposed model poses some challenges. And we've heard from some users that follow software companies that the model may provide for too much accelerated revenue recognition. But those are the types of things the boards will deal with in redeliberations.

Regarding lease accounting, do you think that in your lifetime that FASB will achieve Sir David Tweedie's goal of flying on an airplane that's on the balance sheet of the airline that owns it?

I think the answer is yes. We recently put out jointly with the IASB an exposure draft on lease accounting. Under the so-called right-of-use model proposed in the ED, the right to use the equipment—in this case the airplane—for a period of time would be shown as an asset, and a corresponding liability would be recorded for the present value of payments that are to be paid for that right of use.

I think that is a good approach, but again it's out for comment, and the boards will benefit from the comments they receive and will carefully consider those comments in redeliberations.

If you look ahead five years, do you see U.S. accounting standards converged with the rest of the world's?

That's hard to predict. The SEC staff are currently working their way through a systematic work plan to look at a variety of issues relating to potential incorporation of IFRS into our reporting system. When they've completed that work plan, they will be able to go to the commission with recommendations on whether, when, and how to proceed regarding IFRS for U.S. public companies. In the meantime, I believe it's up to the two boards to continue to work together toward developing standards that foster both convergence and improvement in reporting.

Do you have any plans to rejoin the IASB?

Well, I very much enjoyed my time on the IASB, and I have very much enjoyed working with our colleagues at the IASB. But right now I'm looking forward to new experiences and challenges. I'm 57, and as I look at people I admire, like Paul Volcker and Bill Donaldson, I see that they've contributed in many different ways over their distinguished careers.

So, while I certainly wouldn't rule out returning to accounting standard-setting at some point, right now I'm looking forward to doing new things. I'd like to do a bit of teaching, I'd like to serve on some corporate boards, and I already have been involved with some not-for-profit activities. And I also hope to find ways to continue to contribute to financial reporting, the capital markets, and the public interest.

Proud Accomplishments

I suppose just about everyone who undertakes public service does so from a desire to contribute to the public good—to help make things better. Certainly, that was my reason for spending what has been a sizeable chunk of my career and life in accounting standard setting and related activities involving financial reporting. I consider accounting and financial reporting to be a very important part of the fabric of the capital markets, financial system, and economy.

As I said in a speech at the AICPA 2002 National Conference on Current SEC Developments shortly after becoming Chairman of the FASB,

> Throughout my own career as an accountant, I have believed passionately in the importance of accounting and good financial and corporate reporting to the overall soundness of our capital markets.... It matters! Reporting is a bit like the air we breathe ... as long as it's clean, we kind of take it for granted. But bad reporting, misleading reporting, and fraudulent reporting is like dirty air. It pollutes and clouds—it threatens the health of all those around it and makes people want to stay away from the polluted area.

In the same speech, I outlined some of my thoughts about the elements of sound reporting and key challenges facing the reporting system:

> And, we must regard reporting as an exercise in communication—good communication about performance, financial condition, prospects, and uncertainties and not as, on the one hand, an exercise in mere compliance or, on the other hand, an opportunity to spin, to paint a picture that is more flattering and appealing than the underlying reality. It means reporting that meets the needs of investors and other key users, that is operational, and that faithfully reflects the underlying business and economic realities. It means reporting that satisfies the key qualitative characteristics described in the FASB Conceptual Framework—relevance, reliability, neutrality, timeliness, and understandability. In an era of continuing globalization of business and capital markets, I think it means financial reporting that is comparable across borders. And I think it means looking for ways to modernize and upgrade the whole reporting model to replace some of the traditional but perhaps seldom used information with more meaningful information on cash flows, on key performance indicators and business value drivers

Chapter 7: Looking Back and Moving Forward

and to better harness the power of technology in the reporting and data analyses processes.

These are lofty and, I believe, enduring goals. In assuming the role of Chairman of the FASB, particularly at a moment in history when U.S. financial reporting was in the spotlight and being criticized, I felt both responsible and empowered to try to make forward progress toward these goals, knowing full well it would take a lot of hard work and, most importantly, a team effort involving my fellow Board members and our staff, the support of our trustees and colleagues at the SEC, and many, many other stakeholders in the financial reporting system. In chapter 2, "Charting Course," I discussed how we went about charting a course to try to bring about improvement in accounting standards and the standard-setting process, simplification of the U.S. standard-setting structure and codification of the U.S. GAAP literature, and international convergence.

So, a decade later, where are we in achieving those objectives and in making progress toward the kind of reporting system envisioned in my 2002 speech? By "we," I do not mean just the FASB but everyone with a stake in the financial reporting system. The mission and role of FASB, as important as it is, is limited to the realm of accounting and financial reporting standards, but many other organizations have key roles in the financial reporting supply chain.

Overall, I believe we collectively made significant progress in some areas but not in others. Certainly, through the spread of IFRS around the world and ongoing convergence efforts in major countries, including the United States, we have seen significant progress in achieving greater comparability of reported financial information across the global capital markets. Although we have a way to go, the vision of common, high-quality international accounting standards is, I believe, much closer to becoming a reality than it was one decade ago.

Very importantly, I also believe that new accounting standards and disclosure requirements in important areas have improved the overall relevance and transparency of reported financial information. There have been major new accounting standards on business combinations, employee stock compensation, consolidation of variable interest entities, fair value measurements, and pension and other postretirement obligations, and major new standards on revenue recognition and lease accounting are expected in the near future. There are richer disclosures in areas of particular interest to professional investors and financial analysts, perhaps most notably with respect to derivatives and other financial instruments and involvements with special purpose entities and other off-balance sheet arrangements.

I believe both the FASB and IASB have made important improvements in their standard-setting processes, including expanding and enhancing their outreach activities to stakeholders on proposals and emerging issues. I take considerable pride in the many steps we took to proactively increase and broaden the input that FASB receives from investors and other users of financial information. If imitation is the sincerest form of flattery, then the FASB should feel flattered that the IASB, SEC, and PCAOB also established investor advisory groups. As well, I take great pride in our successful effort to develop the FASB *Accounting Standards Codification*™, which I believe was a major step forward in improving the overall usability of the U.S. GAAP literature. We have also seen progress on using technology in financial reporting through the development and use of eXtensible Business Reporting Language (XBRL).

Although not the subject matter of most of this book, I believe the SEC and the PCAOB have made significant progress in their areas of responsibility relating to the financial reporting system. To their credit, I believe that companies and audit committees have also worked hard to improve the quality of their financial reports, communications with investors, and internal controls over financial reporting. Audit quality has clearly improved from the days before Sarbanes-Oxley.

Perhaps most importantly and notwithstanding the criticisms by some of accounting, auditing, and financial reporting relating to the recent financial crisis, the collective result of all these efforts is that overall public confidence in reported financial information seems to be higher now than it was after the reporting scandals of 2001–02:

> This year's results suggest that confidence about domestic markets may have stabilized and perhaps even begun to rebound. In 2012, investors' confidence in U.S. capital markets increased four percentage points, to 65 percent, after declining or remaining static every year since 2008. Investors' ratings on two other key metrics—confidence in investing in U.S. companies and confidence in audited financial information—remained steady at 71 percent and 69 percent, respectively.[3]

With respect to maintaining confidence in financial reporting, I take pride that we, with the strong support from the FAF trustees and many other parties, were able to maintain the independence and integrity of accounting standard setting in the United States in the face of what were, on occasion, strong attempts to interfere with it through political means.

So, overall, I believe we have seen forward progress and the financial reporting system is in a better place now than it was one decade ago, both in the United States and internationally.

---

[3] Center for Audit Quality, "Main Street Investor Survey," September 2012. www.thecaq.org/newsroom/pdfs/2012MainStreetInvestorSurvey.pdf.

Opportunities for Further Improvement

Even in the areas where progress has been made, there is clearly still much to do in achieving the goal of common high-quality accounting standards around of the world, improving the relevance and overall usefulness of reported financial information and making it less complex and more understandable, achieving greater consistency across the global capital markets in the implementation of accounting standards and the quality of auditing, corporate governance, and regulatory oversight and enforcement of reported financial information, and in more fully harnessing the power of technology in financial reporting. All of these are works in process that I hope will continue to be pursued with focus and vigor.

In some important areas relating to the reporting system, I don't believe there has been much progress during the past decade, including making financial statements less complex and more understandable and expanding corporate reporting to systematically include critical information on key nonfinancial performance indicators, business value drivers, risks, and uncertainties. However, in all fairness to me and my colleagues at the FASB and IASB, the expansion of financial reporting to encompass key nonfinancial information was generally beyond our reach. Nonetheless, this type of information is critical to enhancing the wider realm of corporate reporting. What is in the purview of accounting standard setters, however, is helping to make financial statements more understandable and less complex. With respect to that topic and as discussed in chapter 6, "Complexity," the disclosure framework project of the FASB offers a real opportunity to make meaningful progress.

Similarly, although we have seen a marked and an important increase, particularly outside the United States, in the number of companies providing information on the environmental and social impacts of their activities through triple bottom line, sustainability, and corporate social responsibility reports that are based on the Global Reporting Initiative (GRI) Framework or AccountAbility AA1000 standards, I believe there are significant opportunities to broaden the extent of reporting of such information and to make it more consistent, credible, and effective.

Despite the growing use of XBRL in financial and regulatory reporting around the world, overall, there has been relatively slow progress in using the power of technology to advance financial reporting when compared with many other products and aspects of modern life.

So, the dreamer in me continues to envision a future in which we have a common corporate reporting system for listed companies and other publicly accountable entities that spans the major global capital markets and that, using technology, provides high-quality financial and nonfinancial information on corporate activities in a systematic, consistent, understandable, and timely manner. Imagine a global reporting system in which, for any listed company in the world, you can quickly access consistently prepared, comparable, and understandable financial and key nonfinancial performance information. In short, I continue to believe there are significant opportunities to improve the overall usefulness and usability of financial statements and broader corporate reporting as products in the marketplace.

Many will say, with some justification, that this was an unrealistic vision one decade ago and remains so today, and I concede that the challenges and barriers to achieving such a system are formidable. Yet, I believe that powerful geoeconomic, geopolitical, and global environmental, technological, and social forces have been driving, and will continue to drive, corporate reporting in these directions. The ongoing work of the International Integrated Reporting Council reflects these forces and themes.

Regarding my own leadership of and contributions to the FASB and to broader developments in financial reporting, I look back on these with an overall sense of pride. These were summed up in the FAF's *2010 Annual Report* by FAF Chairman Jack Brennan and FAF President and CEO Terri Polley who wrote,

> Bob's vision, leadership, and strong commitment to the goal of improving and converging accounting standards for the benefit of the global and US capital markets brought the FASB to a new level of excellence. His tenure at the FASB set the direction for the future of financial reporting, and we thank him for his leadership and considerable contributions to the organization and its mission during a critical period in the history of the US capital markets. We will always be grateful for his strong leadership of the FASB.

Commenting in the October 1, 2010, CFO.com article "Herz Closes the Books on FASB Tenure," Arnie Hanish, corporate controller at Eli Lilly, said I had "done a really fine job over the past eight years in leading FASB through a challenging period." Mark Ellis, CFO of Michael C. Fina and a member of the FASB's Small Business Advisory Committee said "Part of [Herz's] legacy is that FASB is [now] such a vibrant organization and that the other members share Bob's intellect and vision." I appreciate those kind words and those of many others concerning my years at the FASB.

Some Regrets, Mistakes, and Disappointments

That's not to say that I do not also have some regrets and some areas of disappointment as I look back. As the Frank Sinatra song "My Way" goes, "Regrets, I've had a few," and I made plenty of mistakes. So what, given the chance, would I try to do over? A few things quickly spring to mind, which I have already alluded to in prior chapters. The first and, I believe, most important is that I regret our not having made more progress in our joint project with the IASB to improve the Conceptual Framework. As I will discuss shortly in my recommendations to those who continue in and will become involved in accounting standard setting in the future, I believe it is essential that the key cross-cutting conceptual issues that have challenged, and continue to challenge, accounting standard setters, be wrestled to the ground. Although not a panacea to resolve all accounting issues, I am convinced it is important for standard setters and the whole financial reporting system, both in the United States and internationally, that there be a more solid Conceptual Framework. Unfortunately but understandably, our experience was that in an era of having to respond to significant financial reporting issues from a very major financial crisis and with the push to complete projects in our Memorandum of Understanding (MoU) on international convergence, the important gave way to the urgent.

In terms of mistakes on my part, perhaps the most significant one was misjudging, in late 2009, the ability of the two boards to expedite progress on the many MoU projects by greatly increasing the number and frequency of joint meetings. As discussed chapter 4, "International Convergence," we did so in response to the September 2009 call from the G20 leaders to redouble our efforts to complete the convergence program by June 2011. This action was also consistent with the recommendations of our Financial Crisis Advisory Group and with the SEC's plan to make a decision in 2011 on the future of IFRS in the United States. Although I was not alone in expecting (or perhaps hoping) that this would enable us to make more rapid progress, as the leader of one of the two boards involved in this effort, I take responsibility for misjudging what was realistically achievable.

With respect to specific standard-setting decisions and actions, with the benefit of hindsight, I would probably try to do some over if I had a time machine. Probably the most important of these relates to the qualifying special purpose entity. Knowing what I know now about how the use of this device was sometimes stretched and became an important element in the growth of the "shadow" banking system leading up to the financial crisis, I certainly would have worked to eliminate it from the standards much earlier. As I said in chapter 5,

"The Financial Crisis," I think it, along with some other notable examples in the history of accounting standards, serves as an example of the perils of creating exceptions that grant highly coveted financial reporting outcomes. Similarly and also with the benefit of hindsight, I wish we had accomplished before the onset of the financial crisis the changes we made in 2009 to the model for consolidation of variable interest entities.

Changes in Financial Reporting—A Challenging but Necessary Process

Accounting and reporting are no different from other aspects of human endeavor; they are all subject to the natural laws of change. I believe that history teaches us that it is important to adapt and move forward or risk becoming irrelevant. Certainly, throughout the last 80 years or so, our reporting system has been subject to many changes that were made in response to changes in the economy and modes of business and finance, changes that may have been strongly opposed at the time but that now, with the benefit of hindsight, most people would view as progress. For example, before the 1930s, many public companies did not report sales and cost of sales information, viewing that as highly proprietary information. Segment reporting was not common or mandatory until the 1970s. For more than 15 years FASB endeavored to develop and put into place improved standards on measuring and reporting obligations and costs relating to defined benefit pension and other postemployment benefits (OPEBs). This effort was protracted and strongly opposed by major auto and other industrial companies that argued the liabilities were not real or too soft to include in financial statements. Indeed, the September 1989 issue of *Business Week* captured the firestorm over FASB's proposal on OPEBs in the article "First Thing We Do is Kill All the Accountants":

> Some time in October, a little-understood group in Norwalk, Conn., will do something that could knock at least 25% off the annual profits of big industrial companies. It may also wipe out one-third of the net worth of all of Corporate America. This is no crazed band of financial guerrillas. This is the green-eyeshade crowd at FASB—the Financial Accounting Standards Board. And all it's really trying to do is to get companies to 'fess up to what they are likely to owe for retiree health benefits. The likely sum is more than a trillion—that's with a T—dollars.[4]

Yet, some 20 years later, I think most people would agree that the pension and OPEB liabilities were quite real and very significant in

---

[4] James R. Norman and Susan Garland, "First Thing We Do Is Kill All the Accountants," *Business Week*, 12 September 1988.

evaluating the long-term prospects and viability of the very companies that argued most vociferously against the accounting changes.

I have chronicled some of the major changes that have occurred in accounting and reporting over the past decade, some of which were quite contentious. Further significant changes in accounting standards and other areas relating to financial reporting are in the works, including new major accounting standards resulting from the FASB-IASB projects, new auditing standards from the PCAOB, the use of XBRL and new technologies in the financial reporting process, and the potential movement to more integrated reporting that addresses a company's performance and prospects across broader financial, nonfinancial, environmental, social, and governance dimensions.

In short, as the worlds of business and finance change, accounting and reporting has needed and will need to continue to evolve to properly reflect these changes. Changes will continue to be made in response to identified problems and shortcomings in financial reporting. Moreover, controversy often accompanies change, both because change can be uncomfortable and disruptive and because those attempting to fend off or delay change often have a vested interest in maintaining the status quo.

That is not to say that all changes proposed by policymakers, including regulators and standard setters, are worthwhile or needed. Certainly, that is not the case. As Winston Churchill said, "There is nothing wrong with change, if it is in the right direction." That's why having a thorough, open, and objective standard-setting process that includes obtaining and carefully considering relevant input on the likely and potential costs, benefits, and unintended consequences of proposed changes is important. An effective system for postimplementation review of major standards, rules, and regulations and mechanisms for surfacing and addressing emerging issues are also important to help ensure that the financial reporting system progresses in the right direction.

However, the due process should not be so excessive that it unduly delays needed improvements in financial reporting. As I noted in chapter 2, the FASB has been subject to criticism, particularly in times of crisis, for being too slow to address issues and improve accounting in key areas. The word *glacial* has sometimes been used by critics to describe what they perceive as an unacceptably slow pace of the FASB (as well as the IASB and other accounting standard setters). For example, in the wake of the Enron scandal, the cover story of the November 25, 2001, issue of *BusinessWeek* commented, "The pace of change at FASB tends to be glacial.... The slow pace means the standard-setters sometimes fail to react to sudden changes in the market."[5] Similarly, as noted in chapter 5, we were criticized by some during the financial crisis for not having responded quickly enough to certain reporting issues. In some cases these criticisms came from the same people who, in other instances, argue that the FASB, IASB, or both, are moving too quickly and that added due process, including extensive field tests, are needed before finalizing changes in accounting standards, changes that may be favored by and viewed as overdue by investors.

Finding the right balance is not easy. Narrower issues and practice problems can be addressed more rapidly, but on major projects that involve potentially pervasive changes to the existing standards, extensive due process is usually needed in order to confirm the overall soundness and cost-benefit of proposed changes in standards. But that process should not seek to try to address every conceivable issue or guarantee ease of implementation of every aspect of a proposed new standard. To do so can unduly delay needed improvements in accounting standards and financial reporting. It can also result in introducing exceptions, compromises, and bright lines that add to the complexity of the standard and the resulting reporting and can dilute the overall effectiveness of a new standard. I share some of the concerns of people such as former FASB Vice Chairman David Mosso in his book *Early Warning and Quick Response: Accounting in the Twenty-first Century*. In chapter 7, "Standard Setting: Undue Process," Mosso discusses what he views as a number of fundamental problems with the current accounting standard-setting process, stating, "The first one is excessive due process. The present form of due process causes delay beyond reason—it takes far too long to complete a standard-setting project. Serious accounting practice problems fester for years while standard setters wrestle with constituents over what is the best way to solve them."

During my years at the FASB, I believe we were able to speed up addressing a number of issues. However, a number of major projects progressed more slowly, subject to extensive due process, and have continued to advance at a measured but deliberate pace since I left the FASB. Many probably view this as quite appropriate, especially on major projects that involve potentially very significant changes in financial reporting. However, some no doubt may view this as excessive due process and unacceptable delay in finalizing overdue improvements in key standards. In that respect, Mosso advocates the adoption of a wealth measurement model as the best way for accounting standard setting to escape what he characterizes in his book as the gargantuan maze of the current due process. I have some sympathy with Mosso's diagnosis and his proposed solution and believe it could

---

[5] Nanette Byrnes and David Henry, "Confused about Earning?" *BusinessWeek*, 25 November 2001.

improve both the process of accounting standard setting and the overall relevance of the resulting standards and financial reporting. However, experience suggests to me that such a change is unlikely to occur in the foreseeable future and that even if it were to occur, it would not provide a panacea to resolve all current and future accounting issues or fend off criticisms of the accounting standard-setting process. Nevertheless and as I have tried to emphasize many times in this book, I do believe there is a real need to get on with the effort to improve the Conceptual Framework.

Some Words of Advice to Colleagues and Successors

So, with the benefit of the lessons I have learned from my many years of involvement in accounting and financial reporting and with a belief that continuing changes and improvements are inevitable and necessary, what advice would I give to those now charged with these responsibilities? Again, those who know me well know that I have some strong views on certain matters regarding accounting standards and financial reporting. I have already discussed some of these in earlier chapters of this book and will not expound further on them. Rather, in the spirit of providing constructive input to those now charged with key roles in the financial reporting system, I will offer a few high-level suggestions recognizing full well that the world has moved on since my time in accounting and standard setting.

First, to my former colleagues at the FASB and IASB, keep going! There are plenty of opportunities to improve existing standards. It is important to complete the major MoU projects and to do them in a way that achieves convergence and genuine improvement in the standards. To me, that includes the projects on financial statement presentation and financial instruments with characteristics of equity. Some, if not many, of the types of changes that were being explored in the financial statement presentation project were supported by many users and the SEC Advisory Committee on Improvements to Financial Reporting (CIFiR). In my view, the issues that were being addressed in the project on accounting for financial instruments with characteristics of equity continue to plague financial reporting. So I strongly believe these projects need to continue to be pursued. If that takes a few more years, so be it. And I feel that other major areas, including accounting for income taxes and intangibles, also need improved and converged standards.

Now, I recognize that "the times they are a-changin," and beyond the completion of the current joint FASB-IASB projects on revenue recognition, lease accounting, financial instruments, and insurance contracts, there is likely to be a change in the way the two boards work together. I also understand that many stakeholders are coping with lots of other challenges and priorities. In my opinion, although those considerations may affect the mode and pace of standard setting, they do not and should not detract from the need to develop improved accounting standards on the other major areas previously cited.

Additionally and very importantly, consistent with my prior comments, I urge you to try to find ways to reenergize and complete the Conceptual Framework project. Fundamental conceptual issues and disagreements continue to hamper standard setting and financial reporting. One thought, certainly not a new one, would be to convene a separate group, like the Constitutional Congress that drafted the U.S. Constitution, to work on the project under the oversight of the boards. Such a group might comprise, for example, former FASB and IASB members, members of national accounting standard-setting boards, and senior representatives of key stakeholder groups.[6] I am glad that the FASB, together with other groups, is proceeding with the disclosure framework project that was started in 2009. Regardless of whether the United States moves to IFRS, this is a very important effort that is needed in order to better organize and streamline the financial statement footnotes, improve their content, make them more readable, and better facilitate the use of XBRL and other technologies.

To the commissioners of the SEC, I offer two bits of advice. First, with respect to the path forward to potential incorporation of IFRS into the U.S. reporting system, you need to provide clarity as soon as possible. The U.S. system should not have to "ride two horses" for an indefinite or a prolonged period, and the world is watching and waiting. Your staff has completed a comprehensive work plan and obtained extensive input that should provide a good basis for making decisions and assessing what actions are needed to deal with the issues that have been identified. The FAF has provided input and suggestions on a possible approach, and the staff of the IFRS Foundation has provided a thoughtful analysis of your staff's findings. Be clear in your decision. If it is to transition to IFRS, through, for example, an endorsement process, be clear on how and when this will occur and outline the process. If you believe actions are needed by the IASB, the IFRS Foundation, or others, be clear on what is expected. Whatever the path forward toward incorporation of IFRS into the U.S. reporting system, I still like the idea of setting forth a "blueprint" that clearly lays out the needed steps, milestones, and projected timelines. If the decision is not

---

[6] In that regard, and as noted in Chapter 4 on International Convergence, in September 2012 the IASB decided to restart work on the Conceptual Framework and has indicated that it intends to actively involve the new proposed Accounting Standards Advisory Forum in this effort. However, it is not clear whether the FASB will participate in this work, for example, through membership in the Accounting Standards Advisory Forum, or whether the FASB will at some point separately resume working on the Conceptual Framework project.

Chapter 7: Looking Back and Moving Forward

to move to or incorporate IFRS, be clear on that and how you see the U.S. financial reporting system moving forward and whether and how the U.S. will continue to participate in the development of IFRS and the international financial reporting system.

Second, to the SEC and its staff, continue to try to implement the major recommendations of CIFiR. A lot of hard work and worthwhile thought went into that effort. Of all the recommendations, the one I that believed should be acted on as soon as possible was establishing something akin to the Financial Reporting Forum envisioned by CIFiR. Therefore, I welcomed and applauded the creation of a Financial Reporting Series of periodic public roundtables by the SEC staff. These roundtables, similar to the recommendation of CIFiR, bring together representatives from the preparer, auditor, investor, and user communities with senior representatives of the SEC staff, FASB, and the PCAOB to, as stated in CIFiR's *Final Report of the Advisory Committee on Improvements to Financial Reporting to the United States Securities and Exchange Commission,* "discuss pressures in the financial reporting system overall, both immediate and long-term." I believe this type of ongoing forum can help bring issues to the surface in the reporting system more promptly and facilitate addressing them in a logical, coordinated, and effective way that will help provide overall strategic direction to the U.S. financial reporting system. It might also help the SEC, FASB, and the PCAOB decide whether and how best to address other key recommendations in the CIFiR report. These key recommendations include those relating to the judgment framework, continuing to harness the power of technology in financial reporting to make financial reports more understandable and useful, and expanding and enhancing the reporting of information on key performance indicators and elements of critical nonfinancial information.

To the IASB, their trustees, constituents of IFRS, and all who believe in a single set of high-quality global accounting standards, I say be patient with the United States. I recognize the frustration among some that the United States hasn't yet signed on to moving to IFRS. Please understand that without the United States, the system cannot be a truly global one. Also recognize that for the United States, which has long enjoyed a high-quality financial reporting system that has been an important component of our capital markets, a decision whether, when, and how to move to international standards is a very important public policy matter. I hope that you should not have to wait much longer to know where the United States stands and is headed.

To the trustees of the FAF, thanks for your service, and I wish you the wisdom of Solomon and the patience of Job in helping guide U.S. accounting standard setting through a challenging period. What you have decided for private company accounting standard setting and the

AICPA FRF for SMEs initiative, together with the SEC's decisions regarding IFRS, may determine not only the future role of the FASB but the direction of the whole U.S. financial reporting system for many years to come.

To the countless individuals and many organizations that spend time and effort supporting and participating in the accounting standard-setting process, I also say, "Thanks." Broad participation by stakeholders is a major strength of the U.S. accounting standard-setting process, one that has served as a model for standard setters around the world, including the IASB. My only words of advice: keep up the support, input, and participation. The FASB and IASB will need to continue to draw upon it in addressing the many continuing challenges they face. Your support is also essential to maintaining private-sector accounting standard setting that operates in an independent manner in the public interest in the face of what can sometimes be significant pressure from special interests and political bodies.

Finally, to everyone involved in the financial reporting system, I recognize that, collectively, we have been through a lot of change over the last decade and that the potential for further significant changes in accounting standards, disclosure requirements, and modes of delivery of financial and corporate information is not, very understandably, a thrilling prospect for many. However, I think it is fair to say that without change, there can be no progress. As Benjamin Franklin said, "When you're finished changing, you're finished." Jack Welch, former CEO of General Electric, put it more bluntly in a trailer for CNBC, "If you're stagnant, you're dead."

So, What Now, Bob?

When I left the FASB, my expectation was that I would continue to have opportunities to contribute to financial and corporate reporting, but as I previously explained, I was also very much looking forward to being able to do some new and different things. First, most importantly and consistent with my hopes and plans, I have been able to spend more time with Louise, our son Michael and his wife Heather, and our daughter Nicole and her husband Cameron. It's been wonderful.

In terms of other activities, I have had three primary criteria in deciding whether to take on a particular role. I have to view it as substantive and a worthwhile expenditure of my time. It has to be something I believe I will find interesting and enjoyable in terms of subject matter and the people I will be working with. I want it to be something in which I believe I can provide some value and also learn some new things. One of my first decisions after leaving FASB was to join the faculty of Columbia Business School. It's a part-time role that has me

Chapter 7: Looking Back and Moving Forward

giving some lectures, advising students on course material and career planning, and working with faculty on research projects, papers, and symposiums. It's invigorating and satisfying and connects me back to my dad, who grew up opposite the Columbia campus on the Upper West Side of Manhattan and was a proud graduate. It has also reunited me with Professors Trevor Harris and Stephen Penman, two of the six members of the accounting academic advisory committee we set up in the 1990s at C&L. (Katherine Schipper, who would later become my fellow FASB Board member, was also a member of that academic advisory committee.) I also continue to serve on the advisory board of the Manchester Business School in England.

I have also continued my not-for-profit activities as a trustee of the Kessler Foundation, one of the nation's largest foundations dedicated to medical research and grant-making in the areas related to rehabilitation of people disabled by severe brain trauma and spinal cord injuries. I have also joined various advisory boards and I am a senior adviser to some promising private companies, including one called WebFilings whose leading-edge, cloud-based product offering is very much in line with my view of making more and better use of technology in corporate reporting. It is a very good product and I work with terrific people there.

When I left the FASB, I was hoping to serve on the boards of a few major companies where my experience and skills might add value, so I was pleased in June 2011 to join the board of directors of Fannie Mae, an organization at the heart of the U.S. housing finance system and deeply involved in helping address the challenges currently facing many homeowners and the overall housing market and in the effort to build a strong, more stable housing finance system in this country. My fellow board members include Phil Laskawy, who chairs the board and who I worked with on the National Steering Committee when he was CEO of Ernst & Young. Phil served for many years on the IFRS Foundation so we also worked together while he was in that role. Also on the board was Denny Beresford (until March 2012), another former Chairman of FASB and whose wise counsel I sometimes sought in my years at FASB. Denny and I also worked together on CiFIR. Finally, David Sidwell, who I have known and worked with when he was at C&L, JP Morgan, Morgan Stanley, and as a fellow member of the EITF and CIFiR, also sits on the board.

I also was pleased to join the board of Morgan Stanley in July 2012. During my career in public accounting, I had extensive experience auditing securities and investment banking firms, including Goldman Sachs and Shearson Lehman Brothers, and worked frequently with investment bankers in my Corporate Finance Advisory Services role. Joining the Morgan Stanley board has also provided me with the opportunity to work again with my friend and former partner and colleague Don Nicolaisen. One of the wonderful things about getting older is being able to renew working relationships with past colleagues while also being able to meet and work with new people.

In the realm of financial and corporate reporting, I have been fortunate to have been sought out as a speaker at numerous conferences, something I have always enjoyed because it enables me to get out and meet with all sorts of people and groups around the country. I was appointed in 2012 to the Standing Advisory Group of the PCAOB, whose members include many former colleagues. I was pleased to be appointed to this group because I strongly believe that audit quality and public confidence in independent audits is absolutely critical to the proper functioning of the capital markets, the financial system, and the economy.

I am also a member of the Accounting Standards Oversight Council of Canada that oversees the establishment of accounting standards in Canada. That has reunited me with many colleagues. Trish O'Malley is a former colleague on the IASB. I worked with Paul Cherry at C&L and PwC and while Paul chaired the Accounting Standards Board of Canada, I chaired the FASB. Bob Muter, another colleague and friend from C&L and PwC, is also on this council. Canada adopted IFRS for its public company financial reporting starting in 2011 and has gone to separate "made in Canada" standards for private companies and not-for-profit entities. Thus, the Canadian experience may provide some important insights for, and a harbinger of, things to come in the U.S. financial reporting system. I continue as a member of the Financial Reporting Faculty Advisory Board of the Institute of Chartered Accountants in England and Wales. I also write a periodic column on financial reporting matters for *Compliance Week*.

It is always satisfying and uplifting to have one's career efforts and accomplishments recognized. While I was Chairman of the FASB, I was included on various annual lists of the top 100 people in accounting, finance, and corporate governance. Although flattering, I think a lot of that comes with the position, but I was proud and quite touched to be named an Outstanding Alumnus and to receive an honorary doctorate from my alma mater the University of Manchester in England. Soon after I left the FASB in 2010, I received the 2010 Berkeley Award for Distinguished Contributions to Financial Reporting from the Haas School of Business at the University of California Berkeley. In 2012, I was elected to the Accounting Hall of Fame as the 89th inductee into a group of leaders who helped shape the accounting profession and the development of accounting and auditing theory and practice over the past century.

Consistent with my continuing passion for trying to improve the broader realm of corporate reporting, I have become involved with a number of interesting and important initiatives, including what is known as integrated reporting. In July 2010, as Chairman of the FASB, I participated in the initial meeting in London of what was then called the International Integrated Reporting Committee (now the International Integrated Reporting Council [IIRC]). The IIRC was established by the Prince of Wales's Accounting for Sustainability Project (A4S) and the GRI and includes representatives from major international corporations, investor groups, nongovernmental organizations, global accounting firms, regulators, and accounting standard setters. The IIRC's mission is explained on its website as follows:

> At present a range of standard setters and regulatory bodies are responsible for individual elements of reporting. No single body has the oversight or authority to bring together the different elements that are essential to the presentation of an integrated picture of an organisation and the impact of environmental and social factors on its performance. Globalisation means that an accounting and reporting framework needs to be developed on an international basis.

In a nutshell, the vision is one of corporate reporting that brings together in an integrated fashion financial reporting, reporting on key nonfinancial performance indicators and value drivers, and reporting on a company's efforts and impacts relating to corporate responsibility and sustainable development.

This is very much in line with the next generation of corporate reporting we envisioned over a decade ago in *The ValueReporting Revolution: Moving Beyond the Earnings Game*, the book I coauthored. Not surprisingly, this and related efforts have reunited me with 2 of my coauthors on that book: Dr. Robert Eccles of Harvard and David Phillips of PwC. A primary task for the IIRC and its working groups has been to develop an overarching framework for integrated reporting and to develop a strategy and path forward for making it a reality. This involves a number of ongoing efforts, including a major pilot program with more than 80 companies from around the world, such as Coca Cola, Microsoft, and Prudential Financial from the United States, HSBC, Marks & Spencer, and Sainsbury from the United Kingdom, Volvo from Sweden, and Tata Steel from India. Also participating in the pilot program are approximately 25 organizations representing institutional investors from various parts of the world.

I have been dubbed an "ambassador" for the IIRC, and it has brought me in contact with many people involved in the burgeoning area of sustainability reporting, including those from the A4S project, the GRI, and AccountAbility, an international organization that establishes standards and provides solutions relating to corporate responsibility and sustainable development. I also serve on AccountAbility's Advisory Council. In addition, I serve on the Advisory Council of the recently established Sustainability Accounting Standards Board, which is developing industry-based standards for reporting on key environmental, social, and governance issues affecting corporate sustainability and whose board of directors is chaired by Dr. Robert Eccles. These activities have brought me in contact with many other organizations and individuals concerned with sustainability and the ongoing depletion and pollution of the world's natural capital of key and finite resources. Through these, I have become much more aware of the potential magnitude and severity of these threats to our ongoing economic, environmental, social, and planetary welfare; of the need for better measurement and reporting as part of the effort to address these critical issues; and of the challenges these issues can pose to the sustainability of individual business enterprises.

These issues and challenges were very forcefully explained by the Prince of Wales in his address to the A4S Forum he hosted on December 15, 2010, at St. James Palace in London:

> Experts tell me that though over a billion people have no ready access to drinkable water and live on less than a dollar a day, we are still consuming, every year, 50 percent more of the planet's natural resources than it can renew. In other words, we are living way beyond the Earth's means. My Accounting for Sustainability project was established to address this issue—to ensure that we are counting everything that counts and measuring everything that matters.... It is clearly a daunting task to value and price natural capital and to broaden our accounting information and reports to include environmental, social and governance factors, while at the same time making accounts simpler and more comprehensible. But it is a task which cannot be ignored or shirked.... Ladies and gentlemen, if I may say so, if governments, businesses, the accountancy profession, regulators and standard-setters do not address the present limitations in our accounting information and reports, then it will be the greatest accounting failure that the world has ever seen.... If we don't take the right decisions now, we will effectively lock our children and grandchildren into a very grim future and throw away the key.... Many people think that accounts and accountancy aren't important, but information is power. And it is the responsibility of accountants to provide the best systems and information so that acting with the long-tem in mind, and serving the best interests of communities and the environment, can also be seen to be the right financial approach.

In this book, I have chronicled what is now my almost 40 years in the accounting profession, from my early days as an articled clerk in England through my years as an auditor and the many other roles I had at Price Waterhouse, C&L, and PwC. I have also discussed my many involvements in professional activities, my years as an accounting standard setter, and the various roles and activities that now keep me

Chapter 7: Looking Back and Moving Forward

busy and engaged. During that period, there have been many changes in the accounting profession and in accounting, auditing, and financial reporting, and I have had the good fortune to have had a front row seat for many of these developments and the opportunity to be an active participant in helping shape some of them. Throughout, I have been proud to be the member of a profession that serves clients and the public interest with skill, knowledge, and objectivity. It has afforded me many opportunities to grow as a professional and person and instilled in me a deep belief in the importance of sound reporting to the proper functioning of capital markets and the economy. Moreover, it has also convinced me that what you measure and report matters—that it affects behavior, actions, and outcomes—and therefore, that it is critical that we measure and report on those things that do matter, in corporate reporting and beyond.

As one who has devoted a good bit of my career to better accounting and reporting and to an abiding belief in the power of transparency and that what you measure matters, the Prince's words ring true, and his call to action demand attention. I am not a "tree hugger" or an environmental activist, just a citizen of this planet concerned about the welfare of future generations. So, as someone with a passion for helping bring about positive changes in accounting and reporting, the realm of integrated reporting and accounting for sustainability represents a new frontier of accounting changes.

People Mentioned in This Book

Abahoonie, Ed
Ackerman, Gary
Allen, Chris
Allen, George
Allen, Tom
Alusik, John
Ameen, Phil
Anderson, Kristofer
Anderson, Rick
Angelides, Phil
Arnold, John
Atkinson, Billy M.
Attmore, Bob
Bachus III, Spencer
Bahnson, Paul R.
Baird, Erica
Baird, Rich
Barker, Holly
Barth, Mary

Batavick, George
Baugh, Ernest
Bazaar, Harvey
Bean, David
Beier, Ray
Beller, Alan
Bement, Ken
Beresford, Denny
Bernstein, Aaron
Beswick, Paul
Bhave, Bob
Bielstein, Suzanne
Bies, Susan
Bishop, John
Blackman, Elaine
Blasi, Joseph R.
Bloomberg, Michael
Boris, Charry
Bossio, Ron

Accounting Changes: Chronicles of Convergence, Crisis, and Complexity

Boxer, Barbara	Defliese, Phil
Breeden, Richard	Delves, Donald
Brennan, John (Jack)	Denham, Robert
Brinkman, Jeff	Derrick, Steve
Brodish, Jay	DeSantis, Bob
Brody, Janet	Dever, Ray
Bruns, Hans-Georg	DiMaggio, Joe
Buck, Daryl	Dimon, Jamie
Buffett, Warren	DiPiazza, Sam
Bullen, Halsey	Dirks, John
Cafini, Regina	Dittmar, Nelson
Cappiello, Nick	Doerr, John
Carnall, Wayne	Donaldson, William
Carney, Gerard	Donoghue, Pat
Carsberg, Bryan	Dottori, Jodi
Cassel, Jules	Doty, James
Cherry, Paul	Dreibelbis, John
Chookaszian, Dennis	Durbin, Dick
Cintron, Ginny	Eccles, Robert
Clements, Phil	Ellis, Mark
Cohen, Brett	Enzi, Michael
Cope, Anthony	Eshoo, Anna
Cosper, Susan	Ferrera, Laura
Cox, Christopher	Fitzgerald, Peter
Crooch, G. Michael	Fitzpatrick, Tom
Crowhurst, Ellen	Flegm, Eugene H.
Dakkduk, Ken	Foster, John (Neal)
Damico, Joe	Frank, Barney
Davis, Roger	Freedman, Gene
Day, Jack	Fritz, George
De Rynck, Stefan	Gabriele, Jane

People Mentioned in This Book

Garnett, Robert
Garrett, Michael
Gelard, Gilbert
Gerson, Jim
Getz, Steve
Gilbert, Gelard
Gingrich, Newt
Glotzer, Paul
Glynn, John
Godwin, Charles
Golden, Russell
Goldschmid, Harvey
Goodrich, David
Graul, Lee
Grayson, Alan
Green, Jim
Greenspan, Alan
Gribble, John
Groves, Ray
Guasp, Karen
Guerrette, Ron
Hand, Jeremy
Hanish, Arnie
Hannon, Neal
Harrington, Jim
Harris, Trevor
Hartig, Jay
Hauser, Jan
Heindel, Steve
Herdman, Bob
Herz, Heather

Herz, James
Herz, Louise
Herz, Michael
Herz, Nicole
Herz, Susan
Hewitt, Conrad
Hinchman, Grace
Hoey, Tom
Hollein, Marie
Hood, Phil
Hoogervorst, Hans
Hope, Tony
Hunt, Sr., Isaac
Hyudic, Mary
Ianieri, Linda
Immelt, Jeff
Inzano, Diane
Jaroszynski, Steve
Jenkins, Ed
Johns, Mike
Johnson, Jeff
Johnson, Manuel
Johnson, Todd
Jones, Sy
Jones, Thomas
Kalina, Bob
Kanjorski, Paul
Kaplan, Dave
Kawanishi, Nobu
Keegan, Dame Mary
Keeshan, Larry

Kelley, Jerry
Kessler, Stuart
Ketz, J. Edward
Kilcran, Michele
Kinney, Catherine
Kirk, Don
Klimek, Christine
Kosminoff, Karen
Kranacher, Mary-Jo
Krause, Ray
Kroeker, James
Kruse, Douglas L.
Kudlow, Lawrence
La Gambina, Joe
Lapolla, Patty
Laskawy, Phil
Leisenring, James
Levin, Carl
Levitt, Jr., Arthur
Linsmeier, Thomas
Lis, Steve
Logan, Scott
Lott, Ronald
Lucas, Frank
Lusniak, Vickie
MacDonald, Linda
Mahoney, Jeff
Marshall, Ken
Matherne, Louis
McCain, John
McCreevy, Charlie

McDonnell, Pat
McDonough, Bill
McGarity, Neal
McGregor, Warren
McLean, David
Mechanick, Jeffrey
Melancon, Barry
Menem, President, Carlos
Miller, Paul B. W.
Miller, Susan
Mills, Adrian
Mishley, Eileen
Monroe, Debby
Mooney, Bill
Mooney, Bob
Moore, Nick
Moran, Don
Moritz, Denise
Morris, David
Moscarello, Louis (Lou)
Moss, Leah
Moss, Stephen
Mosso, David
Muir, Rick
Murray, Ron
Muter, Bob
Nally, Dennis
Nicolaisen, Don
Nussbaum, Ed
Olson, Mark
O'Malley, Patricia (Trish)

People Mentioned in This Book

O'Reilly, Vin
Orenstein, Edith
Parsons, Jack
Paulson, Henry
Penman, Stephen
Perlmutter, Ed
Petrone, Kim
Phillips, David
Pitek, Ray
Pitt, Harvey
Pittu, Lisa
Plank, Roseann
Polley, Teresa (Terri)
Posta, Alicia
Pozen, Robert (Bob)
Prada, Michel
Proestakes, Peter
Quinn, Jim
Reed, Jack
Regan, Ned
Reich, Jules
Ricciardi, Walter
Richards, Brooke
Richter, J.R.
Roberge, Chris
Rogers, Doris
Rokakis, James
Romas, Joanne
Salamone, Denis
Sarbanes, Paul
Schapiro, Mary

Schieneman, Gary
Schipper, Katherine
Schiro, Jim
Schmid, Harry
Schneider, Herman
Schroeder, Hal
Schuetze, Walter
Schwab, Charles
Seidenstein, Tom
Seidman, Leslie
Shelby, Richard
Sidwell, David
Siegel, Marc
Simon, Art
Small, Roberta
Smith, Chandy
Smith, John
Smith, Lawrence
Solo, Judy
Solomon, Miriam
Spencer, Peter
Spindel, Fred
Steinberg, Rick
Stemberg, Tom
Stewart, Cameron
Stewart, John
Stoklosa, Kevin
Stolz, Dick
Storey, Reed K.
Storey, Sylvia
Strauss, Norman

Sullivan, Jenny	Walker, David
Sutay, Stacey	Wallace, Woody
Sutton, Michael	Wallison, Peter
Swieringa, Bob	Weil, Jonathan
Swift, Richard	Weinstock, Lawrence
Switter, Jill	Weltmann, Allen
Tanki, Frank	White, John
Tatore, Len	White, Rick
Taub, Scott	Whittington, Geoffrey
Tovey, Michael	Wilkins, Bob
Trott, Edward	Wilks, Jeff
Turner, Lynn	Winograd, Barry
Tweedie, Sir David	Wintrub, Warren
Upton, Wayne	Wulff, John
Valukas, Anton	Yamada, Tatsumi
Vernuccio, Joe	Young, Donald
Vitray, Randy	Zeff, Stephen
Volcker, Paul	Zeyher, Danielle